# THE
# REDBOOK
# TIMESAVER
# COOKBOOK

# THE
# REDBOOK
# TIMESAVER
# COOKBOOK

by the Editors of *Redbook*

*Compiled by Ruth Fairchild Pomeroy*

❧§§❧

With recipes and menus developed in

*Redbook*'s Test Kitchens

*Saturday Review Press*

NEW YORK

Published simultaneously in Canada by Doubleday Canada Ltd., Toronto.

Library of Congress Catalog Card Number: 72–79036

ISBN 0–8415–0199–8

Saturday Review Press
230 Park Avenue, New York, New York 10017

Printed in the United States of America

Design by Tere LoPrete

# CONTENTS

# FOREWORD

More than fifteen years ago, the editors of *Redbook* magazine began to pay special attention to young married women.

Aware of the keen interest young homemakers had in convenience foods—canned, packaged, or frozen—we in *Redbook*'s Test Kitchens began to develop recipes and meals especially designed to take advantage of these new foods.

True, convenience foods were not entirely new even then. After all, a package of corn flakes or a can of peas can be considered convenience foods. And they had been available for nearly half a century. But many partially prepared or ready-to-heat-and-serve foods were newcomers to the kitchen.

Many of the new foods had the exciting quality of really being ready-made recipes with a flair. They needed little more than a garnish to give them individuality. In cans, women could find chicken Cacciatore, Swedish meatballs, spaghetti and meatballs, chicken fricassee, ready-to-serve puddings. From the frozen-food counters, homemakers would be able to choose crab Newburg, ready-to-heat fried chicken, beef and chicken pot pies, cheese fondue, ready-to-serve apple pie, and eventually an array of seasoned vegetables to boil in a bag. (This innovation allowed busy women to produce fluffy seasoned rice or a smoothly-sauced vegetable with no more equipment than a pan of boiling water, and with no chance of failure.) Dehydrated foods began to appear in greater quantity—soups in many flavors needed only the water replacement and a short cooking time. Rice or rice and pasta combinations came with their own array of seasonings built in. Creamy mashed potatoes, scalloped potatoes, and noodles Romanoff needed no more than replacement of lost liquid and some cooking to produce a finished dish. Many manufacturers began to package meals to use the ubiquitous hamburger. Some depended upon the use of dehydrated starches and sauces; others achieved exotic results with combinations of canned sauces and dehydrated vegetables.

The potential of these products was evident. Women had told us over and over that one of their greatest needs was to save time. Here were products that could help them achieve that goal.

The extent to which a person would use the new convenience foods depended upon a budget—just how much she was willing to pay for time saved—and upon how much creativity in cooking meant to her. We felt the fun of using the new variety of time-saving foods lay in the creative ways they could be combined to make good dishes in a short time.

As a result, our own new ideas about convenience foods evolved into a regular feature in the magazine: "Redbook's Timesaver Cookbook." In it we provided tested examples of how to use convenience foods with originality and flair. Recipes ranged from something as simple as sprinkling sesame seeds on brown-and-serve rolls to the addition of a can of mushrooms, a little cream, and a dash of Worcestershire sauce to spark up a can of corned beef. All were ways in which a creative cook could accomplish her ideal—meals that were tasty and individualized, yet took little time to prepare.

The "Timesaver Cookbook" became an important part of the editorial content of *Redbook*. This book is a collection of the best of those timesaving recipes developed in *Redbook*'s Test Kitchens. When your family and guests admire the meal you've just prepared and served, we hope this book will help you to say honestly and with pride, "Why, it took no time at all!"

Ruth Fairchild Pomeroy
Women's Service Editor,
*Redbook* magazine

# INTRODUCTION

*Redbook's Timesaver Cookbook* is designed to help you prepare easy and inviting meals when the time for cooking them is short. Each recipe is clocked twice—first, for how much of your time it will take to prepare it, and second, for how long it will take the dish to cook, bake, or chill before you serve it. Each of these times appears at the end of every time-tested recipe in this book. You can tell at a glance which one suits your work schedule on any particular day.

These timings allow you to devise your own menus within the time limits you choose for a given meal. If you want to spend no more than fifteen minutes in the kitchen and have dinner ready in less than half an hour, you can take a quick reading on times by checking the *Your Time* and *Cooking Time* entries at the end of each recipe. For example, you might choose Chinese-Style Chicken (page 305) as your main course and find that it takes seven minutes of your time to prepare and twelve minutes to cook. Now you will need to find a vegetable or salad and dessert that will not exceed the balance of your fifteen-minute time limit.

You might end up with a menu that looks like this:

|                                         | My Time  | Cooking or<br>Chilling Time |
|-----------------------------------------|----------|-----------------------------|
| Chilled Cranberry Juice                 |          |                             |
| Scalloped Salmon (page 88)              | 9 min.   | 20 min.                     |
| Peas and Mushrooms (page 151)           | 1 min.   | 8 min.                      |
| Hearts of Lettuce                       |          |                             |
| Prepared French Dressing                |          |                             |
| Coffee-Macaroon Pudding (page 218)      | 4 min.   | 5 min.                      |
| Beverage                                |          |                             |
| Total:                                  | 14 min.  | 33 min.                     |

You'll find your time will total about fifteen minutes in the kitchen, allowing time to pour the chilled juice, put salad on plates, and prepare a beverage (instant coffee would fit the picture perfectly). You can also go further mathematically and figure that the peas and salmon are really cooking at the same time and that the pudding can chill while you eat the main course, so you can reduce your estimated cooking time to 20 minutes.

When you time out a meal, always start with the dish that requires the longest cooking or chilling time and fill in other menu items to correspond. In the Timesaving Menus chapter (starting on page 298) you will find several fifteen-minute meals planned in the sequence of their preparation. Note that in the Steak Diane Dinner, the vegetables are started before the meat.

Since all kitchens are arranged differently, the time you spend getting out ingredients and utensils will of course be individual to yourself. We do not, therefore, include this time in our estimation, and you will need to allow a short while to assemble all your needs.

You might say the master recipe for timesaving dishes is to take ready-prepared foods, season them with ingenuity, and blend them creatively. There are other ways, too, to save time when preparing food. One is to keep the ingredients on hand for several of your favorite quick meals. The Overnight Crab Casserole (page 87) and the Quick Chicken Cacciatore (page 67), for example, use ingredients that you can have on hand on your pantry shelf or in your freezer or your refrigerator. Last-minute company or a late day at your job won't bother you if you know there's an easy dish ready to put together just waiting on the shelf.

In the Timesaving Menus chapter, beginning on page 298, you will find a selection of menus designed to save shopping time. One group of dinners is prepared entirely from foods you can keep on your pantry shelf, while another is prepared from foods you can keep in your freezer. These are reliable safeguards against the day you can't get to the store before it closes. Once you've found favorites among these meals, replenish your supplies so they are always on hand.

Although the use of convenience foods is certainly the quickest and simplest way to save preparation time at a given meal, many homemakers like to rely on some other timesaving techniques. One is what is often described as "going on a cooking binge." It may consist of making quantities of spaghetti sauce or casserole dishes or seasoned meatballs to freeze. Or it may consist of making up several dishes that will hold in the refrigerator until it's time to heat and serve them. Women who prefer this method of timesaving feel it is easier on the budget than relying on convenience foods entirely, because it gives them a chance to take advantage of quantity buying when meats and seasonal vegetables are sale-priced. This method of make-your-own convenience foods also allows for a greater inclusion of family food preferences.

If one appliance could be named a timesaver, it would be the pressure cooker. This is a reliable device for cutting down cooking time, especially for women who want to use the less expensive cuts of meat but feel there is never time for the long cooking involved.

All of these timesaving meal preparation methods are discussed fully in Chapter IX: Other Ways to Save Meal Preparation Time.

When you want to save time, don't overlook the tricks that make any recipe faster to prepare:

If you're going to use a frozen food that needs defrosting, put it out in the morning so it's ready to use at night.

Before you start to put a recipe together, assemble all the ingredients, measuring spoons and cups, and pans you will be needing. Then you won't have to take unnecessary steps while you work.

Think ahead so that you can reuse equipment whenever possible. For instance, if a recipe calls for a tablespoon of flour and a tablespoon of milk, measure the flour first so you can use the same tablespoon for the liquid ingredient. It will save washing and drying the spoon. Or if your recipe calls for dissolving bouillon cubes, do it in the same pan in which you plan to cook your sauce. There's no need to wash two pans.

Be a timesaver when you do your shopping, too. The best way to do this is to match your shopping list to the layout of the store in which you shop. For example, if the dairy counter is first as you progress around the store, put milk, cheese, butter, and eggs at the top of your list. If it's located in the middle of the store, put those items halfway down on your list. You'll save yourself from backtracking.

Some people question the economy of prepared foods, but in many cases it's false economy to say, "I can make it more cheaply from scratch." Packaged puddings and canned soups are notable examples. Government figures show that these are just two of many items you cannot make more cheaply yourself, starting from scratch. What's more, if you, the cook, also have a job, it makes sense to calculate the value of your time against the cost of buying some "built-in maid service." Because often that's exactly what con-venience foods are.

Whether you rely entirely on convenience foods or plan to use make-your-own convenience meals, the recipes that follow will prove that mealtimes can be fast, foolproof, and easy.

# CHAPTER

# I

# *How to Run a Timesaving Kitchen*

It's perfectly possible for two different cooks to come home with a can of soup, a package of ready-to-fry minute steaks, some frozen French fries, a head of lettuce, and a can of pudding—an identical dinner that may take one person twenty minutes to get on the table and the other an hour or more to serve. Why the difference? The answer lies in the organization of each cook's kitchen. If it's an efficiently laid out kitchen, if much-used utensils are right at hand and always in the same place, the time needed to prepare any meal can be considerably lessened.

Running a timesaving kitchen takes original thought and planning. If you've marveled at friends who can calmly and coolly present a sumptuous banquet with nary a sudden crisis or minor failure, whereas you inevitably wind up hurried, harried, and exhausted, the difference is probably in organization and preplanning (experience helps too).

Having your kitchen efficiently organized can make cooking more enjoyable and less time- and energy-consuming, because it frees your mind for the actual processes of cooking, eliminating interruptions to hunt or reach for necessary tools or ingredients, or having to improvise because you can't find—or don't have—what's needed. But working efficiently also means organizing yourself—giving some thought to what habits you should change, because they get you into difficulties, or what habits you should acquire. Maybe it's just a matter of getting yourself to clean up as you go along or of practicing a little with a French knife until you can chop, mince, or dice foods easily.

## Schedules Can Save You Time

One of the best ways to be or become an efficient, unflappable cook is to get in the habit of thinking through and planning each meal. For simple meals that you've fixed before, preparation may be no more than ticking off ingredients and writing a shopping list or checking the supplies on hand. If it's the first try at a new menu, however, you should think through all the steps involved in getting things ready, including how the cooking times or preparation of the various foods will dovetail. This mental run-through will help make the actual preparation go more smoothly and will help you to find and rectify any problems ahead of time.

If timing a meal really stymies you, or if you are planning an important event such as a dinner party, make a written schedule. This will give you a definite timetable, assuring you that everything can and will come out when it should. It also will show how much overlapping of activities must take place.

To make a schedule, start with the time you want to serve the meal and work backward. Include required cooking (or chilling) time, preparation time (be overgenerous with this if it's a new recipe), and whatever other special time requirements there may be for foods such as roasts, which should stand before carving. Fill in obvious gaps in the schedule with jobs that can be done at any time—such as setting the table.

If your work space is limited, extend the preparation time so you can complete and clean up one job before starting another. Move whatever jobs you can out of the kitchen—fill glasses from a pitcher at the table and fill plates at the table too.

## A Well-Stocked Kitchen Is A Timesaver

Making and working with a schedule will help with specific meals, but any meal preparation will go more smoothly if your kitchen is well stocked with the ingredients you use most often. In any kitchen the inventory of staples is the key to good management. A continual check of your inventory helps: first decide what foods or ingredients are "staples" in *your* cooking; then remember to replenish your supplies so that they will be on hand when needed.

As part of your staple supply, include an "emergency shelf" for a quick meal for your family or for unexpected company. It may be as simple as "soup and a sandwich," a quick-to-do casserole, or a more elaborate meal that you wouldn't be embarrassed to serve to special guests. For company, the menu should be one you've done often enough to be able to prepare under pressure and with distractions. Don't forget that the emergency shelf can be in the freezer, with foods ready to go on demand. (Depending on the food and how it's cooked, you may have to allow for thawing time.)

Having the proper tools and equipment in good condition and in adequate supply helps the work go more smoothly. What this means depends on your own cooking habits; if you cook only basic meals and seldom bake or experiment, you may survive very nicely without a flour sifter, using a sieve instead. On the other hand, if your cooking is extensive or involved or if your kitchen is spread out, you probably will want one or more duplicates of certain basic items such as measuring cups and spoons, flexible spatulas, paring, utility, or French knives, and saucepans of the size you use most often. Use drawer dividers, special racks, or other holders to make tools and gadgets easy to find, as well as to keep them from becoming bent, dented, or broken.

Time-tested principles for efficient storage still hold true: store frequently used items where you can reach them easily. Use high or less-accessible storage areas for equipment and supplies that are used infrequently.

When you open a cabinet door you should be able to see, identify, and reach everything stored there, and not have to shove things around. For the least effort in retrieving items, keep stacking to a minimum; stack only items of the same size and shape.

## An Organized Kitchen Is A Timesaver

You can increase efficiency by storing all equipment and supplies—cookware, tools, food, small appliances—right where they are first used. It's a natural tendency to keep all canned goods together, all cookware together and so on, but if they're used in different parts of the kitchen, they should be stored in the area where they are *first* needed. With this kind of storage plan the cleanup also is simpler, and it takes little time and thought to return items where they will be used next.

To organize your cupboards for first-use storage it's easier if you think of your kitchen, as the experts do, subdivided into separate work centers for the various major activities that take place there. These are preparation, cooking, serving, cleanup (or sink center), and storage (including the refrigerator-freezer). Some activities and logical storage needs are obvious; others, not so obvious. A teakettle, double boiler or coffee maker, for example, should be kept at the sink center since the first thing you do when using one is fill it with water.

When either storage space or countertop work space is severely cramped, there are a number of ways to get more use from existing space.

First, check your cabinets to make sure that valuable space isn't taken up by equipment, serving accessories, or foodstuffs that needn't be there—the nine casseroles that came as wedding presents, the cake-decorating set you used once. Anything you haven't used in the past year or so should be discarded, given to someone who will use it, or stored in another part of the house.

With hooks, nails, or a pegboard, use walls to hang up tools, gadgets, cookware—whatever will fit in the space and can be hung. If it won't interfere with traffic patterns, a series of open shelves, either free-standing or attached to the wall, is a relatively inexpensive do-it-yourself project.

## Increased Storage Space Saves Time

There are many inexpensive easy-to-install storage accessories that either create new storage space or put existing space to fuller use. Stacking shelves or turntables can create one or two extra storage levels in tall cabinets. Slide-out drawers or large turntables make storage space in floor-level cabinets more fully or easily accessible. Special racks that attach to the inside of a cabinet or closet door hold spices, cleaning supplies, paper bags, or trash. If you have enough space between the countertop and the cabinets above, there are drawers that can be fastened to the underside of the cabinet, specially made to hold paper towels and kitchen wraps, tools and utensils, flour, and sugar.

Inadequate refrigerator or freezer storage is as serious a handicap as other storage shortages, as the number of foods available in refrigerated or frozen form continues to increase. If it's your own refrigerator or freezer that's inadequate—if it's too small or won't keep foods thoroughly frozen—a new one might be a wise investment. If only the freezer space is inadequate, compact freezers at reasonable prices are now in many stores. (These have a capacity of four to six cubic feet and are often sized to slip under a work counter.) There are storage accessories for both refrigerator and freezer to keep foods neatly filed and viewable.

If you have the floor space, you can create additional storage with inexpensive furniture pieces or cabinets (a cutting board or ceramic slab on top will give additional work space). A rolling cart can be particularly useful for both storage and use of small appliances or for items that go from kitchen to table. If a series of permanent shelves isn't possible, one fold-down shelf will give extra work space in emergencies, such as when you are preparing a large dinner, yet be out of the way when not needed.

If it's countertop work space that's limited, perhaps you're storing things there that, while less conveniently, could be kept elsewhere. (Do you really need or want that canister set on the counter just because it's always been there?) You'll have to decide whether to keep small, portable appliances such as a blender, mixer, toaster, or coffee maker on a counter. They do take up space, but they're often cumbersome to move, and if they're not in an easy-to-reach spot, you're likely to use them less. Some of these appliances—can openers, portable mixers, electric knives—come in versions that can be hung on a wall.

## Less Frequent Shopping Saves Time

"Buy it now, eat it later" is a convenience of modern life that lets you benefit from food bargains and makes meal planning and preparation faster and easier. But how can you be sure that all that food you bring home today is going to be just as appetizing and edible by the time you're ready to prepare it? Shopping for large quantities of food on one trip can save time, but if storage is not thought through, it can be an expensive bargain.

Assuming that the food you buy is of good quality and freshness, these guides will help you determine how much food you can store properly in your kitchen at one time.

The recommended temperature for fresh-food storage in the refrigerator is about 37° F. Vegetable crispers may be a little warmer and meat compartments should be cooler (about 30° F. is best).

All frozen foods should be kept at 0° F., and our suggested storage times are based on this temperature. If you have a freezer or a combination refrigerator-freezer, it should be able to maintain this temperature, whereas the freezing compartment of a conventional refrigerator will not (its temperature is usually about 15° F. to 20° F.). Even though a food package may be frozen hard at these higher temperatures, losses in color, texture, flavor, and nutritive value will occur much more quickly than they do at 0° F. Foods should be stored at temperatures above 0° F. only for short periods—two weeks to a month. (Foods stored for a longer time will still be wholesome; they simply won't be as attractive or nutritious.)

Once a food has thawed completely it should not be refrozen; but if the food is only partially thawed and still has ice crystals, it's safe to refreeze it. Thawing and refreezing will usually affect quality and flavor, so you should use such food quickly.

To maintain the quality of frozen foods, proper packaging or wrapping is extremely important. The foods must be sealed from air, moisture, and vapor. If not properly sealed, the food will deteriorate much more rapidly, the flavor may change or "freezer burn" (drying of the surface of the food) will develop. The food will still be safe to eat; it simply won't taste or look as good.

Moistureproof and vaporproof sheet wrappings that are suitable for freezer use include heavyweight aluminum foil; plastic films such as cellophane, polyethylene, and Saran; heavily waxed freezer paper, and laminated freezer papers. Ordinary wax paper and kraft (wrapping) paper are not moisture- and vaporproof. Containers made of plastic, glass, aluminum, or specially treated paper are suitable if they can be tightly sealed. For taping, use special freezer tape that sticks at very low temperatures. Plastic films can be heat-sealed with a low-temperature iron.

The storage times given below are suggested times for maintaining maximum quality. Although you don't necessarily have to discard a food if it's not used within the time limits, you must be willing to accept a less appetizing product.

## *Breads*

Refrigeration doesn't keep bread from getting stale, but it does prevent mold from forming in hot, humid weather. Prewrapped bread can be refrigerated up to a week in its original wrapper.

*Yeast and quick breads* freeze well. Bakery yeast breads can be frozen up to two weeks in their original wrappers. Homemade yeast breads and rolls and bakery products that have been properly wrapped can be frozen for six to eight months. Quick breads (muffins, biscuits) can be frozen for two to three months.

*Refrigerated dough products* should be used before the expiration date marked on the end of the container. It is better not to store these products in the refrigerator door or directly under the freezer compartment: temperatures in the door are usually too warm; those under the freezer compartment are too cold. These products should *not* be frozen.

# Butter, Shortening, and Oils

*Butter and margarine* will keep about two weeks if tightly covered or wrapped and refrigerated. Many refrigerators have compartments that keep butter at spreading consistency. Only the amount of butter that will be used within two or three days should be stored there. Butter can be frozen up to six months and margarine up to nine months.

*Cooking and salad oils* need not be refrigerated if used quickly, but refrigerating will prevent possible flavor change from overlong storage at room temperature. Some oils may cloud and solidify in the refrigerator, but they will become clear and liquid when warmed to room temperature. *Hydrogenated shortening* can be stored at room temperature for several weeks.

# Cheese

*Hard cheeses* such as Cheddar, blue, Parmesan, and Swiss will keep about a month if wrapped tightly and refrigerated. They can be frozen, either whole or grated, up to six months. Hard cheeses get crumbly if their thawing time is too long, so freeze half-pound or smaller pieces.

*Soft cheeses* such as cottage, cream, or Camembert should be refrigerated tightly covered. Cottage cheese should be used in three to five days; other soft cheeses will keep about two weeks. Most soft cheeses (Camembert is one exception) do not freeze well. Cream cheese freezes satisfactorily when combined with other foods, as in a dip.

*Cheese spreads or foods* should be covered and refrigerated after opening.

# Eggs

Fresh eggs in their shells will keep in the refrigerator about two weeks. Store them, with the small end down, in the original carton or a covered container. (If not covered, the egg can lose moisture through its porous shell.)

Uncooked egg whites can be refrigerated, tightly covered, up to ten days. Uncooked egg yolks can be refrigerated two to three days. Enough water should be added to cover the yolks.

Uncooked egg whites, yolks, or whole eggs (removed from their shells) can be frozen six to nine months. (Whole eggs in their shells should not be frozen, as the eggs expand in freezing and the shells will crack.) Egg whites need no special preparation for freezing other than an airtight container. Sugar or salt must be added to yolks or whole eggs.

Do not freeze hard-cooked eggs or foods containing them—the whites will become tough and rubbery.

# Fruits

Most fresh fruits must be handled carefully and used rather quickly because they are fragile and perishable. Sort fruits before storing and discard bruised or decayed fruit.

*Apples:* Hard or unripe apples should be left at room temperature until they are ready to eat. Ripe or mellow apples should be refrigerated uncovered and used within a week.

*Apricots, avocados, nectarines, peaches, pears, plums, rhubarb:* Store ripe fruit uncovered on a refrigerator shelf and use within three to five days. Allow unripened fruit to ripen at room temperature before refrigerating.

*Bananas:* Store at room temperature and use within a few days. Once bananas have reached the ripeness that you like, they can be refrigerated to hold them for a few days. The skin will turn dark, but taste and texture won't be affected.

*Berries:* Sort before storing and discard any spoiled ones, but do not wash or remove stems until you are ready to use them. Refrigerate berries whole and uncovered in plastic mesh baskets or spread on a plate; use within two days.

*Citrus fruits, melons, pineapples:* Store at cool room temperature (60° to 70° F.). They also can be refrigerated for a short time if the temperature isn't too cold. Use within a week.

Nearly all fresh fruits can be frozen satisfactorily, but most must be prepared in a sugar syrup or dry sugar pack (see *The Redbook Cookbook* for instructions). They will keep for six to sixteen months, depending on the fruit and its preparation.

Commercially frozen fruits can be kept frozen for about a year.

## Mayonnaise and Salad Dressings

After opening, store covered in refrigerator. Do *not* freeze mayonnaise or oil-based salad dressings—they will separate.

## Meats, Poultry, and Fish

### Refrigerator Storage

*Raw* meats should be kept in the coldest part of the refrigerator at a temperature close to freezing (30° to 35° F.). Many refrigerators have special meat-storage compartments at this temperature.

Meat and poultry benefit from some air circulation, so they should be covered loosely. Remove bulky store wrappings and cover with wax paper, foil, or the *inner* wrapping from the butcher. Prepackaged meat can be left in its original film wrapper, as it has "breathing" properties.

Fish also keeps better if wrapped loosely, but its odor may be a problem if it's not used quickly.

Roasts can be stored five to six days; steaks and chops, three to four days; ground meat, variety meat, poultry, and fish, one to two days.

*Home-cooked* meat should be refrigerated immediately. If it is warm when refrigerated, leave it uncovered until it has cooled; then cover loosely to prevent odor transfer and drying of the food.

Whenever possible, separate meat from gravy or sauce and refrigerate separately. Always remove stuffing from poultry and refrigerate it separately.

Use fish within one day. Use gravies and sauces in one to two days and meat cooked in gravy or sauce within three days. Use roasted meats within four to five days, poultry within two to three days, poultry stuffing within two days.

*Cured* meats (ham, bacon) and *ready-to-serve* meats (bologna, frankfurters, and luncheon meats) should be wrapped tightly or left in the unopened package and refrigerated. Bacon, frankfurters, and bologna may be kept five to seven days, and luncheon meats three to five days. A whole ham can be kept for a week; half a ham, three to five days; ham slices, two to three days.

## Freezer Storage

All kinds of fresh meat can be frozen satisfactorily—beef, pork, lamb, veal—including variety meats such as liver, kidneys, sweetbreads, heart, tongue, or brains. Cured and smoked meats or any other salted meat should not be frozen unless absolutely necessary and then only for a short time (one to two months), since they deteriorate rapidly in flavor and quality.

All kinds of poultry—chicken, turkey, geese, game birds—freeze well. Do *not* stuff poultry before freezing or freeze uncooked stuffing. (Uncooked stuffing is a potentially dangerous source for the growth of harmful bacteria.)

Many types of fish and shellfish can be frozen satisfactorily if they are of good quality, are fresh, and are processed quickly.

Many cooked meats can also be frozen, either by themselves or in a prepared dish or casserole.

Storage times and preparation procedures vary widely according to type and cut of meat. For specific information, refer to a good cookbook (such as *The Redbook Cookbook*) or to the instruction book for your freezer.

Commercially frozen meat can be treated like home-frozen meat. Storage times are the same.

# Milk, Cream, and Ice Cream

*Fresh milk and cream* can be kept three days to a week, depending on how fresh they are when first refrigerated. Homogenized milk can be frozen up to three months. Rich, heavy cream can be frozen satisfactorily, but it will not whip well after thawing. Whipped cream, however, freezes well and can be frozen in individual portions for use as dessert toppings.

*Ice cream,* either purchased or homemade, can be kept frozen about a month.

# Nuts

Store shelled or unshelled nuts tightly covered in the refrigerator or freezer to delay development of rancidity (caused by their high fat content). Nuts may be kept for several months refrigerated, and up to a year frozen.

# Vegetables

Sort vegetables before storing; remove discolored or dried leaves and discard bruised or damaged vegetables. The fresher the vegetables are when eaten, the better the quality and food value.

Many vegetables, including *asparagus, broccoli, Brussels sprouts, cabbage, cauliflower, green beans, green onions, carrots, beets, radishes, peppers, and cucumbers,* require moist, cool surroundings to retain their freshness. They should be refrigerated in plastic bags or in the vegetable crisper. Crispers perform best when fairly full. If you have only a few items in the compartment, they'll keep better in plastic bags.

*Lettuce, salad greens, and other leafy green vegetables* such as *spinach* also need to be kept cool and moist. If they are to be used the same day, wash thoroughly, dry carefully, wrap in a towel, and put in the refrigerator to get crisp. If they will be used over several days, rinse, shake dry, and store in the crisper; or protect them with a plastic bag or film, foil, or towel and store on a low shelf in the refrigerator.

Leave *peas and lima beans* in the pod and *sweet corn* in its husk, in the refrigerator, until you're ready to cook them. *Tomatoes* can be ripened at room temperature, then refrigerated uncovered.

*Potatoes, sweet potatoes, dry onions, hard-rind squash, turnips, and eggplant* should be stored in a cool, dry place. If, as is usually the case, you must keep them at temperatures over 60° F., try to use them in about a week.

Fresh vegetables are best when used within the following times:

One to two days: Asparagus, beans (green, wax, or limas), Brussels sprouts, mustard greens, peas, leafy lettuce varieties, spinach, sweet corn, ripe tomatoes.

Three to four days: Cauliflower, collards, kale, Swiss chard, iceberg lettuce, okra, watercress.

One week: Beets, broccoli, cucumbers, eggplant, endive, escarole, kohlrabi, leeks, green onions, green peppers, radishes, romaine, parsley, summer squash.

A week or more: Artichokes, cabbage, carrots, celery, garlic, dry onions, parsnips, potatoes, rutabaga, winter squash, turnips.

Most fresh vegetables can be successfully frozen for from eight to twelve months, but they must be blanched or scalded before packaging. Blanching prevents loss of color, flavor, and nutritive value by stopping enzyme action.

Commercially frozen vegetables can be stored up to a year.

# CHAPTER

# II

# *Appetizers*

No hostess or host should feel helpless about appetizers these days. Not with the cheeses and crackers and the great variety of ready-to-use dips and spreads that are easily available.

But since almost everyone relies on these no-work appetizers, the real problem is coming up with something a little different. Even the definition of an appetizer—something that whets the appetite but doesn't kill it—dictates that appetizers shouldn't be dull. They should be chosen to enhance a menu and never echo the main dishes you plan to serve. For example, if you are having a cheese fondue for your main course, you should avoid cheese as an appetizer.

Ideally, appetizers should keep cocktail guests nibbling happily, perhaps asking something like "What exactly is in this marvelous dip?" That's the sort of reaction you'll get when you start with a can of deviled ham and add just a few ingredients to make the Pink Devil Dip on page 23. Or when you season English muffins, then toast them, to make the Dill-Butter Strips on page 35. You'll be as pleasantly surprised as your guests at how tasty appetizers can become when you take just a little time to give them new character.

Timesaver appetizers like the two we have just described not only make a delightful first course, they're practically a must when you're planning a big party. You'll be able to make them ahead of time, and because they're so easy to prepare, you'll save yourself hours of work.

Planning appetizers for a big party can include a lot of timesaving preparation if you take a little thought. If you're planning several canapés to put on rounds of bread, cut the bread rounds a day ahead and store them in a securely fastened plastic bag in the refrigerator. Have all of the spreads mixed and stored in plastic containers in the refrigerator. Have olive slices, parsley or watercress sprigs, or pimiento strips stored in tightly covered jars in the refrigerator. Making an assorted tray of canapés thus becomes an assembly-line procedure rather than a time-consuming job.

Many hors d'oeuvres will freeze well, especially the pastry-biscuit-based hot ones. Freeze them on a cookie sheet so they are ready to pop in the oven without further handling. Or, if you plan stuffed eggs, cook a quantity of eggs. Divide the hard-cooked yolks into two bowls and season them differently—an easy way to give your guests the impression of variety.

Dips are probably the easiest of all appetizers to make, and they're all-round favorites that help get any social gathering off to a friendly start. They are usually made with sour cream or softened cream cheese, to which any number of seasonings can be added. In these weight-conscious days it's thoughtful to offer an assortment of fresh vegetable sticks along with the usual chips for dipping. In this chapter you'll find recipes for many different dips as well as for an assortment of hot and cold hors d'oeuvres.

# *Dips*

### AVOCADO DIP

| | |
|---|---|
| *2 ripe avocados* | *¼ cup lemon juice* |
| *1 large clove garlic, peeled* | *½ cup olive oil* |
| *⅛ teaspoon crushed red* | *¼ teaspoon salt* |
| *pepper* | *Corn chips* |

Peel and pit avocados (save one pit). Chop the pulp coarsely. Place all ingredients except corn chips in the container of an electric blender. Blend 30 to 60 seconds on high speed. Turn the puréed mixture into a serving bowl; place the reserved pit in center of mixture. Cover and chill in the refrigerator for at least 1 hour. Serve as a dip with corn chips. Makes about 2 cups dip.
Your Time: 15 minutes
Chilling Time: 1 hour

## BOSTON BEAN DIP

1  13-ounce can baked beans
   in molasses sauce
¼ cup bottled barbecue sauce
   with onions and
   mushrooms
2  teaspoons prepared mustard

2  tablespoons finely chopped
   green onions or scallions
3  or 4 drops Tabasco
1  pound fully cooked ham,
   cut into ½-inch cubes

Place beans, barbecue sauce, mustard, onion, and Tabasco in the container of an electric blender. Blend on low speed until thoroughly combined. Cover mixture and chill 30 minutes. Spear ham cubes on toothpicks and serve with dip. Makes about 1½ cups dip.
Your Time: 7 minutes
Chilling Time: 30 minutes

## CREAMY BEAN DIP

1  8-ounce package cream
   cheese, at room
   temperature
1  11½-ounce can condensed
   bean with bacon soup
¼ cup bottled creamy blue
   cheese dressing

¼ teaspoon Worcestershire
   sauce
Few grains of garlic powder
2  teaspoons dried parsley
   flakes
Corn chips or potato chips

In a bowl thoroughly blend softened cream cheese, bean with bacon soup, dressing, Worcestershire, garlic powder, and parsley. Cover and chill 1 hour. Serve as a dip with corn chips or potato chips. Makes about 2½ cups dip.
Your Time: 3 minutes
Chilling Time: 1 hour

## CURRIED LIMA-CHEESE DIP

1  9-ounce package frozen
   lima beans in cheese sauce
3  tablespoons grated
   Parmesan cheese
2  teaspoons instant minced
   onion

¼ teaspoon curry powder
3  tablespoons commercial
   sour cream

Prepare lima beans in cheese sauce as directed on package, but reduce the cooking time to 6 minutes. Pour heated lima beans and sauce into the container of an electric blender. Blend on high speed (or set at Blend) for about 10 seconds, or until lima beans are puréed. Pour into a small bowl. Add Parmesan cheese, onion, curry powder and sour cream; mix well. Cover and chill about 30 minutes. If dip gets too thick, thin with additional sour cream. Serve with potato or corn chips. Makes about 1¼ cups dip.
Your Time: 8 minutes
Cooking Time: 7 minutes
Chilling Time: 30 minutes

### ZESTY CHEESE DIP

1  8-ounce can tomato sauce
1  teaspoon bottled steak
    sauce
Dash Tabasco
1  3-ounce package cream
    cheese, at room
    temperature

2  ounces Roquefort cheese
1  4-ounce package shredded
    Cheddar cheese
Crisp raw vegetables

Place all ingredients except vegetables in the container of an electric blender and blend 1 minute or beat until smooth with electric mixer. Turn the puréed mixture into a serving bowl; cover and chill 1 hour. Serve as a dip with crisp raw vegetables. Makes 1¾ cups dip.
Your Time: 6 minutes
Chilling Time: 1 hour

### LIEDERKRANZ DIP

1  4-ounce package soft,
    ripened Liederkranz
    cheese
1  8-ounce container
    cream-style cottage cheese
    with vegetables
¼ cup milk

2  tablespoons frozen chopped
    chives
1  tablespoon lemon juice
Carrot sticks
Celery sticks
Cherry tomatoes

Let Liederkranz stand at room temperature until softened, about 1 hour. Place cottage cheese, milk, chives, and lemon juice in the

container of an electric blender; blend on low speed about 30 seconds. In a bowl combine softened Liederkranz and cottage cheese mixture. Cover and chill 1 hour. Serve as a dip with carrot and celery sticks and cherry tomatoes. Makes 2 cups dip.
Your Time: 5 minutes
Chilling Time: 1 hour

## ROQUEFORT DIP

*½ pound Roquefort cheese,*
  *crumbled*
*1 8-ounce package cream*
  *cheese, at room*
  *temperature*

*½ cup light cream*
*¼ cup brandy*
*½ cup finely chopped walnuts*
*Crisp raw vegetables*

Place all ingredients except vegetables in a bowl; blend well by hand or beat with an electric mixer until smooth. Turn puréed mixture into a serving bowl; cover and chill 1 hour. Serve as a dip with crisp raw vegetables. Makes 3 cups dip.
Your Time: 10 minutes
Chilling Time: 1 hour

## CORN AND BACON DIP

*1 8-ounce package cream*
  *cheese*
*½ cup commercial sour cream*
*¼ cup mayonnaise or salad*
  *dressing*
*1 8-ounce can whole kernel*
  *corn, drained*

*3 tablespoons imitation bacon*
  *pieces*
*½ teaspoon garlic powder*
*⅛ teaspoon Tabasco*
*Potato chips or crackers*

Place cream cheese in a medium-sized bowl and let stand at room temperature to soften. Blend sour cream and mayonnaise thoroughly with the cheese. Stir in corn, bacon pieces, garlic powder, and Tabasco. Cover mixture and chill in refrigerator until ready to serve, or at least 1 hour. Serve as a dip with potato chips or crackers. Makes 2 cups dip.
Your Time: 4 minutes
Chilling Time: 1 hour

## TOMATO-CLAM DIP

1  pint commercial sour cream       1  7½-ounce can minced
1  1½-ounce envelope                    clams, drained
   spaghetti sauce mix               Potato chips or crackers

Combine all ingredients except potato chips or crackers in a small bowl and blend well. Cover and chill 1 hour. Serve as a dip with potato chips or crackers. Makes 2 cups dip.
Your Time: 4 minutes
Chilling Time: 1 hour

## CLAM DIP

1  8-ounce can minced clams     Few drops Tabasco
1  clove garlic, split                    ½ teaspoon salt
1  8-ounce package cream         Few grains pepper
   cheese, at room                    Potato chips or crisp raw
   temperature                            vegetables
2  teaspoons lemon juice
1½ teaspoons Worcestershire
   sauce

Drain clams and reserve ¼ cup of the liquid. Rub a medium-sized bowl with the cut surface of the garlic clove. Add cheese to clams and beat with a fork until smooth. Mix in the remaining ingredients, including the reserved ¼ cup clam liquid. Cover and chill about 1 hour. Serve as a dip with potato chips or crisp raw vegetables. Makes about 1½ cups dip.
Your Time: 10 minutes
Chilling Time: 1 hour

## DEVILED HAM DIP

1  cup commercial sour cream     Potato chips
1  2¼-ounce can deviled ham
2  teaspoons Worcestershire
   sauce

Place all ingredients except potato chips in a small bowl. Stir until well blended. Serve as a dip with potato chips. Makes 1 cup dip.
Your Time: 3 minutes

## PINK DEVIL DIP

1　cup commercial sour cream　　¼　teaspoon prepared
1　4½-ounce can deviled ham　　　　horseradish
3　tablespoons bottled chili　　　Potato chips or corn chips
　　sauce
1　teaspoon instant minced
　　onion

Combine all ingredients except potato or corn chips in a small bowl
and stir to blend well. Cover and chill 1 hour. Serve as a dip with
potato chips or corn chips. Makes 1 cup dip.
Your Time: 3 minutes
Chilling Time: 1 hour

## LIVER PÂTÉ DIP

1　4¾-ounce can liver spread　　2　egg whites
½　cup small-curd cottage　　　Celery sticks
　　cheese　　　　　　　　　　Carrot sticks
½　teaspoon seasoned salt

Combine liver spread, cottage cheese, and seasoned salt in a small
bowl. Beat egg whites until stiff, but not dry. Fold into liver mixture.
Cover and chill about 1 hour. Serve as a dip with celery and carrot
sticks. Makes about 1½ cups dip.
Your Time: 6 minutes
Chilling Time: 1 hour

## LIVERWURST DIP

1　pound liverwurst, at room　　1　teaspoon Worcestershire
　　temperature　　　　　　　　　sauce
1　8-ounce package cream　　　1　tablespoon instant minced
　　cheese, at room　　　　　　　　onion
　　temperature　　　　　　　　Crackers
½　cup beer

Place liverwurst in the large bowl of an electric mixer and break into
small pieces with a spatula. Add softened cream cheese and beer and
blend on low speed of the mixer, scraping the sides of the bowl often
with a spatula. As mixture blends, increase the speed of the mixer to

medium. Beat until mixture is fairly smooth and creamy, about 3 minutes. Stir in Worcestershire and minced onion. Cover and chill 30 minutes. Serve as a dip with crackers. Makes 3½ cups dip.
Your Time: 7 minutes
Chilling Time: 30 minutes


## SOUR CREAM-HERB DIP

2  *cups commercial sour cream*     ½ *teaspoon salt*
¼ *cup freeze-dried chives*          *Potato chips*
1  *teaspoon dried dillweed*

Combine all ingredients except potato chips in a small bowl and refrigerate, covered, 1 hour or longer. Serve as a dip with potato chips. Makes 2 cups dip.
Your Time: 3 minutes
Chilling Time: 1 hour


## TUNA-ONION DIP

1  *6½-ounce can tuna, well*          8  *slices crisp-fried bacon,*
   *drained and flaked*                  *crumbled*
2  *cups commercial sour cream*      1  *large tomato, finely*
1  *envelope onion soup mix*            *chopped*
1  *medium-sized cucumber,*          *Crackers or corn chips*
   *unpeeled and finely*
   *chopped*

Place tuna, sour cream, and onion soup mix in a medium-sized bowl and mix until blended. Add cucumber, bacon, and tomato and mix until blended. Cover and chill 1 hour. Serve as a dip with crackers or corn chips. Makes 4½ cups dip.
Your Time: 15 minutes
Chilling Time: 1 hour

## TUNA DIP

1 8-ounce package cream
  cheese, at room
  temperature
2 tablespoons crumbled blue
  cheese
1 6½-ounce can tuna, drained
½ cup commercial sour cream

2 teaspoons instant minced
  onion
1 whole canned pimiento
Few grains garlic powder
1 tablespoon lemon juice
1 tablespoon water
Crackers or potato chips

Place all ingredients except crackers or potato chips in the container of an electric blender. Blend on high speed about 1 minute or until mixture is well blended. Pour mixture into a bowl; cover and chill at least 1 hour. Serve as a dip with crackers or potato chips. Makes 2½ cups dip.
Your Time: 8 minutes
Chilling Time: 1 hour

## VEGETABLES WITH CURRY DIP

2 cups mayonnaise or salad
  dressing
¼ cup chili sauce
2 tablespoons white vinegar
1½ teaspoons curry powder
½ teaspoon salt
1 teaspoon paprika

¼ teaspoon ground pepper
1 head cauliflower, cleaned
2 medium-sized green
  peppers
2 bunches radishes
½ pound fresh mushrooms,
  washed

Combine mayonnaise, chili sauce, vinegar, curry powder, salt, paprika, and pepper in a medium-sized bowl and blend well. Cover and refrigerate 3 hours. Near serving time, separate cauliflower into flowerets. Clean and cut green peppers into thin strips. Clean radishes and slice mushrooms. Place dip in a bowl and place in the center of a large serving platter. Arrange vegetables in groups around dip on platter. Makes 2 cups dip.
Your Time: 12 minutes
Chilling Time: 3 hours

# *Cold Appetizers*

### PARSLEY-CHEESE BALL

6 ounces blue cheese, at room
 temperature
2 5-ounce jars pasteurized
 process bacon-cheese
 spread, at room
 temperature
4 3-ounce packages cream
 cheese, at room
 temperature
2 tablespoons instant minced
 onion
1 teaspoon Worcestershire
 sauce

½ teaspoon monosodium
 glutamate
¼ cup finely chopped walnuts
1 tablespoon dried parsley
 flakes
1 cup finely chopped fresh
 parsley
Crisp crackers
Sliced ripe olives (optional)
Sliced pimiento (optional)

Combine cheeses, onion, Worcestershire, and monosodium glutamate in the large bowl of an electric mixer. Mix at medium speed until well blended and smooth. With a spoon, stir in nuts and parsley flakes. Line a 1½-quart mixing bowl with aluminum foil. Pack the cheese mixture into the bowl, smoothing the top flat. (The flat part will be the bottom when the cheese ball is turned out.) Cover bowl tightly and refrigerate at least 4 hours, or overnight, until well chilled and hardened. One hour before serving time, remove cheese ball from bowl and peel off aluminum foil. Pat parsley on rounded side of cheese ball to cover it evenly. Place cheese ball on a large platter and surround with a variety of crisp crackers. The top of the ball may be decorated with sliced ripe olives and pimiento, if desired. Makes about 5 cups dip.
Your Time: 12 minutes
Chilling Time: 4 hours or overnight

### GOLDEN CARROT CIRCLES

2 large carrots, scraped
1 2¼-ounce can deviled ham

Parsley sprigs

Cut carrots into round slices ¼-inch thick. Mound ham on each carrot slice. Top each circle with a sprig of parsley. Chill for 30 minutes. Makes 16 to 20 appetizers.
Your Time: 8 minutes
Chilling Time: 30 minutes

## CURRIED CHICKEN SPREAD

2 4¾-ounce cans chicken
   spread
⅓ cup finely chopped celery
¼ cup mayonnaise or salad
   dressing

¼ cup slivered blanched
   almonds
½ teaspoon curry powder
Crisp crackers

In a small bowl blend together chicken spread, celery, mayonnaise, almonds, and curry powder. Cover mixture and chill in refrigerator 1 hour. Serve as a spread with crackers. Makes 1½ cups spread.
Your Time: 6 minutes
Chilling Time: 1 hour

## GINGER-CHICKEN SPREAD

1 3-ounce package cream
   cheese, at room
   temperature
1 4¾-ounce can chicken
   spread

2 teaspoons finely chopped
   crystalized ginger
2 tablespoons slivered
   blanched almonds
Crackers

Combine all ingredients except crackers in a small bowl. Cover and chill at least 1 hour. Serve as a spread with crackers. Makes about 1 cup spread.
Your Time: 3 minutes
Chilling Time: 1 hour

## CHEESE-STUFFED BOLOGNA WEDGES

2 3-ounce packages cream
   cheese, at room
   temperature

6 slices bologna
6 slices cooked salami

Spread some of the cream cheese on three slices of the bologna. Cover each with a slice of salami; spread salami slices with more of the cheese. Add a slice of bologna to each stack and spread bologna slices with the remaining cheese. Top each stack with remaining salami slices. Wrap stacks individually in waxed paper or plastic wrap. Chill 1 hour or overnight. Cut each stack into 8 wedges and serve wedges with toothpicks. Makes 24 wedges.
Your Time: 3 minutes
Chilling Time: 1 hour or overnight

## LIVERWURST CANAPÉS

1 4¾-ounce can liver spread
1 3-ounce package cream cheese, at room temperature
2 tablespoons packaged dry onion soup mix
¼ cup chopped celery
1 tablespoon diced pimiento
6 slices white bread
¼ cup butter or margarine, melted

Heat oven to 375° F. In a small bowl combine liver spread, cream cheese, onion soup mix, celery, and pimiento and blend well. Cover and chill. Trim crusts off bread and cut each slice into square quarters. Brush both sides of each quarter with melted butter. Insert a quarter slice in each cup of two 1¾-inch muffin pans (12 cups in each). Bake 10 to 12 minutes, or until golden brown. Cool on wire cake racks. Place a heaping teaspoonful of liverwurst mixture in each toast cup. Makes 24 appetizers.
Your Time: 9 minutes
Baking Time: 10 to 12 minutes

## RIBBON MEAT STACKS

1 6-ounce package sliced chopped pressed ham
2 6-ounce packages pimiento cream cheese, at room temperature
1 6-ounce package sliced olive-and-pickle loaf

Spread 1 slice of the chopped pressed ham with a thick layer of cream cheese. Place a slice of the olive-and-pickle loaf on top. Repeat layers twice, using 4 slices of meat and 3 layers of cheese for each stack. Wrap stack in plastic wrap. Repeat with remaining meat and

cheese. (You will have 3 meat stacks.) Chill stacks until firm, about 3 hours. At serving time remove meat stacks from plastic wrap. Cut each stack into 4 strips and cut each strip crosswise into 4 pieces. Stick a toothpick in each piece. Makes 36 appetizers.
Your Time: 14 minutes
Chilling Time: 3 hours

## SARDINE-CREAM CHEESE CANAPÉS

1  3-ounce package cream cheese, at room temperature
1  4⅜-ounce can skinless and boneless sardines, well drained

Soft butter or margarine
4 to 6 thin slices white or rye bread
Pimiento-stuffed olives

In a bowl blend together cream cheese and sardines. Butter bread slices lightly. Spread each with an equal amount of the cream cheese mixture. Cut each slice into 4 triangles. Garnish with slivers of olives in a decorative design. Makes 16 to 24 canapés, or 4 to 6 servings.
Your Time: 15 minutes

## JELLIED SHRIMP

1  12-ounce can vegetable juice
1  envelope unflavored gelatine
¼  cup cold water
5  drops Tabasco

1  teaspoon prepared horseradish
2  dozen cooked, shelled, deveined, and chilled shrimp
Packaged Melba toast rounds

Empty juice into a small saucepan. In a small bowl sprinkle gelatine over water to soften. Add to juice with the Tabasco and horseradish. Heat mixture to boiling over moderate heat (about 250° F.). Stir until gelatine is dissolved. Pour mixture into an 8-inch-square pan. Chill until mixture begins to set. Arrange shrimp in rows in jelly. Chill until completely set. To serve, cut gelatine in cubes with a shrimp in each and place on Melba toast rounds. Makes 2 dozen.
Your Time: 5 minutes
Chilling Time: 2 hours

## SEASONED WALNUT SNACKS

1  *8-ounce can shelled walnut*   *Variety of seasoning salts*
    *halves*    *(garlic salt, onion salt,*
2  *tablespoons melted butter*   *celery salt, or seasoned*
    *or margarine*    *salt)*

Heat oven to 350° F. Fill a medium-sized saucepan half full with water and bring to a boil over moderate heat (about 250° F.). Drop walnuts into the boiling water. Boil 3 minutes. Drain well. Spread nuts evenly in the bottom of a 12¾-x-9-x-2-inch baking pan. Bake 15 to 20 minutes, stirring frequently, or until nuts are golden brown. Immediately brush nuts lightly with butter and sprinkle with desired seasonings. If variety is desired, divide nuts and sprinkle each group with a different seasoning. Cool before serving. Snacks will keep well if stored covered tightly in refrigerator. Makes about 1 cup snacks.
Your Time: 3 minutes
Cooking Time: 23 minutes

# *Hot Appetizers*

## BACON CURLS

2  *5-ounce cans water*    2  *tablespoons lemon juice*
    *chestnuts*    6  *slices raw bacon, cut in*
1  *tablespoon seasoned salt*    *halves*
1  *tablespoon Worcestershire*
    *sauce*

Drain water chestnuts and place in a small bowl; sprinkle with salt, Worcestershire, and lemon juice. Wrap each in a half slice of bacon and secure with a toothpick. Place on broiler rack about 4 inches from heat and broil 2 minutes on each side, or until bacon is crisp. Serve hot. Makes 4 to 5 servings.
Your Time: 7 minutes
Broiling Time: 4 minutes

## BACON-CHICKEN BITES

6 slices white sandwich bread   8 slices raw bacon, cut into
1 4¾-ounce can chicken              thirds
    spread
⅛ teaspoon Worcestershire
    sauce

Heat oven to 400° F. Trim crusts from bread and discard; flatten bread slightly with a rolling pin. Combine chicken spread and Worcestershire in a small bowl and spread mixture on bread slices. Cut each slice into square quarters. Fold each square in half, spread side in, and wrap with a piece of bacon. Place on a broiler pan. Bake 40 minutes, turning halfway through the baking. Drain on paper towels. Serve warm. Makes 2 dozen appetizers.
Your Time: 11 minutes
Baking Time: 40 minutes

## CHEESE AND BEEF APPETIZERS

¼ cup coarsely chopped          ¼ cup mayonnaise or salad
    dried beef                        dressing
1 4-ounce package shredded    24 buttery round crackers
    Cheddar cheese

Heat oven to 350° F. Place dried beef in a small bowl. Pour enough boiling water over beef to cover. Let stand 5 minutes; then drain. In a medium-sized bowl, combine cheese, dried beef, and mayonnaise and blend well. Spread mixture generously on crackers. Place crackers on a cookie sheet. Bake 6 to 8 minutes, or until cheese is melted and lightly browned. Serve hot. Makes about 24 appetizers.
Your Time: 6 minutes
Standing and Baking Time: 11 to 13 minutes

## FLAKY CHEESE PINWHEELS

1 small package piecrust mix    Water and ice
½ cup grated Parmesan cheese   Garlic salt
¼ cup catsup                    Poppy seeds
¼ cup milk

Heat oven to 400° F. In a large mixing bowl combine piecrust mix, Parmesan cheese, catsup, and milk. Toss lightly with a fork just until blended and mixture forms a ball. Roll out pastry on a floured board or pastry cloth into a 15-x-12-inch rectangle. Cut into 1-x-3-inch strips. Place strips in a large bowl of water with ice and soak 10 minutes. Remove strips from ice water and pat dry with paper towels. Sprinkle each strip with garlic salt and poppy seeds. Roll up strips. Place rolls, flat side down, on greased cookie sheets; bake 10 to 12 minutes, or until golden brown. Serve hot. Makes about 3 dozen snacks.

Your Time: 11 minutes
Baking Time: 10 to 12 minutes

## CHEESE TWISTS

1 cup (4 ounces) coarsely shredded Swiss cheese    1 small package piecrust mix
1 teaspoon salt

Heat oven to 425° F. Add cheese to piecrust mix and prepare according to package directions. Roll out dough on a floured board or pastry cloth to a thickness of ¼ inch. Sprinkle dough with salt and cut in strips 5 x ½ inches. Twist strips by holding both ends and turning in opposite directions. Place twists on ungreased cookie sheet and bake 15 minutes, or until crisp and golden brown. Serve hot. Makes 3 dozen twists.

Your Time: 9 minutes
Baking Time: 15 minutes

## POLKA-DOT CHEESE BITS

2 tablespoons butter or margarine
½ cup packaged shredded Cheddar cheese
2 tablespoons imitation bacon pieces
¼ cup packaged frozen chopped green pepper

1 teaspoon instant minced onion
2 tablespoons chopped canned pimiento
1 8-ounce container refrigerated biscuits (10 biscuits)

Heat oven to 400° F. Grease an 8-inch round cake pan with unsalted shortening. In a medium-sized saucepan melt butter over moderately low heat (about 225° F.). Add cheese, bacon pieces, green pepper, onion, and pimiento. Stir until cheese melts; remove from heat. Open biscuit container according to' label directions. Cut each biscuit in quarters. Drop a few pieces at a time into the cheese mixture and toss lightly with a fork. Arrange biscuit pieces in prepared pan. Bake 18 to 20 minutes, or until golden brown. Serve warm. Makes 40 appetizers.

Your Time: 9 minutes
Baking Time: 18 to 20 minutes

## CRAB CRISPS

1 7½-ounce can Alaska king crab
1 cup commercial sour cream
½ cup (2 ounces) coarsely shredded Swiss cheese
½ package dry onion soup mix
Packaged Melba toast rounds

Preheat broiler. Drain crab and flake. Combine crab, sour cream, cheese, and dry soup mix in a medium-sized bowl. Place about 1 tablespoonful on each toast round and spread to the edges with a spatula. Place rounds on cookie sheets. Broil about 4 inches from source of heat 4 to 5 minutes, or until tops are bubbly and lightly browned. Serve immediately. Makes about 3 dozen appetizers.

Your Time: 4 minutes
Broiling Time: 4 to 5 minutes

## CLAM CANAPÉS

1 8-ounce can minced clams
1 teaspoon instant minced onion
1 tablespoon freeze-dried chives
½ cup cream cheese, at room temperature
2 tablespoons finely chopped green pepper
1 container refrigerated crescent dinner rolls

Drain clams and reserve liquid. Mix onion with 1 teaspoon of the clam liquid and let stand 1 minute. (Use leftover clam liquid in tomato juice or soups.) Grease a cookie sheet with unsalted shortening. Mix clams, onion, chives, cream cheese, and green pepper. Heat oven to 400° F. Open roll container according to label directions and unroll on a floured board. Separate dough into 4

rectangles. Pinch dough together at the diagonal cuts. Roll each rectangle with a floured rolling pin into a square 6 x 6 inches; cut into 4 squares. Spoon about 1 tablespoon filling on center of each square and fold in half to make a turnover. Press edges together with tines of a fork and prick top of turnover. Repeat with remaining sections of dough. Place turnovers on prepared cookie sheet and bake 10 minutes. If desired, cut each turnover in half. Serve hot. Makes 16 large or 32 small canapés.
Your Time: 25 minutes
Baking Time: 10 minutes

## SPICY CLAM APPETIZER

2 8-ounce containers
  refrigerated tender flaky
  biscuits (24 biscuits)
1 10½-ounce can minced
  clams, drained

¼ cup chili sauce
¼ cup commercial sour cream
Shredded process American
  cheese

Heat oven to 400° F. Open biscuit container according to label directions. Separate each biscuit into two layers. Place on ungreased cookie sheets. Combine minced clams, chili sauce, and sour cream in a small bowl. Spread about 2 teaspoons clam mixture on each biscuit half; sprinkle with a little cheese. Bake 10 to 12 minutes, or until golden brown. Serve warm. Makes 48 halves.
Your Time: 11 minutes
Cooking Time: 10 to 12 minutes

## HOT DEVILED BISCUITS

1 5-ounce jar pimiento-cheese
  spread
1 4½-ounce can deviled ham

1 8-ounce container
  refrigerated biscuits
  (10 biscuits)

Heat oven to 450° F. Grease a 9-inch pie plate with unsalted shortening. Combine cheese spread and deviled ham in the bottom of prepared pie plate. Place in oven for about 5 minutes to melt mixture. Remove pan from oven and stir mixture again, spreading it evenly over bottom of pan. Open biscuit container according to label directions. Snip each biscuit into quarters and arrange pieces close together on ham-cheese mixture. Return pan to oven and bake 10 minutes, or until biscuits are browned. Let stand a few minutes

before inverting pan onto a serving plate. Remove pan. Pull biscuits apart with 2 forks and serve warm. Makes about 40 appetizers.
Your Time: 6 minutes
Baking Time: 15 minutes


## DILL-BUTTER STRIPS

4 English muffins
⅓ cup soft butter or margarine

2 teaspoons ground dillseed
⅛ teaspoon pepper

Cut muffins in half and place on broiler rack. Toast muffins lightly under preheated broiler 4 inches from heat for about 2 minutes. Combine soft butter, dill, and pepper in a small bowl. Spread butter mixture liberally over muffin halves. Return to broiler and broil about ½ minute longer, or until browned and bubbly. Cut each muffin half into 3 strips. Serve hot. Makes 24 strips.
Your Time: 6 minutes
Broiling Time: 2½ minutes


## BARBECUED FRANKS

¾ cup bottled barbecue sauce
3 tablespoons prepared
   mustard

¼ teaspoon Tabasco
1 pound skinless frankfurters
   (about 8 to 10)

Place barbecue sauce, mustard, and Tabasco in a small bowl and mix until blended. Set sauce aside. Cut each frankfurter into 4 equal parts. Place in a cold skillet over moderately high heat (about 375° F.) and fry frankfurters until lightly browned, about 5 minutes, stirring frequently. Reduce heat to moderate (about 250° F.). Add sauce mixture to frankfurters and cook, stirring frequently, until frankfurters are well coated with sauce. Turn mixture into a serving dish and serve hot with cocktail picks. If necessary, frankfurters may be reheated in top of double boiler over boiling water. Makes 32 to 40 pieces.
Your Time and Cooking Time: 18 minutes

## HOT HAM PUFFS

| | |
|---|---|
| 1  4½-ounce can deviled ham | 1  egg white, stiffly beaten |
| 3  tablespoons dry red wine | 2  tablespoons mayonnaise |
| Few grains pepper | ½ teaspoon prepared mustard |
| Sliced bread | |

Combine ham, wine, and pepper in a small bowl. Cut bread into 36 1½-inch rounds. Spread ham mixture on rounds. Combine egg white, mayonnaise, and mustard in a small bowl. Spread egg white mixture over ham. Place rounds on broiler rack. Broil in preheated broiler about 4 inches from heat about 3 minutes, or until lightly browned. Serve hot. Makes about 3 dozen puffs.
Your Time: 6 minutes
Broiling Time: 3 minutes

## MAYONNAISE PUFFS

| | |
|---|---|
| ¼ cup mayonnaise | ⅛ teaspoon dry mustard |
| ½ cup packaged shredded Cheddar cheese | 1  egg white, at room temperature |
| ¼ teaspoon Worcestershire sauce | Crisp crackers |

Heat oven to 350° F. Combine mayonnaise, cheese, Worcestershire, and mustard in a small bowl. Beat egg white until stiff but not dry. Fold mayonnaise mixture into beaten egg white. Spoon ½ to 1 teaspoon of the mixture onto each cracker. Place on ungreased cookie sheet. Bake about 10 minutes, or until puffy and golden brown. Serve warm. Makes about 1½ to 2 dozen puffs.
Your Time: 12 minutes
Baking Time: 10 minutes

## PARTY ONION APPETIZERS

| | |
|---|---|
| ¼ cup mayonnaise or salad dressing | 2  tablespoons grated Parmesan cheese |
| 24  slices party rye bread | |
| 1  Spanish onion, cut into very thin slices or slivers | |

Spread mayonnaise over slices of rye bread. Arrange slivers of onion over mayonnaise and sprinkle with cheese. Place slices on a cookie sheet. Place in a preheated broiler 4 inches from heat. Broil 1 to 2 minutes, or until cheese and edges of bread are lightly browned. Serve hot. Makes 24 appetizers.
Your Time: 9 minutes
Broiling Time: 1 to 2 minutes

## PARTY SNACK

*¼ cup butter or margarine*  *1 6½-ounce can mixed nuts*
*2 cups packaged seasoned*  *½ teaspoon hickory-smoked*
*croutons*  *salt*
*2 cups fish-shaped crackers*  *¼ teaspoon garlic salt*
*2 cups thin pretzel sticks*

Melt the butter in a large skillet over low heat (about 200° F.) and add croutons, crackers, pretzels, and nuts; toss to combine. Sprinkle with the hickory-smoked salt and garlic salt. Heat over moderate heat (about 250° F.) until thoroughly heated, stirring occasionally. Makes about 7 cups mix.
Your Time: 3 minutes
Cooking Time: 6 minutes

## POPPY-SEED MORSELS

*1 container refrigerated*  *¼ cup packaged shredded*
*crescent dinner rolls*  *Cheddar cheese*
*1 2¼-ounce can deviled ham*  *1 teaspoon poppy seeds*

Heat oven to 375° F. Lightly grease a cookie sheet. Open roll container according to label directions, remove dough, and unroll. Separate the dough into 4 rectangles. Pinch together the diagonal cuts in each rectangle. Spread 2 of the rectangles with deviled ham and sprinkle with the cheese. Top each with the 2 remaining rectangles and pat together lightly. Sprinkle with poppy seeds. Starting at the narrow end of each rectangle, cut into 3 long equal strips. Cut longer side into 6 equal strips to make 18 squares from each rectangle. Place on a lightly greased cookie sheet. Bake about 10 to 12 minutes, or until browned. Serve hot. Makes about 36 appetizers.
Your Time: 10 minutes
Baking Time: 10 to 12 minutes

## SALAMI APPETIZERS

*24  thin slices hard salami     2  tablespoons grated*
*Parmesan cheese*

Arrange salami on broiler rack and sprinkle slices lightly with cheese. Place in a preheated broiler 5 inches from heat. Broil 3 to 4 minutes, or until cheese and edges of salami slices are lightly browned. Serve hot. Makes 24 appetizers.
Your Time: 3 minutes
Broiling Time: 3 to 4 minutes

## BROILED SHRIMP MARINADE

*1  12-ounce package frozen        ½ teaspoon dry mustard*
*shelled and deveined              ½ teaspoon salt*
*shrimp                            ¼ cup olive oil*
*1  clove garlic, peeled and       Juice of ½ lemon*
*finely minced*
*2  tablespoons chopped fresh*
*parsley*

Thaw shrimp so that they separate easily. Mix all other ingredients in a shallow pan. Spread shrimp in marinade; let stand 2 hours. When ready to serve, arrange shrimp on broiler pan. Place in preheated broiler 5 inches from source of heat. Broil 6 to 7 minutes, or until shrimp are pink and tender. Serve hot. Makes 4 to 5 servings.
Your Time: 10 minutes
Marinade Time: 2 hours
Broiling Time: 6 to 7 minutes

## SAUSAGE ROLLS

*1  8-ounce package              1  container refrigerated*
*brown-and-serve sausage         crescent dinner rolls*
*links                        Melted butter or margarine*

Heat oven to 375° F. In a skillet over moderately high heat (about 350° F.) cook sausage links for 2 to 3 minutes, or until brown on all sides. Remove from heat and drain sausages on paper towels. Open roll container according to label directions, remove dough, and unroll. Place pieces of dough together on a floured board to form a

rectangle. Pinch together diagonal cuts in dough. Roll dough with a rolling pin into a 6-x-15-inch rectangle. Cut dough into 3-inch squares. Place a sausage link in center of each square and wrap dough around sausage. Cut each sausage roll crosswise into thirds. Place the sausage rolls on cookie sheet and brush tops with butter. Bake 10 to 15 minutes, or until golden brown. Serve hot. Makes 30 rolls.
Your Time: 9 minutes
Baking Time: 10 to 15 minutes

## CHEESE-DIPPED VIENNA SAUSAGES

*3  4-ounce cans Vienna
   sausages
½ pound process American
   cheese*

*¼ cup dry white wine
1  teaspoon prepared mustard
½ teaspoon Worcestershire
   sauce*

Cut sausages in halves, crosswise; spear each piece with a toothpick. Melt cheese in the top of a double boiler over boiling water. Stir in wine, mustard, and Worcestershire. Serve cheese in a chafing dish set over a candle warmer. Guests dip sausages in it. Makes about 4 dozen appetizers.
Your Time: 4 minutes
Cooking Time: 5 minutes

# CHAPTER

# III

# *Soups*

A repertoire of quick and appetizing soups can rescue you from many mealtime emergencies. Combined with a salad or a sandwich, soups can turn a hurried lunch into something special, and when you start a dinner with a cup of soup with an elusive flavor, you are off to a good start.

The base of all the soups in this chapter is either a canned condensed soup, a ready-to-serve soup, or a dehydrated soup. The condensed soups are usually prepared for serving by adding water, milk, or a combination in a quantity equal to the soup from the can. In some recipes you will note that the recipe calls for a particular soup undiluted. This means you do not add the liquid called for on the can. Ready-to-serve soups are heated just as they come from the can. Dehydrated soups call for an addition of liquid and several minutes of cooking time to allow the dried vegetables and/or pasta to regain the water needed to make them soft. Follow package directions carefully to reconstitute any dehydrated soups.

Soups can serve so many purposes; the hearty ones make a quick, nourishing meal. Served with bread and fruit or cheese they make a classic luncheon or a late supper. The variety of vegetable soups— from asparagus and black bean to tomato and vegetable beef—give such a broad choice of flavors, it's easy to use them to enhance whatever sandwich your leftover roast dictates. Clear soups and cold soups, jellied soups and combination-flavor soups all make tantalizing first courses for a meal.

Once prepared according to certain directions, soups may be flavored or garnished in a number of ways to make them more exciting or more the homemaker's individual creation.

One easy way to make soups more interesting is to combine canned, packaged, or frozen soup flavors. We do this in one of our special favorites, the Soup Medley on page 49. Or the addition of unexpected flavoring like a slice of orange in beef broth, a sprinkling of curry in cream of chicken soup, or a dollop of sherry in green turtle soup will make family and guests admire your creativity.

Garnishes add appeal to the appearance of soup. As always, they should be edible. Choose garnish flavors that will enhance the soup being served. These are a dozen ideas that look and "eat" well:

On jellied madrilène, drop a rounded tablespoon of commercial sour cream; sprinkle chopped chives or dollop a little red caviar on the sour cream.

On black bean soup, float a thin slice of lemon and sprinkle with hard-cooked egg white and yolk, sieved separately.

On onion soup, float a slice of toasted French bread and sprinkle the bread with grated Parmesan cheese.

On cream of celery soup, float a thin slice of cucumber centered with a sprig of parsley.

On cream of asparagus soup, sprinkle circles of sliced ripe olives.

On clear chicken broth, cover the broth with minced watercress leaves.

On any hot cream soup, drop carrot curls just before serving.

On green pea soup, drop a spoonful of unsweetened whipped cream. Sprinkle with grated cheese if desired.

On vichyssoise, sprinkle a liberal portion of freshly snipped chives.

On fish chowders, float seasoned packaged croutons.

On clam chowder, float some finely chopped fresh dillweed.

On mushroom soup, float crisp radish slices.

In this chapter you'll find a section on cold soups, one on hot soups, and a third on hearty soups and chowders that make perfect late-night supper dishes.

Cold soups are particularly welcome in warm weather, although they also provide an appetizing contrast to a hot sandwich meal.

Hot soups, always an easy first course for formal dinners, do equally well on informal occasions. Serve them in pretty pottery cups or mugs, for example, at a buffet party. While your guests are enjoying soup in the living room this way, you can be assembling the rest of the meal.

Many of the hearty soups and chowders, like the Hearty Beef Chowder on page 53 and the Bouillabaisse Americana on page 53, can be used as a main supper dish. Add a crusty loaf of bread and some fruit or cheese for dessert to make a particularly rewarding meal.

# Cold Soups

### CHILLED BLACK-BEAN SOUP

| | |
|---|---|
| 1  10½-ounce can condensed black-bean soup | 1  soup can water |
| 1  10½-ounce can condensed beef consommé | 1½ tablespoons dry sherry |
| | Lemon slices |

In a bowl, combine bean soup, consommé, water, and sherry. Chill soup thoroughly, for about 1 hour. Serve soup garnished with lemon slices. Makes about 3½ cups, or 4 to 5 servings.
Your Time: 5 minutes
Chilling Time: 1 hour

### CHILLED BORSCHT

| | |
|---|---|
| 1  beef bouillon cube | 3  tablespoons commercial sour cream |
| 1  cup boiling water | ¾ teaspoon salt |
| 2  4½-ounce jars strained beets (baby food) | Few grains pepper |
| 2  teaspoons lemon juice | Commercial sour cream |
| Pinch of crushed, dried thyme leaves | Snipped fresh dill |
| 2  teaspoons finely chopped onion | |

Dissolve bouillon cube in boiling water. Place half the bouillon in the container of an electric blender; add strained beets, lemon juice, thyme, onion, the 3 tablespoons sour cream, the salt, and pepper. Cover and blend 30 seconds at high speed. Stir in remaining bouillon. Chill soup until ice-cold, or about 2 hours. Top each serving with a

spoonful of sour cream and some of the dill. Makes 3 to 4 servings.
Your Time: 5 minutes
Chilling Time: 2 hours

## SPICY JELLIED CONSOMMÉ

*1 10½-ounce can condensed
  beef consommé, undiluted
1 tablespoon lemon juice
2 tablespoons chili sauce
Few drops Worcestershire
  sauce*

*Few grains paprika
¼ cup chopped unpeeled
  cucumber
2 tablespoons chopped
  radishes
¼ cup commercial sour cream*

In a bowl blend consommé, lemon juice, chili sauce, Worcestershire, and paprika; fold in cucumber and radishes. Chill 2 to 3 hours, or until set, stirring occasionally. Spoon jellied consommé into soup cups and top each with some of the sour cream. Makes 1⅔ cups, or 2 to 3 servings.
Your Time: 7 minutes
Chilling Time: 2 to 3 hours

## CHILLED CURRY SOUP

*1½ tablespoons cornstarch
1½ teaspoons curry powder
1 teaspoon lemon juice
Few grains of salt
1 13¾-ounce can clear
  chicken broth*

*1½ cups light cream
Toasted coconut or ground
  cinnamon*

Combine cornstarch, curry powder, lemon juice, and salt in a saucepan; stir in chicken broth. Cook over moderately low heat (about 225° F.) until mixture boils. Remove pan from heat. Add cream gradually to the hot mixture, stirring constantly. Cool about 15 minutes at room temperature. Stir. Chill soup thoroughly until ice-cold, at least 3 hours. Serve garnished with coconut or cinnamon. Makes 4 to 5 servings.
Your Time: 5 minutes
Cooking Time: 3 minutes
Chilling Time: 3 hours

## CREAMY MADRILÈNE

2  12½-ounce cans jellied
   consommé madrilène
1  cup commercial sour cream
1  tablespoon lemon juice

2  tablespoons snipped chives
Sliced stuffed green olives or
   watercress

Place madrilène, sour cream, lemon juice, and chives in a bowl. Beat with a rotary beater until mixture is well blended. Chill soup several hours or overnight. Serve garnished with olive slices or watercress. Makes 4 to 6 servings.
Your Time: 2 minutes
Chilling Time: Several hours or overnight

## CHILLED STRAWBERRY-PEACH SOUP

2  chicken bouillon cubes
1¼ cups boiling water
1  10-ounce package frozen
   sliced strawberries, in
   quick-thaw pouch
1  12-ounce package frozen
   sliced peaches, in
   quick-thaw pouch

½ cup unsweetened
   pineapple juice
2  tablespoons sugar
½ cup commercial sour
   cream
2  tablespoons chopped
   toasted almonds

Dissolve bouillon cubes in boiling water in a small bowl. Place strawberries, peaches, and the juice from each package in the container of an electric blender. Cover and blend 30 seconds at high speed. Add bouillon, pineapple juice, and sugar. Cover and blend 10 seconds at low speed. Chill soup until ice-cold, or about 2 hours. Serve soup garnished with a spoonful of sour cream and a sprinkling of nuts. Makes 4 to 6 servings.
Your Time: 5 minutes
Chilling Time: 2 hours

## COLD TOMATO-CREAM SOUP

1  10¾-ounce can condensed
   tomato soup
1  10½-ounce can condensed
   cream of mushroom soup

1½ cups cold milk
½ cup commercial sour
   cream

In a bowl combine soup; beat until smooth. Stir in milk. Chill soup thoroughly, for about 1 hour. Garnish each serving with some of the sour cream. Makes 6 servings.

Your Time: 4 minutes
Chilling Time: 1 hour

## CHILLED TOMATO-WINE SOUP

1 10¾-ounce can condensed
   tomato soup, undiluted
½ cup tomato vegetable juice
½ cup commercial sour cream

¼ cup dry white wine
Sour cream (optional)
Snipped chives (optional)

In a bowl combine all ingredients with a rotary beater or wire whip until thoroughly blended. Chill at least 1 hour before serving time. Top each serving with additional sour cream and chives, if desired. Makes 2½ cups, or 3 to 4 servings.

Your Time: 3 minutes
Chilling Time: 1 hour

## VICHYSSOISE

1 13¾-ounce can clear
   chicken broth
2 10½-ounce cans condensed
   cream of potato soup,
   undiluted
2 cups light cream

1 teaspoon onion powder
Few grains pepper
¾ teaspoon Worcestershire
   sauce
Snipped chives

Place chicken broth and potato soup in the container of an electric blender; cover and blend for 30 seconds at low speed. Stir in cream, onion powder, pepper, and Worcestershire. Mix thoroughly. Chill soup until ice-cold, or about 2 hours. Serve garnished with chives. Makes 6 servings.

Your Time: 3 minutes
Chilling Time: 2 hours

# Hot Soups

### APPLE-BEEF BROTH

1  10½-ounce can condensed        ½ soup can apple juice
   beef broth                              Ground cinnamon

Combine beef broth and apple juice in a small saucepan. Cook over
moderate heat (about 250° F.) until heated through. Serve soup with
a sprinkle of cinnamon on top. Makes 2 to 3 servings.
Your Time: 1 minute
Cooking Time: 5 minutes

### TANGY BEEF SOUP

1  10½-ounce can condensed        2  egg yolks
   beef broth                              2  tablespoons lemon juice
Water                                    Chopped fresh parsley
1  tablespoon dry white wine
   (optional)

Pour soup into saucepan; add 1 soup can water and the wine. Heat to
boiling over moderately low heat (about 225° F.). Beat egg yolks and
lemon juice together with a rotary beater; gradually add ½ cup of the
soup mixture, stirring until blended. Gradually pour egg mixture into
soup in saucepan. Serve at once with a sprinkle of parsley. Makes
about 3 cups, or 3 to 4 servings.
Your Time: 5 minutes
Cooking Time: 5 minutes

### BUTTERED BLACK-BEAN SOUP

1  10½-ounce can condensed        2  tablespoons butter or
   black-bean soup                            margarine
1  soup can water                    Lemon slices
½  teaspoon Worcestershire
   sauce

Combine soup, water, Worcestershire, and butter in a saucepan. Heat
over moderate heat (about 250° F.), stirring frequently, until soup
bubbles. Put a thin lemon slice in each soup dish. Pour hot soup over

lemon to serve. Makes 2½ cups, or 3 to 4 servings.
Your Time: 4 minutes
Heating Time: 5 minutes

## QUICK HOT BORSCHT

*1 16-ounce can julienne beets*
*1 10½-ounce can condensed*
*onion soup*
*½ soup can water*
*½ teaspoon salt*

*⅛ teaspoon pepper*
*Few grains sugar*
*2 tablespoons lemon juice*
*Commercial sour cream*

In a saucepan combine beets with liquid from can, onion soup, water, salt, pepper, and sugar. Place over moderate heat (about 250° F.) and heat until mixture boils. Remove pan from heat and add lemon juice. Serve hot, topped with sour cream. Makes 6 servings.
Your Time: 3 minutes
Heating Time: 10 minutes

## CLAM-CHICKEN BROTH

*2 8-ounce cans minced clams,*
*undrained*
*1 13¾-ounce can chicken*
*broth*

*1 10½-ounce can condensed*
*chicken with rice soup,*
*undiluted*
*Chopped fresh parsley*

Combine clams, chicken broth, and soup in the container of an electric blender. Blend 1 minute on low speed. Pour mixture into a saucepan and heat to serving temperature over low heat (about 200° F.). Serve garnished with parsley. Makes 4 to 6 servings.
Your Time: 4 minutes
Heating Time: 10 minutes

## CONSOMMÉ REINE

*2 13¾-ounce cans chicken*
*broth*
*½ cup cold water*
*¼ cup packaged precooked*
*rice*

*2 egg yolks, beaten*
*¼ cup warm heavy cream*

Put consommé, water, and rice in a saucepan; bring to a boil over moderately high heat (about 300° F.). Turn off heat, cover pan, and let stand 5 minutes. Stir in beaten egg yolks and cream. Reheat slowly. Makes 4 cups of light cream soup, or 5 to 6 servings.
Your Time: 5 minutes
Cooking Time: 18 minutes


## EGG DROP SOUP

1  10½-ounce can condensed          1  egg, slightly beaten
   beef broth                        ⅛ teaspoon salt
1  soup can water

Heat soup and water to boiling over moderately low heat (about 225° F.). Beat egg and salt together in a small bowl until blended. Pour through a fine strainer into the boiling soup, moving strainer back and forth so egg falls into soup in fine threads. Cook 1 minute. Serve at once. Makes 2½ cups soup, or 3 to 4 servings.
Your Time: 3 minutes
Cooking Time: 3 minutes


## GREEK LEMON SOUP

2  10½-ounce cans condensed         2  tablespoons lemon juice
   chicken with rice soup           1  teaspoon finely chopped
2  soup cans water                     watercress or fresh parsley
2  eggs

Combine soup and water in a saucepan. Heat over moderately low heat (about 225° F.) just until it reaches the boiling point, stirring frequently. Beat eggs, lemon juice, and watercress together in a bowl until blended. Slowly add about ⅓ of the hot soup to egg mixture, stirring constantly; pour soup–egg mixture back into remaining soup in saucepan. Heat soup over moderate heat (about 250° F.) 2 or 3 minutes, stirring constantly, until heated through. Serve immediately. Makes 6 servings.
Your Time: 7 minutes
Cooking Time: 5 to 6 minutes

## SOUP MEDLEY

1  10¾-ounce can condensed
   tomato soup
1  11¼-ounce can condensed
   green pea soup
1  10½-ounce can condensed
   beef broth

2½ cups water
¼ cup dry sherry
Commercial sour cream
Shredded Cheddar cheese

Combine soups and water in a saucepan. Heat slowly over moderately low heat (about 225° F.), stirring frequently, until mixture boils. Stir in sherry. Top each serving with a spoonful of sour cream sprinkled with some of the cheese. Makes 8 servings.
Your Time: 3 minutes
Heating Time: 4 minutes

## QUICK ONION SOUP

½ cup butter or margarine
4 cups frozen chopped
   onions (about 1 pound),
   unthawed
3 10½-ounce cans condensed
   beef broth
3 cups water
1 teaspoon Worcestershire
   sauce
1 teaspoon sugar

½ teaspoon salt
Few grains pepper
1 cup dry white wine
8 ½-inch-thick slices French
   bread
1½ tablespoons softened
   butter or margarine
3 tablespoons grated
   Parmesan cheese

Melt the ½ cup butter in a large saucepan or Dutch oven over moderately low heat (about 225° F.). Add onions and cook 20 minutes, or until tender, stirring frequently. Add beef broth, water, Worcestershire, sugar, salt, and pepper. Cover and cook over low heat (about 200° F.) for 30 minutes, stirring occasionally. Add wine and heat 5 minutes. While soup is heating, arrange bread slices on a cookie sheet; spread the 1½ tablespoons butter over slices and sprinkle each with cheese. Place in a preheated broiler about 4 inches from heat for 2 to 3 minutes, or until lightly browned. Serve soup in bowls topped with a slice of bread. Makes about 2 quarts, or 8 servings.
Your Time: 14 minutes
Cooking Time: 57 to 58 minutes

## FLEMISH PEA SOUP

1  11¼-ounce can condensed    2  thin orange slices, cut into
   green pea soup                 quarters
1  soup can water or milk
⅛ to ¼ teaspoon ground
   nutmeg

Combine soup, water, and nutmeg in a saucepan. Place over
moderately low heat (about 225° F.) and cook, stirring occasionally,
until blended and heated. Serve in soup cups garnished with
orange slices. Makes 3 to 4 servings.
Your Time: 3 minutes
Cooking Time: 10 minutes

## PEANUT SOUP

1  10½-ounce can condensed    ½ teaspoon chili powder
   beef broth                 ½ teaspoon salt
1  soup can water            Commercial sour cream
½ cup salted peanuts            (optional)
1  cup light cream

Combine beef broth and water. Place peanuts and 1 cup of the broth
in the container of an electric blender; blend on medium speed (or
set at Purée) for about 1 minute, until peanuts are finely puréed.
Pour peanut mixture into a saucepan; add the rest of the beef broth
and the remaining ingredients. Cook and stir the mixture over
moderate heat (about 250° F.) until soup reaches boiling point.
Reduce heat to low (about 200° F.) and heat 15 minutes, stirring
occasionally. Top each serving with a spoonful of sour cream, if
desired. Makes 3 cups, or 4 servings.
Your Time: 5 minutes
Cooking Time: 15 minutes

## POTATO-CHEESE SOUP

1  cup boiling water          1  10½-ounce can condensed
2  chicken bouillon cubes        cream of celery soup
1  9-ounce package frozen     ⅛ teaspoon paprika
   French fried potatoes      ⅛ teaspoon pepper
2  teaspoons instant minced   2  4-ounce packages shredded
   onion                          Cheddar cheese
3  cups milk                  Fresh parsley (optional)

In a medium-sized saucepan combine hot water, bouillon cubes, and French fried potatoes. Bring mixture to a boil over moderately low heat (about 225° F.) and simmer 5 minutes, or until potatoes are quite soft. Remove from heat. Beat mixture with a rotary beater until smooth. Add onion, milk, celery soup, paprika, and pepper. Cook until mixture just reaches the boiling point. Add cheese and cook, stirring occasionally, until cheese is melted. Garnish servings with parsley, if desired. Makes 4 to 5 servings.
Your Time: 6 minutes
Cooking Time: 20 minutes

## PUMPKIN SOUP

1 16-ounce can pumpkin
1 10½-ounce can condensed
   cream of celery soup
1 chicken bouillon cube
½ cup boiling water
¼ teaspoon instant minced
   onion
2 cups light cream
Celery salt (optional)

Combine pumpkin and soup in a saucepan. In a small bowl dissolve bouillon cube in boiling water. Add minced onion and let stand 2 to 3 minutes. Slowly add bouillon liquid to pumpkin mixture; mix thoroughly. Slowly add light cream, stirring constantly, until thoroughly blended. Cook mixture over moderately low heat (about 225° F.) 8 to 10 minutes, stirring frequently, until soup is heated through. Soup may be served immediately, lightly sprinkled with celery salt, if desired. Or soup may be served chilled, adding a little more light cream if a thinner consistency is desired. Makes 6 servings.
Your Time: 6 minutes
Cooking Time: 8 to 10 minutes ·
Chilling Time: 2 hours

## TOMATO SOUP TROPICAL

3 10¾-ounce cans condensed
   tomato soup
1½ cups milk
1½ cups light cream
¾ cup orange juice
Thin orange slices

Combine tomato soup, milk, and cream in a saucepan. Cook mixture over moderately low heat (about 225° F.) until smooth and blended. Gradually blend in orange juice and heat gently for a few minutes.

Do not boil. Serve in soup cups. Garnish with half slices of orange.
Makes 10 servings.
Your Time: 5 minutes
Cooking Time: 7 minutes

### HOT TURTLE SOUP

2 *20-ounce cans green turtle*    1¼ *cups water*
  *soup with sherry*          *Thin strips lemon peel*
1 *11¼-ounce can condensed*
  *green pea soup*

Combine soups and water in a saucepan; blend thoroughly. Cook
mixture over moderately low heat (about 225° F.) 10 to 12 minutes,
stirring frequently, until heated through. Serve immediately. Garnish
with lemon peel. Makes 10 servings.
Your Time: 6 minutes
Cooking Time: 10 to 12 minutes

### WATERCRESS-CELERY SOUP

1 *10½-ounce can condensed*     ⅛ *teaspoon dried basil leaves*
  *cream of celery soup*         *Few grains pepper*
1 *soup can milk*                *Watercress sprigs (optional)*
¼ *cup coarsely broken*
  *watercress (about ¼*
  *bunch)*

Combine all ingredients in the container of an electric blender. Blend
at high speed 30 seconds. Pour soup into a medium-sized saucepan
and cook over moderate heat (about 250° F.), stirring occasionally,
until soup is heated through. Garnish with sprigs of watercress, if
desired. Makes 3 to 4 servings.
Your Time: 2 minutes
Cooking Time: 5 minutes

# *Hearty Soups and Chowders*

## HEARTY BEEF CHOWDER

1 tablespoon instant minced
   onion
1 24-ounce can beef stew
1 35-ounce can Italian-style
   tomatoes, undrained
1 10½-ounce can condensed
   cream of celery soup

1 12-ounce can
   vacuum-packed
   whole-kernel corn
1 teaspoon seasoned salt

Combine instant minced onion, beef stew, tomatoes, celery soup, corn, and seasoned salt in a large saucepan. Place over moderately high heat (about 275° F.) and heat until mixture comes to a boil, stirring occasionally. Makes 4 main-dish servings.
Your Time: 2 minutes
Heating Time: 10 minutes

## BOUILLABAISSE AMERICANA

2 tablespoons vegetable oil
¾ cup frozen chopped onion
½ cup diced celery
1 cup cold water
1 package instant meat
   marinade
1 16-ounce package frozen
   cod fillets, thawed and cut
   into 1-inch pieces
1 7-ounce can minced clams,
   undrained

1 16-ounce can tomatoes,
   undrained
⅛ teaspoon garlic powder
1 bay leaf
1 5-ounce can shrimp, drained
   and rinsed
4 slices toasted French bread,
   buttered
Grated Parmesan cheese

Heat oil in a large saucepan over moderate heat (about 250° F.). Add onion and celery and cook until tender. Combine the water and instant meat marinade in a small bowl and add the mixture to the

onion and celery in the saucepan. Add cod pieces, minced clams, tomatoes, garlic powder, and bay leaf; stir to blend. Place mixture over moderate heat (about 250° F.) and simmer about 10 minutes, or until cod is easily flaked with a fork. Add shrimp during the last few minutes of cooking. Sprinkle toasted French bread with Parmesan cheese and serve with soup. Makes about 5 cups, or 4 main-dish servings.
Your Time: 11 minutes
Cooking Time: 15 minutes

## CORN CHOWDER

2  *tablespoons butter or margarine*
½  *cup thinly sliced peeled onion*
1  *10½-ounce can condensed cream of celery soup, undiluted*
1  *16-ounce can cream-style corn*
1  *12-ounce can vacuum-packed whole-kernel corn with sweet peppers*

½  *cup light cream*
1  *envelope instant chicken broth mix*
¾  *cup water*
¼  *teaspoon salt*
⅛  *teaspoon ground ginger (optional)*
1  *tablespoon dried parsley flakes*

Melt butter in a saucepan over moderately low heat (about 225° F.). Add onion and cook until crisp-tender, about 3 minutes. Stir in remaining ingredients, except parsley, and heat to serving temperature. Serve garnished with parsley. Makes 3 to 4 main-dish servings.
Your Time: 6 minutes
Cooking Time: 15 minutes

## CURRIED CORN-AND-MUSHROOM CHOWDER

1  *10½-ounce can condensed cream of mushroom soup*
½  *soup can water*
½  *soup can milk*
¼ *to ½ teaspoon curry powder*

1  *teaspoon instant minced onion*
1  *8-ounce can cream-style golden corn*

Prepare cream of mushroom soup in a saucepan, according to directions on the can, using the ½ soup can water and the ½ soup can milk. Blend in remaining ingredients; cook and stir the mixture over moderately low heat (about 225° F.) for 10 minutes. Makes 3½ cups, or 3 to 4 main-dish servings.
Your Time: 5 minutes
Cooking Time: 10 minutes

### CRAB-AVOCADO SOUP

1 10½-ounce can condensed cream of chicken soup, undiluted
1 cup light cream
1 teaspoon instant minced onion
1 teaspoon dried parsley flakes
¼ teaspoon salt
Few grains pepper
1 7½-ounce can Alaska king crab, drained and flaked
1 small avocado, peeled and diced

Combine soup, cream, onion, parsley, salt, and pepper in a saucepan. Add crab and avocado. Place over moderately low heat (about 225° F.) and heat just until mixture bubbles around edges. Makes 2 main-dish servings.
Your Time: 6 minutes
Cooking Time: 10 minutes

### CHUCK-WAGON SOUP

1 29-ounce can meatball stew
1 10¾-ounce can condensed tomato soup
¾ cup water
1 8½-ounce can baby lima beans, undrained
1 teaspoon instant minced onion
¼ teaspoon dried thyme leaves
1 teaspoon white vinegar
1 teaspoon chili powder

Combine all the ingredients in a large saucepan. Blend well and bring mixture to a boil over moderate heat (about 250° F.), stirring occasionally. Simmer 5 minutes. Makes 3 to 4 main-dish servings.
Your Time: 2 minutes
Cooking Time: 7 minutes

## EMERALD FISH CHOWDER

1   9-ounce package frozen                ½ teaspoon celery salt
   creamed spinach                        ⅛ teaspoon dried thyme leaves
2   tablespoons butter or                 Few grains cayenne pepper
   margarine                              1   12-ounce package frozen
¾  cup frozen chopped onion              haddock fillets, thawed
1   10½-ounce can cream of               Commercial sour cream
   potato soup                            Paprika
3   cups milk
¼  teaspoon Worcestershire
   sauce

Cook spinach according to package directions. Melt butter in a large
saucepan over moderately low heat (about 225° F.). Add onion and
cook until tender. Add creamed spinach, potato soup, milk,
Worcestershire, celery salt, thyme, and cayenne pepper. Cut fish
fillets into 1-inch pieces and add to mixture. Place over moderate
heat (about 250° F.) and simmer 10 minutes, until fish is easily
flaked with a fork. Top each serving with a spoonful of sour cream
and sprinkle with paprika. Makes about 6 cups, or 4 to 5 main-dish
servings.
Your Time: 9 minutes
Cooking Time: 30 minutes


## HEARTY PEA SOUP

1   tablespoon butter or                  1   10½-ounce can condensed
   margarine                                 cream of potato soup
2   frankfurters, thinly sliced           1   soup can milk
1   11¼-ounce can condensed            1   soup can water
   green pea soup

Melt butter in a large, heavy saucepan over moderate heat (about
250° F.). Add frankfurter slices and cook until lightly browned. Add
remaining ingredients and cook, stirring occasionally, until soup is
smooth and hot. Makes 2 to 3 main-dish servings.
Your Time: 5 minutes
Cooking Time: 7 minutes

## NEW ORLEANS GUMBO SOUP

1 tablespoon instant minced
    onion
2 tablespoons water
2 tablespoons butter or
    margarine
¼ cup chopped green pepper
1 4-ounce can sliced
    mushrooms, drained
1 10½-ounce can condensed
    chicken gumbo soup

1 10¾-ounce can condensed
    vegetarian vegetable soup
2 soup cans water
1 cup chopped cooked
    chicken
1 4½-ounce can shrimp,
    drained
Few dried tarragon leaves
Melba toast rounds (optional)

Mix minced onion and the 2 tablespoons water in a small bowl and let stand 5 minutes. Melt butter in saucepan over moderately low heat (about 225° F.); add green pepper and mushrooms and cook about 5 minutes, until tender. Add onion, chicken gumbo and vegetable soups, water, chicken, shrimp, and tarragon; heat soup to serving temperature. Serve with Melba toast rounds, if desired. Makes 3 to 4 main-dish servings.

Your Time: 7 minutes
Cooking Time: 15 minutes

## SEAFOOD CHOWDER

1 10¾-ounce can condensed
    tomato soup
1 10½-ounce can condensed
    cream of mushroom soup
1 cup milk
1 16-ounce can white
    potatoes, drained and
    quartered
1 9-ounce can peas, undrained

1 6½-ounce can tuna, drained
1 6½-ounce can crab meat,
    drained
2 tablespoons instant minced
    onion
1 cup light cream
½ cup dry sherry
Salt and pepper

Combine tomato soup, mushroom soup, and milk in a large saucepan. Stir until the mixture is smooth. Add potatoes, peas, tuna, crab meat, and onion. Cook over moderately low heat (about 225° F.), stirring occasionally; until soup is hot. Add cream and sherry; return to heat for 1 minute. Season to taste; serve immediately. Makes 4 main-dish servings.

Your Time: 8 minutes
Cooking Time: 15 minutes

## HEARTY TRIO SOUP

1  10½-ounce can condensed          1  12-ounce can
   cream of mushroom soup             vacuum-packed
1  10½-ounce can condensed             whole-kernel corn
   cream of chicken soup            3  soup cans water
1  10¾-ounce can condensed
   tomato rice soup

Empty soups into a large saucepan. Stir until the soups are
thoroughly combined and smooth. Add corn and water; heat over
moderate heat (about 250° F.), stirring occasionally, until soup
comes to a boil. Makes 4 main-dish servings.
Your Time: 4 minutes
Cooking Time: 15 minutes

## VEGETABLE FRANKFURTER CHOWDER

2  tablespoons butter or            1  10½-ounce can condensed
   margarine                          cream of mushroom soup
4  frankfurters, cut crosswise      2  soup cans milk
   into ½-inch slices               1  8½-ounce can mixed
¼  cup frozen chopped onions           vegetables
1  11¼-ounce can condensed
   green pea soup

Melt butter in a saucepan over moderate heat (about 250° F.). Add
frankfurter slices; cook about 3 minutes, just until they begin to
brown slightly. Add onions and continue to cook and stir until
onions are transparent, 2 to 3 minutes. Remove pan from heat. Stir
in soups; combine thoroughly. Gradually stir in milk and undrained
vegetables. Place over moderate heat (about 250° F.) until soup is
thoroughly heated, stirring constantly. Makes 3 main-dish servings.
Your Time: 18 minutes
Cooking Time: 15 to 16 minutes

# CHAPTER

# IV

# *Main Dishes*

The term *main dish* used to conjure up the image of a cook busy in the kitchen for hours, deep in elaborate preparations for a hearty meal. That's not so any longer. Today's homemaker can fix a main dish for dinner and still have time left to finish a crossword puzzle, take a nap, or rearrange the living room. That's because there are so many possibilities for timesaving main dishes. Think of all the possibilities of things you can do with a package of frozen fish balls: for example, you might warm them in the oven until they are hot and crisp and serve with a bottled tartar sauce for a quick entrée. Or you might add some frozen French fries to the warming tray and serve fish and chips for supper. And if you arrange the same hot fish balls over a bed of spinach, top them with a white sauce made from a mix, sprinkle with cheese, and slide it all under the broiler until it's golden brown, you've turned out a delicious, quick version of Fish Florentine.

These varying and creative ways to use convenience foods are what led us to develop a variety of appetizing timesaving main-dish recipes in our *Redbook* Test Kitchens. Many that you'll find in this chapter involve meat, fish, or poultry. We combine them with a pasta or with vegetables so they are a satisfying meal in themselves. Others are all-in-one main dishes like the Sausage-Corn Escallop on page 118, which makes an ideal family supper. And some, like the Company

Seafood Casserole on page 95, are designed for easy but impressive entertaining.

To help you take advantage of shopping specials, we have divided our main-dish recipes by types of meat or fish. If you know what the current best buy is in your neighborhood market, you can choose a recipe to match. For meatless meals, you'll find the section on cheese and eggs extremely useful.

The frozen, boil-in-a-bag, or partially prepared types of main dishes may intrigue you, but don't sell canned convenience foods short. Here, under fish and chicken, you'll find recipes using canned products; there's even an entire section on making the most of canned meats. Canned foods can be your emergency insurance because they require no special storage. With them on hand, you can always count on turning out reliable meals in a crisis. Make sure, when you shop, to select the ingredients for one or two of these emergency main dishes and keep them ready. In our chapter on Timesaving Menus (starting on page 298) you will find a special section on emergency meals from your pantry shelf as well as one on emergency meals from your freezer.

Usually, in menu planning, you select the main dish first, to use meat, fish, or poultry you may have on hand, to take advantage of what's on sale at the market, or simply to fit what sounds good to you for tonight. We definitely expect you, in using this book, to look for timesaving ideas that allow you to put together a meal in fifteen, twenty, or thirty minutes. But in your concern for time, don't overlook the guidelines that ensure a balanced menu. If, for example, there's a pasta in your main-dish combination, you'll need no other starch. If your main dish is relatively white or pale in color, think of golden carrots or green peas or yellow squash to add color to your plate. If your main dish is soft in texture, choose crisp greens or crunchy bread or snapping-fresh cucumber wedges to add texture to your meal. Timesaving plans shouldn't abandon the time-honored rules for good menu-making.

# Cheese and Eggs

## CARROT-CHEESE PIE

| | |
|---|---|
| 7  slices thinly sliced white bread | 1  4-ounce package shredded Cheddar cheese |
| Softened butter or margarine | 3  eggs |
| 1  16-ounce can julienne carrots, drained | 1½ cups milk |
| | ½ teaspoon seasoned salt |

Heat oven to 325° F. Spread one side of each bread slice with the butter. Cut bread slices in half and line the bottom and sides of a 10-inch pie plate with the bread, buttered sides down. Gently press carrots between paper towels to remove excess liquid. Place carrots and cheese in a layer over bread in pie plate. In a medium-sized bowl combine eggs, milk, and seasoned salt; beat until blended. Pour over carrot-cheese mixture. Bake, uncovered, 55 to 60 minutes, or until a knife inserted in center comes out clean. Serve cut into wedges. Makes 6 to 8 servings.
Your Time: 7 minutes
Cooking Time: 55 to 60 minutes

## CHEESE-NOODLE CASSEROLE

| | |
|---|---|
| 8 ounces medium-wide noodles | 1 tablespoon grated peeled onion |
| Boiling salted water | ¼ teaspoon Tabasco |
| 1 cup large-curd cottage cheese | 2 tablespoons chopped canned pimiento |
| 1 teaspoon Worcestershire sauce | 1 tablespoon chopped green pepper |
| ½ teaspoon salt | ½ cup packaged shredded sharp Cheddar cheese |
| 1 cup commercial sour cream | |

Heat oven to 350° F. Butter a deep 2-quart casserole. Cook noodles in boiling salted water as package directs. Drain. Combine noodles, cottage cheese, Worcestershire, salt, sour cream, onion, Tabasco, pimiento, and green pepper in a large bowl. Turn into prepared casserole. Sprinkle top with Cheddar cheese. Bake, uncovered, 25 to 30 minutes, or until thoroughly heated and top is brown. Makes 8 servings.
Your Time: 5 minutes
Cooking Time: 33 to 38 minutes

## CHEDDAR CHEESE FONDUE

| | |
|---|---|
| 1 clove garlic, peeled and cut in half | 2 cups coarsely shredded Swiss cheese (about ½ pound) |
| ½ cup water | |
| 1 cup dairy half-and-half | 2¾ cups packaged shredded Cheddar cheese |
| 2 packages white sauce mix (each making 1 cup) | ½ cup dry white wine |
| 2 teaspoons prepared mustard | 1 loaf French bread, cut into bite-size pieces |

Rub inside of a saucepan or electric skillet with cut garlic clove. Place water and half-and-half in the pan. Mix in white sauce mix and prepare according to package directions over moderately low heat (about 225° F.). Blend in mustard. Gradually add cheeses and stir until blended. Continue cooking, stirring constantly, until cheeses are melted. Gradually add enough wine to give a good consistency for dipping bread. Fondue may be served in a chafing dish at the table. If an electric skillet is used, set heating control at Warm for serving. Add a little additional wine to fondue if it thickens as it stands. Makes 6 servings.
Your Time: 17 minutes
Cooking Time: 12 minutes

## BAKED CHEESE FONDUE

| | |
|---|---|
| 1  loaf brown-and-serve       French bread | ¼  cup pasteurized process      cheese spread |
| 2  tablespoons anchovy paste | |

### SAUCE

| | |
|---|---|
| 1  10½-ounce can condensed      cream of mushroom soup,      undiluted | ¼  cup pasteurized process      cheese spread |
| | 2  tomatoes, sliced |

Heat oven to 350° F. Slash unbaked French bread lengthwise almost to bottom crust. Slice in fifths crosswise, again almost to bottom crust. Spread anchovy paste and the ¼ cup cheese spread between cuts. Bake bread, uncovered, on ungreased cookie sheet 12 minutes. While bread is baking, combine undiluted soup and the ¼ cup cheese spread in a saucepan. Heat over moderately low heat (about 225° F.), stirring until smooth. Break bread into serving-size pieces and top each with some of the hot sauce. Garnish with tomato slices. Makes 3 to 4 servings.
Your Time: 10 minutes
Baking Time: 12 minutes

## SWISS CHEESE FONDUE

1 *package cheese sauce mix*     1 *loaf French bread, broken*
   *(makes 1 cup)*             *into chunks*
¾ *cup dry white wine*
1 *cup coarsely shredded Swiss*
   *cheese*

Place cheese sauce mix in a medium-sized saucepan. Slowly add wine, stirring constantly until blended. Cook over moderate heat (about 250° F.), stirring constantly, until mixture thickens and comes to a boil. Add Swiss cheese and cook just until melted. Serve in a small fondue pot with chunks of French bread for dipping. Makes 1½ cups; 3 to 4 servings.
Your Time: 10 minutes
Cooking Time: 10 minutes

## EASY CHEESE SOUFFLÉ

1 *10¾-ounce can condensed*     6 *eggs, separated, at room*
   *Cheddar cheese soup,*           *temperature*
   *undiluted*
1 *4-ounce package shredded*
   *Cheddar cheese*

Heat oven to 400° F. Grease a 2½-quart soufflé dish with unsalted shortening. Place soup and cheese in a small saucepan over moderately low heat (about 225° F.); heat until cheese is melted, stirring constantly. Remove from heat. Beat egg whites with an electric mixer until stiff but not dry. Beat egg yolks until thick and lemon-colored; gradually stir into soup mixture. Fold soup mixture into beaten egg whites. Pour into prepared soufflé dish. Bake, uncovered, 30 to 35 minutes, or until golden brown. Makes 4 to 6 servings.
Your Time: 14 minutes
Baking Time: 30 to 35 minutes

## QUICK QUICHE LORRAINE

1 *container refrigerated*
   *crescent dinner rolls (8*
   *rolls)*
2 *eggs*
1 *13-fluid-ounce can*
   *evaporated milk, undiluted*
¾ *teaspoon salt*
¾ *teaspoon Worcestershire*
   *sauce*

¾ *cup shredded Swiss cheese*
¾ *cup shredded Gruyère*
   *cheese*
3 *tablespoons jarred imitation*
   *bacon bits*
⅔ *cup canned French-fried*
   *onion rings*

Heat oven to 325° F. Open roll container according to label directions. Unroll dough and separate into 4 rectangular pieces; roll lightly with a rolling pin to flatten slightly. Place dough pieces on the bottom and sides of an ungreased shallow 2-quart baking dish (11¾-x-7½-x-1¾-inches), pressing pieces together to form a crust. Bake 15 minutes. Combine eggs, evaporated milk, salt, and Worcestershire sauce in a medium-sized bowl. Stir in cheeses and bacon bits. Pour egg mixture into crust. Bake, uncovered, 50 minutes, or until set. Sprinkle with onion rings and bake 5 minutes longer. Let stand about 5 minutes before cutting into squares. Makes 6 to 8 servings as a luncheon entrée.
Your Time: 9 minutes
Baking Time: 70 minutes

## SCRAMBLED EGGS AND HAM TRIANGLES

1 *container refrigerated*
   *crescent dinner rolls (8*
   *rolls)*
2 *tablespoons butter or*
   *margarine*
8 *eggs*

½ *cup milk*
1 *teaspoon salt*
*Few grains pepper*
1 *4½-ounce can deviled ham*
½ *cup packaged shredded*
   *Cheddar cheese*

Heat oven to 375° F. Open dinner roll container according to label directions; unroll dough and separate into 8 triangles. Place on ungreased cookie sheet and bake 10 to 12 minutes, or until golden brown. While rolls are baking, prepare scrambled eggs. Melt butter in skillet over moderately low heat (about 225° F.). Beat eggs, milk, salt, and pepper together slightly in a bowl. Pour into skillet and cook, lifting eggs with a spoon from the bottom and sides as the mixture thickens. Cook until mixture is thickened, but still moist.

Spread deviled ham on baked triangles. Spoon scrambled eggs over ham and sprinkle with cheese. Serve immediately. Makes 4 servings.
Your Time: 17 minutes
Cooking Time: 12 to 14 minutes

## EGGS FLORENTINE

2 10-ounce packages frozen
    chopped spinach
1 tablespoon vegetable oil
¼ cup frozen chopped onion
1 8-ounce can tomato sauce
    with cheese

8 eggs
Grated Parmesan cheese
Salt and pepper

Cook spinach according to package directions. Drain thoroughly. Heat oil in a 10-inch skillet over moderate heat (about 250° F.); add onions and cook until tender. Remove skillet from heat; add tomato sauce. Spoon spinach into 4 mounds in skillet; break eggs one at a time and pour into skillet around spinach. Sprinkle with Parmesan cheese, salt, and pepper. Cover and cook over moderately low heat (about 225° F.) 5 to 10 minutes, or until eggs are cooked to desired doneness. Makes 4 to 6 servings.
Your Time: 10 minutes
Cooking Time: 25 to 30 minutes

## BAKED EGGS SUPREME

1 4½-ounce can deviled ham
¼ cup packaged corn flake
    crumbs
4 large tomato slices, ½ inch
    thick

4 to 8 eggs
Salt and pepper
Buttered toast slices, cut in
    half diagonally

Heat oven to 350° F. Combine deviled ham and corn flake crumbs in a small bowl; spread on tomato slices. Lightly butter 4 individual shallow baking dishes or ramekins. Break 1 or 2 eggs into each dish. Sprinkle eggs lightly with salt and pepper. Cut each tomato slice in half crosswise; arrange 2 pieces on edge on opposite sides in each of the baking dishes. Bake 20 minutes, or until the eggs are the desired degree of doneness. Serve with toast points. Makes 4 servings.
Your Time: 7 minutes
Baking Time: 20 minutes

# *Chicken*
# *Fresh or Frozen*

## CHICKEN WITH BRANDIED MUSHROOM SAUCE

1  *2½-to-3-pound broiler-fryer*      ⅓ *cup brandy*
    *chicken, cut up*
1  *10½-ounce can condensed*
    *cream of mushroom soup,*
    *undiluted*

Heat oven to 375° F. Wash and pat chicken pieces dry and place in an ungreased shallow 2-quart baking dish. Beat soup with a fork until smooth; spread over chicken. Cover and bake 45 minutes. Stir brandy into gravy and bake, uncovered, 20 to 25 minutes, or until chicken is fork-tender. Makes 4 servings.
Your Time: 4 minutes
Baking Time: 65 to 70 minutes

## BAKED CHICKEN ITALIENNE

1  *8-ounce can tomato sauce*    ⅓ *cup grated Parmesan*
¼ *teaspoon garlic salt*          *cheese*
¼ *teaspoon salt*              1  *2½-pound broiler-fryer*
⅛ *teaspoon pepper*               *chicken, cut up*
1¼ *cups packaged instant*     ¼ *cup butter or margarine*
    *whipped potato flakes*

Heat oven to 400° F. In a small bowl combine tomato sauce, garlic salt, salt, and pepper; blend well. In another small bowl combine potato flakes and Parmesan cheese. Wash and pat chicken pieces dry. Dip chicken pieces in tomato sauce mixture, then roll in the potato-cheese mixture to coat well. Set aside. Place butter in a 12¾-x-9-x-2-inch baking pan and place in oven until butter melts, about 4 to 5 minutes. Arrange chicken in baking dish, skin side up. Bake, uncovered, about 1 hour, or until chicken is fork-tender. Makes 3 to 4 servings.
Your Time: 4 minutes
Baking Time: 65 minutes

## CHICKEN BREASTS PARMESAN

½ cup packaged pancake mix
¼ teaspoon salt
⅛ teaspoon pepper
4 whole chicken breasts, split (about 3½ pounds)
1 10½-ounce can condensed cream of mushroom soup, undiluted

⅓ cup dry onion soup mix
⅓ cup milk
½ cup grated Parmesan cheese
Parsley sprigs

Heat oven to 375° F. In a medium-sized bowl combine pancake mix, salt, and pepper. Wash and pat chicken dry. Roll chicken breasts in the pancake mix mixture a few at a time to coat well. Place chicken in an ungreased shallow 3-quart baking dish, overlapping slightly if necessary. Combine mushroom soup, onion soup mix, and milk in a small bowl and blend until smooth. Pour over chicken. Cover dish tightly with aluminum foil. Bake 1 hour. Remove foil and sprinkle cheese on top. Bake uncovered 15 minutes longer. Garnish with parsley. Makes 4 to 6 servings.
Your Time: 8 minutes
Baking Time: 1 hour 15 minutes

## QUICK CHICKEN CACCIATORE

2 10-ounce packages frozen, fully cooked fried chicken halves
1 8-ounce package spaghetti dinner
1 8-ounce can tomato sauce

Water
½ cup chopped green pepper
1 4-ounce can sliced mushrooms, drained
Parmesan cheese

Heat oven to 425° F. Bake chicken according to package directions. Prepare spaghetti sauce as directed on package, using tomato sauce and water; add green pepper. Simmer sauce for 20 minutes over moderately low heat (about 225° F.). Add mushrooms and heat 5 minutes. While sauce is cooking, prepare spaghetti from package according to package directions. Serve chicken over cooked spaghetti; top with sauce and Parmesan cheese. Makes 4 servings.
Your Time: 8 minutes
Cooking Time: 30 minutes

## CHEDDAR-BAKED CHICKEN

1  *2½-pound broiler-fryer*          2  *tablespoons chopped*
   *chicken, cut up*                    *canned pimiento*
2  *tablespoons melted butter*       ½  *teaspoon chili powder*
   *or margarine*                     1½ *teaspoons dried parsley*
1  *10¾-ounce can condensed*            *flakes*
   *Cheddar cheese soup,*
   *undiluted*

Heat oven to 400° F. Wash and pat chicken dry. Arrange chicken
pieces in a single layer, skin side down, in an ungreased shallow
2-quart baking dish. Pour butter over chicken. Bake, uncovered, 20
minutes. Turn chicken skin side up. Bake 20 minutes longer. In a
small bowl combine cheese soup, pimiento, and chili powder. Pour
mixture over chicken. Sprinkle with parsley. Bake 20 minutes longer,
until chicken is fork-tender. Makes 4 servings.
Your Time: 9 minutes
Baking Time: 1 hour

## BAKED CHICKEN IN CHEESE SAUCE

2  *whole chicken breasts, split*     ½  *cup light cream*
2  *tablespoons flour*                ¼  *cup dry white wine*
¼  *cup shortening*                    ½  *teaspoon dried rosemary*
1  *10¾-ounce can condensed*             *leaves*
   *Cheddar cheese soup,*            1  *9-ounce package frozen*
   *undiluted*                          *artichoke hearts, thawed*

Heat oven to 350° F. Wash and pat chicken dry. Coat chicken with
flour. Melt shortening in skillet over moderate heat (about 250° F.);
brown chicken lightly on all sides. Place chicken in an ungreased
shallow 3-quart baking dish. Blend cheese soup, cream, wine, and
rosemary in a bowl; pour mixture over chicken. Cover dish and bake
30 minutes. Remove cover and place artichokes over chicken. Bake,
uncovered, 15 minutes, or until chicken is fork-tender. Makes 4
servings.
Your Time: 10 minutes
Cooking Time: 55 minutes

## QUICK COQ AU VIN

2 packages mushroom gravy
   mix (each making 1 cup)
2 cups water
1 cup dry red wine
1 3-ounce can sliced broiled
   mushrooms; undrained
1 16-ounce can small whole
   onions, drained

⅛ teaspoon dried thyme leaves
2 10-ounce packages frozen,
   fully cooked fried chicken
   halves, thawed
Dried parsley flakes

Place mushroom gravy mixes in a large saucepan; gradually stir in water. Add wine, mushrooms, onions, and thyme leaves; stir to blend thoroughly. Arrange chicken pieces in mixture. Place over moderate heat (about 250° F.) and simmer, covered, about 20 minutes, or until chicken is heated and sauce is thickened. Sprinkle chicken with parsley flakes. Makes 4 servings.
Your Time: 5 minutes
Cooking Time: 20 minutes

## EASY CHICKEN CASSEROLE

1 cup uncooked rice
1 10½-ounce can condensed
   cream of mushroom
   soup, undiluted
1 envelope onion soup mix

1½ soup cans milk
1 3-to-3½-pound
   broiler-fryer chicken, cut
   up
Salt and pepper

Heat oven to 250° F. Mix together rice, soups, and milk in a shallow 3-quart casserole. Wash and pat chicken pieces dry. Place chicken pieces, skin side down, over rice; sprinkle lightly with salt and pepper. Bake casserole, uncovered, for 3 hours. Turn chicken after about 1½ hours of cooking. Makes 4 servings.
Your Time: 3 minutes
Baking Time: 3 hours

## HONEY-BAKED CHICKEN AND SWEET POTATOES

*1  3-pound broiler-fryer          ¼ teaspoon dried tarragon*
*   chicken, quartered               leaves*
*Salt and pepper to taste        1  16-ounce can sweet*
*¼ cup honey                        potatoes, drained*
*¼ cup bottled clear French*
*   dressing*

Heat oven to 375° F. Lightly butter a shallow rectangular 3-quart baking dish. Wash and pat chicken dry. Sprinkle chicken with salt and pepper to taste. Place chicken pieces skin side down in the prepared baking dish. Mix together honey, French dressing, and tarragon in a small bowl; brush chicken lightly with some of the mixture. Bake chicken, uncovered, 30 minutes, brushing occasionally with the honey mixture. Turn chicken skin side up and brush lightly with honey mixture; bake 10 minutes longer. Add sweet potatoes and bake 10 to 15 minutes longer, brushing chicken and potatoes occasionally with remaining honey mixture. Serve chicken and potatoes with pan juices. Makes 4 servings.
Your Time: 14 minutes
Baking Time: 50 to 55 minutes

## HONEYED CHICKEN

*2  tablespoons butter or       1  teaspoon salt*
*   margarine                    1  teaspoon curry powder*
*½ cup honey                     1  3-pound broiler-fryer*
*¼ cup prepared mustard            chicken, cut up*

Heat oven to 375° F. Melt butter in a shallow 3-quart baking dish over moderately low heat (about 225° F.). Stir in honey, mustard, salt, and curry. Wash and pat chicken dry. Roll chicken pieces in honey mixture and arrange in a single layer in the baking dish. Bake, uncovered, 1 hour, or until fork-tender. Makes 4 or 5 servings.
Your Time: 7 minutes
Baking Time: 1 hour

## CHICKEN MARENGO

| | |
|---|---|
| 1 3-pound broiler-fryer chicken, cut up | 1 8-ounce can boiled onions, drained |
| Salt and pepper | 1 4-ounce can sliced mushrooms, drained |
| 3 tablespoons vegetable oil | Cooked noodles (optional) |
| 1 15½-ounce can spaghetti sauce with meat | |

Wash and pat chicken pieces dry. Sprinkle with salt and pepper. Heat oil in a skillet over moderately high heat (about 350° F.). Add chicken pieces and brown well on all sides. Arrange chicken pieces in an ungreased shallow 3-quart casserole. Pour spaghetti sauce over chicken. Cover with aluminum foil. Bake in a 375° F. oven 45 minutes. Add onions and mushrooms to casserole and bake, uncovered, another 15 minutes. Serve with cooked noodles, if desired. Makes 4 to 6 servings.
Your Time: 14 minutes
Baking Time: 1 hour

## ITALIAN-STYLE OVEN-BAKED CHICKEN

| | |
|---|---|
| 1 3-to-3½-pound broiler-fryer chicken, cut up for frying | ½ teaspoon salt |
| | Few grains pepper |
| 1 cup prepared buttermilk biscuit mix | ½ cup evaporated milk, undiluted |
| ¼ cup grated Parmesan cheese | ½ cup melted butter or margarine |
| 1 teaspoon paprika | |
| ½ teaspoon celery salt | |

Heat oven to 400° F. Wash and pat chicken pieces dry. Combine biscuit mix, cheese, paprika, celery salt, salt, and pepper in a small bowl. First dip chicken in evaporated milk and then roll in dry mixture. Place chicken, skin side up, in an ungreased large, shallow baking pan. Sprinkle chicken with the leftover dry mixture. Pour melted butter over chicken. Bake, uncovered, 55 to 60 minutes, or until chicken is fork-tender. Makes 4 to 5 servings.
Your Time: 4 minutes
Baking Time: 55 to 60 minutes

## OVEN-FRIED CHICKEN

| | |
|---|---|
| 1 cup prepared buttermilk biscuit mix | 1 3-to-3½-pound broiler-fryer chicken, cut up for frying |
| 1½ teaspoons salt | ½ cup evaporated milk, undiluted |
| 1 teaspoon paprika | |
| 1½ teaspoons poultry seasoning | ½ cup melted butter or margarine |
| ½ cup finely chopped pecans or walnuts | |

Heat oven to 400° F. Combine biscuit mix, salt, paprika, poultry seasoning, and finely chopped nuts in a medium-sized bowl. Wash and pat chicken pieces dry. Dip chicken first in evaporated milk and then in dry ingredients. Place chicken in a single layer in an ungreased shallow pan, skin side up. Pour butter over chicken. Bake, uncovered, 55 to 60 minutes, or until chicken is fork-tender. Makes 4 to 5 servings.
Your Time: 8 minutes
Baking Time: 55 to 60 minutes

## CRISP ONION-CHICKEN BAKE

| | |
|---|---|
| ½ cup bottled Italian salad dressing | 1 envelope onion soup mix |
| ¼ cup water | 1 2½-pound broiler-fryer chicken, cut up |

Heat oven to 375° F. In a shallow roasting pan combine salad dressing, water, and onion soup mix and blend well. Wash and pat chicken pieces dry. Add chicken to pan and turn each piece to coat well. Bake, uncovered, 1 hour, or until chicken is tender and golden brown. Makes 3 to 4 servings.
Your Time: 3 minutes
Baking Time: 1 hour

## SOUTHERN BAKED CHICKEN

| | |
|---|---|
| 1 10½-ounce can condensed cream of chicken soup, undiluted | 1 cup packaged corn bread stuffing |
| ¼ cup milk | 2 tablespoons melted butter or margarine |
| 1 2½-pound broiler-fryer chicken, cut up | ½ cup milk |

Heat oven to 400° F. Combine ⅓ cup of the undiluted soup and the ¼ cup milk in a small bowl. Wash and pat chicken dry. Dip chicken pieces in soup mixture and roll in dry stuffing to coat. Place in a single layer in an ungreased large shallow baking dish. Pour butter over chicken. Bake, uncovered, 1 hour. Combine the remaining soup and the ½ cup milk in a saucepan. Place over moderately low heat (about 225° F.) and cook, stirring occasionally, until heated. Serve as a gravy over chicken. Makes 3 to 4 servings.
Your Time: 10 minutes
Baking Time: 1 hour

## SEASONED BAKED CHICKEN

*½ cup lemon juice*
*1 cup bottled Italian salad dressing*
*2 2½-pound broiler-fryer chickens, quartered*

*1½ cups packaged corn flake crumbs*
*1½ teaspoons salt*
*½ cup melted butter or margarine*

Mix lemon juice and salad dressing in a small bowl. Wash and pat chicken dry. Place chicken in a double plastic bag; add dressing mixture and chill about 4 hours, turning bag occasionally. Heat oven to 350° F. Mix corn flake crumbs and salt on a piece of waxed paper. Coat chicken pieces with crumb mixture and place on a cookie sheet covered with aluminum foil. Pour melted butter over chicken. Bake, uncovered, 1 hour and 15 minutes, or until chicken is fork-tender. Makes 8 servings.
Your Time: 10 minutes
Chilling Time: 4 hours
Baking Time: 1 hour 15 minutes

## CHICKEN AND ZUCCHINI CASSEROLE

*3 medium-sized zucchini (about 1 pound), washed*
*2½ to 3 pounds chicken pieces*
*Salt and pepper to taste*
*⅔ cup bottled barbecue sauce*

*1 teaspoon dried oregano leaves*
*1 tablespoon lemon juice*
*1 teaspoon instant minced onion*

Heat oven to 400° F. Slice unpeeled zucchini crosswise into slices about ¼ inch thick. Arrange slices along bottom of an ungreased

shallow 3-quart baking dish. Wash and pat chicken dry. Sprinkle chicken with salt and pepper. Place chicken skin side up over zucchini. In a small bowl combine remaining ingredients and pour evenly over chicken. Bake, uncovered, for 30 minutes. Baste chicken with sauce from the bottom of the dish and return to oven for an additional 30 minutes, or until chicken is tender. Makes 4 servings.
Your Time: 8 minutes
Baking Time: 1 hour

## Chicken
## Canned

### CONTINENTAL CHICKEN CASSEROLE

1 14-ounce package noodles with sour-cream-and-cheese-sauce mix
1 5-ounce can boned chicken, diced
1 4-ounce can mushroom stems and pieces, drained
⅓ cup milk
¼ teaspoon salt
Few grains pepper
¼ cup sliced blanched almonds

Heat oven to 350° F. Cook noodles as directed on package. Butter a deep 1-quart casserole. Add the amount of milk and butter or margarine called for on noodle package. Mix chicken, mushrooms, the ⅓ cup milk, salt, and pepper in a bowl; fold into noodles. Pour mixture into prepared casserole. Sprinkle with almonds. Bake, uncovered, 25 to 30 minutes, or until mixture is bubbling at the sides. Makes 4 to 6 servings.
Your Time: 11 minutes
Cooking and Baking Time: 50 to 55 minutes

### QUICK CHICKEN TETRAZZINI

8 ounces thin spaghetti
3 5-ounce cans boned chicken, cubed
1 4-ounce can sliced mushrooms, undrained
1 envelope cheese sauce mix (makes 1 cup)
1 envelope chicken gravy mix (makes 1 cup)
2 cups milk
2 tablespoons dry sherry (optional)
3 tablespoons grated Parmesan cheese

Cook spaghetti according to package directions; drain. Heat oven to 400° F. Grease a deep 2-quart casserole with unsalted shortening. Combine chicken, mushrooms, cheese sauce mix, chicken gravy mix, milk, and sherry in a medium-sized bowl; fold into spaghetti. Pour into prepared casserole. Sprinkle with grated Parmesan cheese. Cover and bake 30 to 35 minutes, or until mixture bubbles at sides. Makes 6 servings.

Your Time: 9 minutes

Cooking and Baking Time: 32 to 37 minutes

## JAPANESE CHICKEN CASSEROLE

1  10-ounce package frozen
    Japanese-style vegetables
2⅔ cups cooked packaged
    precooked rice
2  4¾-ounce cans chicken
    spread

¼ cup sliced water chestnuts
⅓ cup thinly sliced celery
2  tablespoons soy sauce
Soy sauce (optional)

Heat oven to 350° F. Cook vegetables according to package directions. In a bowl combine 3 tablespoons of the sauce from the vegetables with the rice. Combine chicken spread, water chestnuts, and celery in another small bowl. In an ungreased deep 1½-quart casserole layer half the rice, then the chicken spread mixture, then the remaining rice, and top with the vegetables. Sprinkle soy sauce over vegetables. Cover and bake 30 minutes. Serve with additional soy sauce if desired. Makes 4 to 6 servings.

Your Time: 12 minutes

Cooking and Baking Time: 45 minutes

## CHICKEN-RICE CASSEROLE

1  8-ounce package
    chicken-flavored rice and
    vermicelli mix
1  teaspoon dried basil leaves
2  tablespoons butter or
    margarine
½ cup packaged frozen
    chopped onion

2  4-ounce cans sliced
    mushrooms, drained
1  5-ounce can water
    chestnuts, drained and
    sliced
2  4¾-ounce cans chicken
    spread

Heat oven to 400° F. Grease a deep 1½-quart casserole with unsalted shortening. Prepare rice mix according to package directions. Add ½ teaspoon of the basil to rice and blend well. Melt butter in a skillet over moderately low heat (about 225° F.). Add onion and mushrooms and cook until tender, or about 5 minutes. Remove skillet from heat. In a small bowl combine water chestnuts, chicken spread, and the remaining ½ teaspoon basil. Stir in onion-mushroom mixture and blend well. Place half the rice mixture in the prepared casserole. Spread chicken mixture over rice mixture. Top with remaining rice. Bake 15 minutes, or until heated through. Makes 4 servings.
Your Time: 10 minutes
Cooking and Baking Time: 40 minutes

# *Chicken Livers*

## BARBECUED CHICKEN LIVERS

3 tablespoons butter or margarine
1 pound chicken livers
½ cup packaged frozen chopped onion
1 8-ounce can tomato sauce with mushrooms
3 tablespoons creamy peanut butter
1 tablespoon white vinegar
1 teaspoon Worcestershire sauce
4 slices toast

Melt butter in a large skillet over moderate heat (about 250° F.). Add chicken livers and onion and cook about 5 minutes, or until onion is tender and chicken livers are no longer pink inside. In a small bowl combine tomato sauce and peanut butter and blend well. Pour over chicken livers. Add vinegar and Worcestershire and blend well. Heat thoroughly. Serve over toast slices. Makes 4 servings.
Your Time: 6 minutes
Cooking Time: 10 minutes

## CRUSTED CHICKEN LIVERS

1 10½-ounce can mushroom
  gravy
2 tablespoons dry sherry
1 cup prepared buttermilk
  biscuit mix

½ teaspoon dried dillweed
1 pound chicken livers
1 egg, well beaten
5 tablespoons butter or
  margarine

Pour mushroom gravy into a small saucepan and blend in the sherry. Bring to a boil over moderate heat (about 250° F.), stirring frequently. Reduce heat to moderately low (about 225° F.) and simmer 5 minutes. Meanwhile, combine biscuit mix and dillweed in a medium-sized bowl. Dip chicken livers in the beaten egg, then into the biscuit mixture, coating all sides well. Set aside on a plate. Melt the 5 tablespoons butter in a large skillet over moderately low heat (about 225° F.). Increase heat to moderately high (about 325° F.); add chicken livers and cook, uncovered, 10 to 15 minutes, or until tender and golden brown, turning once. Serve with the gravy. Makes 4 servings.
Your Time: 9 minutes
Cooking Time: 15 to 20 minutes

## CHICKEN LIVERS TARRAGON

2 tablespoons butter or
  margarine
⅓ cup finely chopped onion,
  fresh or frozen
¼ cup finely chopped celery
2 8-ounce packages frozen
  chicken livers, thawed
1 10½-ounce can mushroom
  gravy

2 tablespoons dry white wine
½ teaspoon dried tarragon
  leaves
¼ teaspoon salt
Few grains pepper
3 cups hot cooked rice

Melt butter in a skillet over moderate heat (about 250° F.); add onion and celery and cook until tender. Add chicken livers and cook about 5 minutes, until lightly browned. Add mushroom gravy, wine, tarragon, salt, and pepper. Cook until mixture is thoroughly heated, stirring occasionally. Serve over rice. Makes 4 servings.
Your Time: 6 minutes
Cooking Time: 8 minutes

## CHICKEN LIVER SAUTÉ

*½ cup butter or margarine*　　*¼ teaspoon Tabasco*
*½ cup frozen chopped onion*　*¼ teaspoon dried basil leaves*
*¼ teaspoon garlic powder*　　*1 tablespoon flour*
*1½ pounds chicken livers*　　*½ cup beer*
*2 4-ounce cans sliced*　　　*2 cups packaged precooked*
  *mushrooms, drained*　　　　*rice*

Melt butter in skillet over moderate heat (about 250° F.); add onion
and cook until tender. Add garlic powder, chicken livers,
mushrooms, Tabasco, and basil; cook until chicken livers are lightly
browned. Stir in flour. Gradually add beer; cook and stir until sauce
is thickened. Prepare rice according to package directions. Mound
rice in center of serving plate and spoon chicken livers around it.
Makes 6 servings.
Your Time: 9 minutes
Cooking Time: 15 minutes

# Fish
## *Fresh or Frozen*

## CHEESE FISH BAKE

*1 pound frozen fish fillets,*　　*1 tablespoon instant minced*
  *flounder, or any white*　　　　*onion*
  *fish, thawed*　　　　　　　*1 teaspoon dried parsley*
*1 10¾-ounce can condensed*　*Pinch of ground marjoram*
  *Cheddar cheese soup,*
  *undiluted*

Heat oven to 400° F. Grease a shallow 1½-quart baking dish with
unsalted shortening. Arrange fish in prepared baking dish. Blend
soup, onion, parsley, and marjoram together. Pour over fish. Bake,
uncovered, 30 minutes. Makes 4 servings.
Your Time: 4½ minutes
Baking Time: 30 minutes

## FILLETS BAKED WITH SOUR CREAM

1½ pounds fresh or frozen
   fish fillets, thawed
¾ cup commercial sour
   cream
2 tablespoons grated
   Parmesan cheese
1 teaspoon paprika
¼ teaspoon dried tarragon
   leaves

½ teaspoon salt
1 tablespoon fine dry bread
   crumbs
1 tablespoon butter or
   margarine
Lemon wedges

Heat oven to 350° F. Arrange fish fillets on an ungreased ovenproof platter or broiler pan. Mix sour cream, Parmesan cheese, paprika, tarragon, and salt in a small bowl; spread over fish. Sprinkle with bread crumbs and dot with butter. Bake, uncovered, 15 to 20 minutes, or until fish flakes easily. Serve with lemon wedges. Makes 4 servings.

Your Time: 6 minutes
Baking Time: 15 to 20 minutes

## FISH-STICK GARDEN MEDLEY

1 10-ounce package frozen
   mixed vegetables, slightly
   thawed
1 teaspoon salt
¼ teaspoon pepper

2 tablespoons butter or
   margarine
1 8-ounce can tomato sauce
1 8-ounce package frozen fish
   sticks (10), thawed

Heat oven to 350° F. Spoon vegetables into bottom of an ungreased shallow 1½-quart baking dish. Sprinkle vegetables with salt and pepper; dot with butter. Pour tomato sauce over vegetables. Arrange fish sticks over vegetables. Bake, uncovered, 40 minutes. Makes 4 servings.

Your Time: 4 minutes
Baking Time: 40 minutes

## FISH STICKS BAKED WITH VEGETABLES

| | |
|---|---|
| 1  *9-ounce package frozen French-style green beans* | 1  *8-ounce package frozen fish sticks (10)* |
| 1  *16-ounce can chop suey, drained* | 1  *tablespoon melted butter or margarine* |
| 1  *10½-ounce can condensed cream of mushroom soup, undiluted* | 1  *teaspoon soy sauce* |

Heat oven to 375° F. Prepare beans according to package directions but cook only 4 minutes after bringing to a boil; drain. Combine beans, chop suey, and cream of mushroom soup in a medium-sized bowl and blend well. Pour into an ungreased shallow 1½-quart baking dish. Arrange fish sticks on top. Combine butter and soy sauce in a small bowl. Brush top of fish sticks with some of butter–soy sauce mixture. Bake, uncovered, 25 to 30 minutes, until golden brown. Brush fish sticks once again with remaining butter mixture while baking. Makes 4 servings.
Your Time: 8 minutes
Cooking and Baking Time: 30 to 35 minutes

## COMPANY HALIBUT

| | |
|---|---|
| 2  *8-ounce cans tomato sauce with tomato bits* | 2  *12-ounce packages frozen halibut steaks, thawed* |
| ½  *cup drained sweet pickle relish* | *Seasoned salt* |
| 1  *tablespoon prepared mustard* | *Seasoned pepper* |
| 1  *teaspoon Worcestershire sauce* | ¼  *cup chopped scallions or green onions* |

Heat oven to 450° F. Grease a shallow 2-quart baking dish with unsalted shortening. Combine tomato sauce, pickle relish, mustard, and Worcestershire in a medium-sized bowl and blend well. Place halibut steaks in prepared baking dish. Sprinkle fish lightly with seasoned salt and pepper. Pour sauce over fish. Bake, uncovered, 25 to 30 minutes, or until fish flakes easily. Sprinkle top with scallions. Makes 6 servings.
Your Time: 4 minutes
Baking Time: 25 to 30 minutes

## BAKED HALIBUT STEAKS

4 halibut steaks (about 2
 pounds)
3 tablespoons soy sauce
1 tablespoon lemon juice
⅛ teaspoon powdered ginger

3 tablespoons instant minced
 onion
Few grains pepper
Lemon wedges

Heat oven to 375° F. Grease a shallow 2-quart baking dish with unsalted shortening. Place steaks in prepared dish. Pour soy sauce and lemon juice over steaks. Sprinkle tops with ginger, onion, and pepper. Bake, uncovered, 25 to 30 minutes. Serve with lemon wedges. Makes 4 servings.
Your Time: 4 minutes
Baking Time: 25 to 30 minutes

## LOBSTER TETRAZZINI

1 5.5-ounce package noodles
 with sour cream and
 cheese sauce mix
1 11½-ounce package frozen
 lobster Newburg, thawed

2 tablespoons melted butter
 or margarine
¼ cup fine dry bread crumbs
1 tablespoon grated Parmesan
 cheese

Heat oven to 350° F. Prepare noodles according to directions on package. Fold in lobster Newburg. Pour into an ungreased shallow 1½-quart baking dish. Mix butter, bread crumbs, and Parmesan cheese; sprinkle over casserole. Bake, uncovered, 20 minutes. Makes 3 to 4 servings.
Your Time: 4 minutes
Cooking and Baking Time: 28 minutes

## QUICK LOBSTER THERMIDOR

2 8-ounce packages frozen
  lobster tails
1 teaspoon dried parsley
  flakes
½ cup milk
1 tablespoon butter or
  margarine
1 4-ounce can sliced
  mushrooms, drained
Few grains garlic powder
1 10¾-ounce can condensed
  Cheddar cheese soup,
  undiluted

1 tablespoon lemon juice
1 tablespoon dry sherry
2 tablespoons fine dry bread
  crumbs
1 teaspoon grated Parmesan
  cheese
Few grains paprika
2 teaspoons melted butter or
  margarine

Cook lobster tails in boiling salted water as directed on package. Sprinkle parsley over milk in a small bowl and let stand 5 minutes. Remove lobster meat from shells and dice. (Reserve shells for serving thermidor.) Melt the 1 tablespoon butter in skillet over moderately low heat (about 225° F.); add mushrooms and cook until lightly browned. Add garlic powder, cheese soup, milk and parsley mixture, lemon juice, and sherry; mix well. Fold in lobster and spoon mixture into lobster shells. Toss together bread crumbs, Parmesan cheese, paprika, and the 2 teaspoons melted butter. Sprinkle over lobster mixture. Place on rack in broiler pan. Broil 3 to 4 inches from heat about 5 minutes, or until lightly browned. Makes 4 servings.
Your Time: 21 minutes
Cooking Time: 10 minutes

## SHRIMP DE LUXE

1 tablespoon butter or
  margarine
¾ cup frozen chopped onion
1 clove garlic, peeled and
  crushed
1 10½-ounce can condensed
  cream of mushroom soup,
  undiluted
1 cup commercial sour cream

¼ cup catsup
1 4-ounce can sliced
  mushrooms, drained
1 16-ounce package
  ready-to-cook frozen
  shrimp, prepared
  according to package
  directions
2 cups hot cooked rice

In a large skillet over moderate heat (about 250° F.) melt butter. Add onion and garlic and cook until onion is lightly browned. In a bowl combine soup, sour cream, and catsup; blend well and stir into onion mixture. Stir in drained mushrooms and cooked shrimp. Heat to serving temperature, stirring occasionally. Serve over cooked rice. Makes 4 servings.
Your Time: 18 minutes
Cooking Time: 10 minutes

## STIRRED SHRIMP IN SHERRY

2 tablespoons butter or
  margarine
1 16-ounce package frozen
  shelled and deveined
  shrimp, cooked
1 tablespoon cornstarch

1 teaspoon salt
2 tablespoons freeze-dried
  chives
⅛ teaspoon paprika
¼ cup dry sherry
2 tablespoons water

Melt butter in heavy skillet over moderately low heat (about 225° F.); add shrimp. Combine cornstarch, salt, chives, and paprika in a small bowl; add sherry and water and stir until smooth. Add to shrimp and cook 5 to 7 minutes, stirring constantly, until shrimp is pink and sauce is thickened and clear. Makes 4 servings.
Your Time and Cooking Time: 7 to 9 minutes

## SHRIMP RAMEKINS

2 tablespoons butter or
  margarine
½ cup sliced celery
1 10½-ounce can condensed
  cream of mushroom
  soup, undiluted
½ cup commercial sour
  cream
⅓ cup milk

1½ cups cooked shrimp,
  cut up
1 14-ounce can asparagus,
  drained
2 tablespoons water
2 tablespoons melted butter
  or margarine
¾ cup fine dry seasoned
  bread crumbs

Heat oven to 400° F. Butter 4 individual shallow baking dishes. Melt the 2 tablespoons butter in saucepan over moderate heat (about 250° F.); add celery and cook until tender. Remove pan from heat.

Blend in undiluted soup and sour cream until smooth. Slowly stir in milk. Add shrimp. Place 4 to 5 asparagus spears in each of the prepared dishes. Divide shrimp mixture among the 4 dishes. Combine water, the 2 tablespoons melted butter, and bread crumbs; sprinkle about ⅓ cup over each baking dish. Bake, uncovered, for 15 minutes, or until hot and bubbly. Makes 4 servings.
Your Time: 13 minutes
Cooking and Baking Time: 20 minutes

### ONION-BAKED SOLE

1 *cup bottled creamy onion salad dressing*
1½ *cups packaged herb-seasoned croutons*
1 *4-ounce can sliced mushrooms, drained*
1 *tablespoon dried parsley flakes*

2 *16-ounce packages frozen fillet of sole, thawed*
*Paprika*
*Parsley sprigs (optional)*
*Lemon slices (optional)*

Heat oven to 400° F. Butter a shallow 2-quart baking dish. In a small bowl combine ¼ cup of the onion dressing with the seasoned croutons, mushrooms, and parsley; blend well. Separate thawed fillets. Place some of the stuffing on one end of each fillet and roll up. Secure with a toothpick. Place rolled fillets side by side in the prepared baking dish. Spoon the remaining ¾ cup onion dressing over fillets. Sprinkle fillets lightly with paprika. Bake, uncovered, 20 minutes, or until fish flakes easily with a fork. If desired, garnish with parsley sprigs and lemon slices. Makes 6 servings.
Your Time: 5 minutes
Baking Time: 20 minutes

### STUFFED WHOLE TROUT

¼ *cup bottled French dressing*
2 *tablespoons chopped frozen onion*
½ *cup sliced almonds*
1 *cup packaged corn bread stuffing*

1 *canned pimiento, finely chopped*
1 *teaspoon lemon juice*
½ *cup water*
2 *10-ounce packages frozen whole trout, thawed*

Heat oven to 400° F. Grease an ovenproof platter with unsalted shortening. Heat 2 tablespoons of the dressing in a skillet over moderately high heat (about 275° F.). Add onion and almonds and cook, stirring occasionally, until almonds are lightly browned, or about 5 minutes. Remove skillet from heat and add corn bread stuffing, pimiento, and lemon juice; gradually add water, tossing with a fork to mix. Cut along the backbone of each fish to form a pocket. Fill pockets with stuffing. Arrange trout, stuffing side up, in prepared platter. Place any remaining stuffing on platter. Bake, uncovered, 15 minutes. Makes 4 servings.
Your Time: 12 minutes
Cooking and Baking Time: 20 minutes

# Fish
## Canned

### CREAMED CRAB

1  7½-ounce can Alaska king crab
1  10½-ounce can condensed cream of celery soup, undiluted
⅓ cup commercial sour cream
¼ green pepper, diced
1  tablespoon instant minced onion

1  tablespoon lemon juice
1  teaspoon Worcestershire sauce
½ teaspoon prepared mustard
2  tablespoons butter or margarine
½ cup fine dry bread crumbs

Heat oven to 350° F. Drain crab and slice larger pieces. Mix soup, sour cream, green pepper, onion, lemon juice, Worcestershire, and mustard together in a medium-sized bowl; fold in crab. Spoon mixture into ungreased individual casseroles. Mix butter and bread crumbs together in a small bowl; sprinkle over casseroles. Bake, uncovered, 25 minutes. Makes 4 servings.
Your Time: 9 minutes
Cooking Time: 25 minutes

## CRAB FLORENTINE CASSEROLE

1 *9-ounce package frozen*          1 *cup commercial sour cream*
   *creamed chopped spinach*        2 *6½-ounce cans crab meat,*
⅓ *cup packaged precooked*             *drained and flaked*
   *rice*                           2 *tablespoons brandy*
1 *10-ounce package frozen*         2 *tablespoons grated Romano*
   *peas and carrots, thawed*          *cheese*

Heat oven to 375° F. Grease a deep 1½-quart casserole with unsalted
shortening. Prepare creamed spinach according to package directions.
Drain well. Pour cooked spinach into prepared casserole and add rice,
stirring to blend. Blend in peas and carrots, sour cream, crab meat,
and brandy. Sprinkle the top with Romano cheese. Bake, uncovered,
for 30 minutes. Makes 6 servings.
Your Time: 8 minutes
Cooking and Baking Time: 45 minutes

## CRAB TOASTIES

1 *7½-ounce can Alaska king*        1 *cup canned peas, drained*
   *crab*                           2 *hard-cooked eggs, shelled*
1 *10½-ounce can condensed*            *and sliced*
   *cream of mushroom soup,*        ⅛ *teaspoon ground marjoram*
   *undiluted*                      4 *English muffins, split*
½ *cup milk*                        *Softened butter*

Drain crab and cut into bite-sized pieces. Combine soup and milk in a
saucepan. Add crab, peas, and sliced eggs. Place over moderately low
heat (about 225° F.) and heat thoroughly, stirring once or twice.
Toast and butter English muffin halves. Allow 2 muffin halves and a
fourth of the crab mixture per serving. Makes 4 servings.
Your Time: 6½ minutes
Cooking Time: 8 minutes

## CRAB MEAT SUPREME

2 *6½-ounce cans crab meat,*        3 *tablespoons dry sherry*
   *flaked*                         1 *3-ounce can crisp chow*
1 *10¾-ounce can chicken*              *mein noodles*
   *gravy*

Combine the first 3 ingredients in a heavy saucepan. Cook over moderately low heat (about 225° F.) until sauce starts to bubble and crab meat is hot, or about 5 minutes. Serve over noodles. Makes 4 servings.

Your Time: 4 minutes
Cooking Time: 5 minutes

## OVERNIGHT CRAB CASSEROLE

1 *7½-ounce can Alaska king crab*
1 *cup uncooked shell macaroni*
1 *4-ounce package shredded Cheddar cheese*
2 *hard-cooked eggs, shelled and coarsely chopped*

1 *10½-ounce can condensed cream of mushroom soup, undiluted*
1 *cup milk*
1 *tablespoon frozen chopped chives*
*Paprika*

Drain crab and flake coarsely. Combine crab, macaroni, cheese, eggs, undiluted soup, milk, and chives in an ungreased deep 1-quart casserole. Cover and refrigerate at least 8 hours or overnight. Bake, covered, in a 350° F. oven for 1 hour. Sprinkle with paprika. Makes 4 to 6 servings.

Your Time: 9 minutes
Chilling Time: 8 hours or overnight
Baking Time: 1 hour

## TOMATO-CRAB RAREBIT

1 *10¾-ounce can condensed Cheddar cheese soup, undiluted*
1 *8-ounce can tomato sauce with cheese*
½ *teaspoon Worcestershire sauce*

½ *teaspoon dry mustard*
1 *7½-ounce can Alaska king crab, drained and flaked*
4 *slices white bread or 4 English muffins, split*
*Frozen chopped chives*

Pour soup into a medium-sized saucepan and stir until smooth. Stir in tomato sauce, Worcestershire, and mustard and blend well. Cook over moderate heat (about 250° F.) until heated through, about 5 minutes. Stir in crab and simmer 2 to 3 minutes over moderately low

heat (about 225° F.). Meanwhile, toast bread or muffins. Cut each bread slice in half. Spoon rarebit over top. Sprinkle each serving with chives. Makes 4 servings.
Your Time: 3 minutes
Cooking Time: 9 to 10 minutes

### CREAMED SALMON IN BISCUIT RING

1  *16-ounce can salmon,
    drained and coarsely
    flaked*
1  *10½-ounce can condensed
    cream of mushroom soup,
    undiluted*
1  *cup frozen peas, thawed*
1  *cup milk*
2  *tablespoons dry sherry*

¼  *teaspoon salt*
1  *8-ounce container
    refrigerated biscuits
    (10 biscuits)*
2  *tablespoons melted butter
    or margarine*
2  *teaspoons dried parsley
    flakes*

Heat oven to 425° F. In a large bowl gently combine salmon, soup, peas, milk, sherry, and salt. Pour mixture into an ungreased deep 2-quart casserole. Open biscuit container according to label directions and separate biscuits. Brush melted butter over tops of biscuits and sprinkle with parsley. Arrange biscuits in a ring with sides touching on top of the salmon mixture. Bake, uncovered, 15 to 20 minutes, or until mixture is bubbling and the biscuits are golden brown. Makes 4 to 5 servings.
Your Time: 11 minutes
Baking Time: 15 to 20 minutes

### SCALLOPED SALMON

1⅓ *cups packaged seasoned
    bread stuffing*
⅓ *cup melted butter or
    margarine*
1  *16-ounce can salmon*
3  *hard-cooked eggs, chopped*
1  *10½-ounce can condensed
    cream of mushroom
    soup, undiluted*

1  *tablespoon instant minced
    onion*
1  *tablespoon dried parsley
    flakes*

Heat oven to 400° F. Grease a shallow 1-quart baking dish with unsalted shortening. Combine bread stuffing and butter in a medium-sized bowl. Set aside ⅓ cup of the mixture. Drain liquid from salmon and reserve. Remove skin and bones from salmon and flake coarsely. Add enough water to salmon liquid to make ¾ cup. Combine the 1 cup crumb mixture with the salmon, salmon liquid, eggs, soup, onion, and parsley flakes. Spoon into prepared baking dish. Sprinkle with reserved crumbs. Bake, uncovered, 20 minutes. Makes 4 to 6 servings.
Your Time: 9 minutes
Baking Time: 20 minutes

## SALMON WITH CORN BREAD TOPPING

1 16-ounce can red salmon
2 10½-ounce cans condensed cream of mushroom soup, undiluted
¼ cup milk
1 10-ounce package frozen peas, cooked and drained
1 12-ounce package corn muffin mix
½ teaspoon salt
½ teaspoon celery seed
¼ teaspoon ground thyme
¼ teaspoon instant minced onion
1 egg
⅓ cup milk
2 whole canned pimientos, chopped
¼ cup finely chopped green pepper

Heat oven to 400° F. Drain liquid from salmon and reserve. Remove skin and bones from salmon. Combine soup, liquid from salmon, and the ¼ cup milk in a saucepan, heat over moderate heat (about 250° F.) until boiling. Remove pan from heat. Break salmon into chunks and add to soup mixture along with cooked peas. Pour into ungreased shallow 2½-quart casserole. Combine corn muffin mix, salt, celery seed, thyme, and onion in a medium-sized bowl. Combine egg and the ⅓ cup milk in a cup; add to muffin mix and combine thoroughly. Stir in pimiento and green pepper. Drop by spoonfuls over hot mixture in casserole. Bake, uncovered, 30 minutes, or until mixture bubbles at the edges and topping is lightly browned. Makes 6 servings.
Your Time: 11 minutes
Cooking and Baking Time: 37 minutes

## ZESTY SHRIMP

1  cup ice-cold water
2  tablespoons lemon juice
2  4½-ounce cans shrimp,
    drained
1  10¾-ounce can condensed
    tomato soup, undiluted
1  tablespoon prepared
    horseradish
1  tablespoon lemon juice

½  teaspoon mixed herb
    seasoning
2  teaspoons dried parsley
    flakes
1  8-ounce can cut green
    beans, drained
1  3-ounce can chow mein
    noodles

Mix water and the 2 tablespoons lemon juice; pour over shrimp in a bowl and let stand 15 minutes. Mix soup, horseradish, the 1 tablespoon lemon juice, herb seasoning, and parsley in a saucepan; place over moderately low heat (about 225° F.) and heat 5 minutes, stirring occasionally. Drain shrimp and add with beans to saucepan; cook 5 minutes, stirring occasionally. Serve over noodles. Makes 4 servings.
Your Time: 8 minutes
Cooking Time: 10 minutes

## BAKED STUFFED AVOCADO

3  medium-sized ripe avocados
1  6½-ounce can tuna, drained
    and flaked
¼  teaspoon salt
¾  cup finely chopped celery
1  tablespoon frozen chopped
    chives
2  tablespoons bottled Italian
    salad dressing

¼  cup mayonnaise
Boiling water
1  to 2 tablespoons grated
    Parmesan cheese
⅓  cup coarsely crushed potato
    chips

Heat oven to 400° F. Cut avocados in half lengthwise. Remove pits, but do not peel avocados. In a large bowl combine tuna, salt, celery, chives, Italian dressing, and mayonnaise. Toss lightly to blend well. Spoon mixture into unpeeled avocado halves. Arrange stuffed halves in an ungreased shallow 1½-quart baking dish. Pour ½ inch boiling water in the bottom of the dish. Sprinkle tops of avocado halves with Parmesan cheese. Bake, uncovered, 15 minutes, or until lightly browned. Serve sprinkled with crushed potato chips. Makes 6 servings.
Your Time: 10 minutes
Baking Time: 15 minutes

## TUNA BAKED IN FOIL

1  *10-ounce package frozen asparagus spears, partially thawed*
2  *6½-ounce cans tuna, drained and flaked*
1  *teaspoon bottled lemon juice*
½  *cup bottled tartar sauce*
½  *teaspoon instant minced onion*

Heat oven to 375° F. Break apart partially thawed asparagus spears. Arrange 4 12-inch squares of heavy aluminum foil on a flat surface. Divide asparagus evenly among the 4 pieces of foil. Place ¼ of the tuna on each piece of foil. Place ¼ teaspoon lemon juice, 2 tablespoons tartar sauce, and ¹8 teaspoon instant minced onion on each portion. Fold up each packet, sealing well, and place on a cookie sheet. Bake 30 minutes, or until asparagus is tender. Makes 4 servings.
Your Time: 8 minutes
Baking Time: 30 minutes

## CREAMED TUNA IN PATTY SHELLS

1  *package frozen patty shells*
2  *7-ounce cans tuna, drained and flaked*
1  *10½-ounce can condensed cream of mushroom soup, undiluted*
3  *tablespoons milk*
1  *5-ounce can water chestnuts, drained and sliced*
½  *cup commercial sour cream*
3  *tablespoons dried parsley flakes*

Bake patty shells according to package directions. In a saucepan combine tuna, mushroom, soup, milk, and water chestnuts; place over moderate heat (about 250° F.) and cook 5 minutes, stirring occasionally. Remove from heat; fold in sour cream and parsley. Serve immediately in patty shells. Makes 6 servings.
Your Time: 13 minutes
Baking and Cooking Time: 35 minutes

## TUNA JAMBALAYA

3  tablespoons butter or
   margarine
½  cup frozen chopped onion
½  cup finely chopped green
   pepper
1  4-ounce can sliced
   mushrooms, drained
1  10¾-ounce can condensed
   tomato soup, diluted
2  tablespoons water

1  teaspoon Worcestershire
   sauce
Few grains pepper
1  6½-ounce can tuna,
   drained and flaked
½  cup sliced green olives
1⅓ cups packaged precooked
   rice, prepared according
   to package directions

Melt butter in skillet over moderate heat (about 250° F.); add onion, green pepper, and mushrooms and cook about 5 minutes, or until tender. Fold in soup, water, Worcestershire, pepper, tuna, and olives; cook, stirring constantly, until heated. Serve over hot cooked rice. Makes 4 servings.
Your Time: 12 minutes
Cooking Time: 15 minutes

## TUNA ORIENTAL CASSEROLE

1  24-ounce can double-pack
   mushroom chow mein
1  13-ounce can tuna, drained
   and flaked
1  5-ounce can water
   chestnuts, drained and
   quartered

⅔ cup milk
2  teaspoons soy sauce
1  3-ounce can chow mein
   noodles

Heat oven to 350° F. Lightly butter a deep 2-quart casserole. Remove tape from cans and open vegetable can; drain vegetables and rinse with cold water. Combine vegetables with tuna, water chestnuts, mushroom sauce from remaining can, milk, and soy sauce in a large bowl. Turn into prepared casserole. Sprinkle top with the chow mein noodles. Bake, uncovered, 35 to 40 minutes, or until mixture bubbles. Makes 6 to 8 servings.
Your Time: 9 minutes
Baking Time: 35 to 40 minutes

## PEACH-TUNA CASSEROLE

1  16-ounce can cling peach halves
2  packages cream of mushroom sauce mix (each making 1 cup)
2  7-ounce cans tuna, drained
1  10-ounce package frozen peas, thawed
1  3½-ounce can French fried onion rings

Heat oven to 350° F. Drain peaches and reserve liquid. Prepare sauce mixes according to package directions, using peach liquid plus enough water to make 2 cups. Break tuna into chunks and combine with the mushroom sauce, peas, and ½ cup of the onion rings in a medium-sized bowl. Pour into an ungreased 1½-quart casserole. Arrange peach halves on top of casserole. Bake, uncovered, 25 minutes, or until bubbling. Sprinkle remainder of onion rings around edge of casserole. Bake 4 to 5 minutes longer, or until onions are brown. Makes 4 to 6 servings.
Your Time: 7 minutes
Baking Time: 30 minutes

## TUNA PIE

1½ cups packaged precooked rice
1  6½-ounce can tuna, drained and coarsely flaked
⅓ cup sliced stuffed green olives
½ cup milk
2  eggs, slightly beaten
1  envelope Hollandaise sauce mix
⅓ cup mayonnaise or salad dressing
Paprika

Heat oven to 350° F. Butter a 9-inch pie plate. Prepare rice according to package directions. Mix rice, tuna, olives, milk, and eggs in a medium-sized bowl; spread evenly in prepared pie plate. Prepare Hollandaise sauce according to package directions and cook until thickened. Blend in mayonnaise. Spread over rice mixture and sprinkle with paprika. Bake, uncovered, 25 to 30 minutes, or until topping is lightly browned. Makes 4 servings.
Your Time: 9 minutes
Baking Time: 30 to 35 minutes

## TUNA-CHEESE PIE

1 *frozen 9-inch pastry shell*     1 *tablespoon fine dry bread*
1 *package cheese sauce mix*          *crumbs*
   *(makes 1 cup)*                 1 *6½-ounce can tuna, drained*
2 *teaspoons flour*                   *and flaked*
⅔ *cup milk*                       2 *tablespoons drained pickle*
2 *eggs, slightly beaten*             *relish*

Thaw pastry shell for about 10 minutes. Heat oven to 450° F. Bake
pastry shell 8 minutes and remove from oven. Lower oven
temperature to 350° F. Combine cheese sauce mix and flour in a
saucepan; gradually stir in milk. Place over moderately low heat
(about 225° F.) and cook, stirring constantly, until mixture is
thickened and smooth. Cool slightly. Add eggs and mix well.
Sprinkle bread crumbs over bottom of pastry shell; arrange tuna and
pickle relish in pastry shell. Pour sauce mixture over tuna. Bake,
uncovered, 40 minutes, or until a knife inserted near the center
comes out clean. Let stand a few minutes before serving. Cut into
wedges. Makes 4 to 6 servings.
Your Time: 10 minutes
Baking and Cooking Time: 50 minutes

## SEAFOOD PIZZA

1 *8-ounce container*              1 *6½-ounce can tuna, drained*
   *refrigerated biscuits (10*        *and flaked*
   *biscuits)*                     ¾ *cup canned tomato sauce*
¾ *cup grated Parmesan cheese*     ½ *teaspoon dried oregano*
½ *cup milk*                          *leaves*
¼ *teaspoon garlic salt*

Heat oven to 450° F. Open biscuit container according to label
directions. Arrange biscuits in a circle on ungreased cookie sheet.
With flour-dipped fingertips, press biscuits together to form a crust
11 inches in diameter. Bake 5 minutes. Remove from oven. Loosen
biscuit crust from sheet with a spatula. Blend together Parmesan
cheese, milk, and garlic salt in a small bowl. Spread cheese mixture
over crust to within ½ inch of edge. Sprinkle tuna over cheese; pour
on tomato sauce and sprinkle with oregano. Return to oven and bake
10 minutes, or until crust is lightly browned and topping is hot.
Loosen crust immediately after removing from oven. Cut into
wedges. Makes 4 servings.
Your Time: 9 minutes
Baking Time: 15 minutes

## SEAFOOD ROMANOFF

6 cups salted water
1 5.5-ounce package egg
  noodles with sour
  cream-cheese sauce mix
2 tablespoons butter or
  margarine
½ cup milk
1 4-ounce package shredded
  Cheddar cheese

1 7½-ounce can crab meat or
  1 7-ounce can tuna,
  drained and flaked
1 tablespoon instant minced
  onion
1 tablespoon dried parsley
  flakes
1 teaspoon Worcestershire
  sauce

Bring 6 cups salted water to a boil in a large covered saucepan over moderate heat (about 250° F.). Add noodles from package, reserving sour cream-cheese sauce mix, and simmer noodles 8 minutes. Drain. Meanwhile, in the top of a double boiler combine the contents of package of sauce mix, the butter, milk, cheese, crab, onion, parsley, and Worcestershire and blend well. Cover and cook over simmering water about 5 minutes until heated through and cheese is melted. Add drained noodles; cover and continue to cook until thoroughly heated. Makes 4 servings.
Your Time: 12 minutes
Cooking Time: 21 minutes

## COMPANY SEAFOOD CASSEROLE

2 9-ounce packages frozen
  artichoke hearts
Garlic salt
2⅔ cups packaged precooked
  rice
1 5-ounce can lobster,
  drained and flaked
1 6½-ounce can tuna,
  drained and flaked
1 7½-ounce can crab meat,
  drained and flaked

2 10½-ounce cans condensed
  cream of mushroom
  soup, undiluted
1½ soup cans water
½ soup can dry sherry
3 slices process American
  cheese, cut crosswise into
  triangles
Chopped fresh parsley

Heat oven to 400° F. Butter a deep 3-quart casserole. Place artichoke hearts in the bottom of prepared casserole. Sprinkle generously with garlic salt. Cover with rice. Combine lobster meat, tuna, and crab meat lightly with a fork in a medium-sized bowl; spread flaked seafood over rice. Blend soup, water, and sherry in a large bowl. Pour soup mixture over ingredients in casserole. Cover and bake about 40 minutes, or until bubbly. Top with cheese during the last few minutes of baking. Remove from oven and sprinkle with chopped parsley before serving. Makes 8 servings.

Your Time: 10 minutes

Cooking Time: 40 minutes

## SEAFOOD SUPREME

2 tablespoons butter or margarine

¼ cup chopped green pepper

1 10½-ounce can condensed cream of mushroom soup, undiluted

1¼ cups evaporated milk, undiluted

2 tablespoons instant minced onion

1 teaspoon Worcestershire sauce

2 drops Tabasco

Few grains pepper

1 6½-ounce can tuna, drained and flaked

1 4½-ounce can shrimp, drained

⅔ cup chopped ripe olives

Patty shells or toast

Melt butter in skillet over moderate heat (about 250° F.); add green pepper and cook about 5 minutes, or until tender. Add mushroom soup, evaporated milk, onion, Worcestershire, Tabasco, and pepper; cook and stir until mixture is smooth and bubbly. Add tuna, shrimp, and olives; heat. Serve in patty shells or on toast. Makes 5 to 6 servings.

Your Time: 14 minutes

Cooking Time: 15 minutes

# *Beef*

## BEEF PATTIES PARMESAN

1 pound ground beef chuck

½ cup prepared buttermilk biscuit mix

⅓ cup tomato juice

¼ cup frozen chopped green pepper

1 egg, slightly beaten

1 small garlic clove, peeled and minced

1 teaspoon salt

Few grains pepper

½ teaspoon Worcestershire sauce

8 teaspoons grated Parmesan cheese

Buttered noodles (optional)

Heat oven to 400° F. Grease a shallow 2-quart baking dish with unsalted shortening. In a large bowl combine beef, biscuit mix, tomato juice, green pepper, egg, garlic, salt, pepper, and Worcestershire. Toss lightly to blend well. Shape mixture into 4 patties. Arrange in prepared baking dish. Bake, uncovered, 20 minutes. Sprinkle each patty immediately with 2 teaspoons Parmesan cheese. If desired, serve on a bed of buttered noodles. Makes 4 servings.
Your Time: 6 minutes
Baking Time: 20 minutes

## QUICK CHILI

| | |
|---|---|
| 1 tablespoon butter or margarine | ½ cup finely chopped onion |
| 1 pound ground beef | 1 tablespoon flour |
| 1 15½-ounce can chili with beans | 1 cup evaporated milk, undiluted |
| | ½ cup chili sauce |

Heat butter in a skillet; add beef. Cook and stir over moderate heat (250° F.) until meat is lightly browned. Add chili and onion. In a bowl blend flour, milk, and chili sauce. Stir into hot meat mixture. Cook, stirring constantly, until thickened and smooth. Makes 4 servings.
Your Time: 4 minutes
Cooking Time: 5 minutes

## BEEF-NOODLE SKILLET DINNER

| | |
|---|---|
| 1¼ pounds ground beef | ¼ teaspoon pepper |
| 4 beef bouillon cubes | 4 cups boiling water |
| 2 tablespoons catsup | 8 ounces medium or narrow egg noodles |
| 1 tablespoon dried parsley flakes | 1 10-ounce package frozen mixed vegetables, thawed |
| 1 teaspoon salt | |
| ½ teaspoon onion salt | |

Place beef in a large skillet; break up with a fork. Cook over moderately high heat (about 325° F.) for 5 minutes, stirring frequently. Remove skillet from heat; mix in bouillon cubes, catsup, parsley, salt, onion salt, and pepper. Stir in boiling water; cook over

moderate heat (about 250° F.) until mixture comes to a boil and bouillon cubes are dissolved, stirring occasionally. Stir in noodles and sprinkle vegetables over mixture in skillet. Cover and cook over moderately low heat (about 225° F.) for 10 to 15 minutes, or until noodles and vegetables are cooked and all of the liquid is absorbed. Makes 6 servings.
Your Time: 9 minutes
Cooking Time: 25 to 30 minutes


## BEEF-RICE SPECIAL

*1 pound ground beef*
*1 package onion soup mix*
*1½ cups boiling water*
*¾ cup uncooked rice*

*1 16-ounce can tomatoes, undrained*
*1 4-ounce package shredded Cheddar cheese*

Place beef in a medium-sized skillet; break up with a fork. Cook over moderately high heat (about 325° F.) for 5 minutes, stirring frequently. Remove skillet from heat; stir in onion soup mix, water, rice, and tomatoes. Cover and cook over moderately low heat (about 225° F.) for 25 minutes, or until rice is tender. Sprinkle cheese over top of rice mixture; cover and cook for about 2 minutes to melt cheese. Makes 4 to 6 servings.
Your Time: 7 minutes
Cooking Time: 32 minutes

## SPICY BACON BURGERS

*2 pounds ground beef chuck*
*3 tablespoons chopped frozen onion*
*¾ cup fine dry seasoned bread crumbs*
*1 egg*

*⅓ cup milk*
*¼ teaspoon salt*
*1 package dry spaghetti sauce mix*
*8 slices raw bacon*

Heat oven to 375° F. In a bowl mix together beef, onion, bread crumbs, egg, milk, and salt with a fork. Shape meat mixture into 8 patties about 1 inch thick. Pour spaghetti sauce mix into a pie plate and coat patties well all around. Place patties on a shallow baking or broiler pan. Wrap a slice of bacon around edge of each patty and secure with a toothpick. Sprinkle with any leftover sauce mix. Bake, uncovered, 20 to 25 minutes, or until meat is cooked to the desired degree of doneness. Remove toothpicks before serving. Makes 4 to 6 servings.

Your Time: 10 minutes
Baking Time: 20 to 25 minutes

## GAUCHO CASSEROLE

1 *tablespoon vegetable oil*
1 *pound ground beef chuck*
1 *2¼-ounce package chili seasoning mix*
½ *cup water*
1 *16-ounce can tomatoes in tomato purée*
1 *20-ounce can kidney beans, undrained*

1 *8-ounce container refrigerated biscuits (10 biscuits)*
1 *tablespoon melted butter or margarine*
½ *cup chopped salted peanuts*

Heat oven to 450° F. Heat oil in a large skillet over moderately high heat (about 275° F.). Add meat and cook and stir until meat is browned and crumbly. Combine browned meat, chili mix, water, tomatoes, and kidney beans in an ungreased shallow 2-quart baking dish and stir to blend well. Bake, uncovered, 15 minutes, stirring once. Open biscuit container according to label directions. Place biscuits on top of hot meat mixture. Brush tops of biscuits with the melted butter. Sprinkle nuts on top. Continue to bake according to directions on biscuit package about 10 to 12 minutes, or until biscuits are well browned. Makes 4 to 6 servings.

Your Time: 10 minutes
Baking Time: about 25 minutes

## HERO BURGER

1½ *pounds ground beef round*
1 *10¾-ounce can condensed tomato soup, undiluted*
⅓ *cup frozen chopped onion*
1 *tablespoon prepared mustard*
1 *tablespoon Worcestershire sauce*
1 *teaspoon prepared horseradish*
1 *teaspoon salt*

1 *medium-sized loaf French bread*
2 *medium-sized tomatoes, cut into thin slices*
1 *4-ounce package shredded Cheddar cheese*
*Onion rings (optional)*
*Pickle fans (optional)*
*French fried potatoes (optional)*

Preheat broiler. Combine ground beef, tomato soup, onion, mustard, Worcestershire, horseradish, and salt in a large bowl. Cut French bread in half lengthwise. Spread meat mixture over cut surfaces, spreading to the edges. Place open-faced sandwiches on a cookie sheet. Place in a preheated broiler with top of sandwich 4 inches from heat. Broil about 2 minutes. Arrange tomato slices on meat mixture and sprinkle with cheese. Return to broiler until cheese melts. Cut each into thirds. If desired, serve with onion rings, pickle fans, and French fried potatoes. Makes 4 to 6 servings.
Your Time: 12 minutes
Broiling Time: 14 minutes

## HUNGARIAN-STYLE BEEF

2 *tablespoons butter or margarine*
½ *cup frozen chopped onion*
¼ *cup chopped green pepper*
1 *pound ground beef*
1 *10½-ounce can condensed cream of mushroom soup, undiluted*
½ *cup commercial sour cream*
½ *teaspoon paprika*
*Few grains pepper*
2 *3-ounce cans chow mein noodles*

Melt butter in skillet over moderate heat (about 250° F.). Add onion and green pepper and cook until tender, stirring occasionally. Add ground beef and cook and stir until lightly browned. Stir in mushroom soup, sour cream, paprika, and pepper. Heat and serve over noodles. Makes 4 servings.
Your Time: 7 minutes
Cooking Time: 20 minutes

## SKILLET MACARONI-BEEF DINNER

2 *tablespoons vegetable oil*
¼ *cup frozen chopped onion*
¼ *cup chopped green pepper*
1 *pound ground beef round*
2 *cups cooked elbow macaroni (1 cup uncooked)*
1 *teaspoon prepared mustard*
½ *teaspoon Worcestershire sauce*
1 *10¾-ounce can condensed tomato soup, undiluted*
½ *cup commercial sour cream*
*Salt to taste*
*Grated Parmesan cheese*

Heat oil in a large skillet over moderately high heat (about 300° F.). Add onion and pepper and cook until lightly browned. Stir in ground beef and brown lightly, stirring frequently. Drain off any excess fat. Stir in macaroni, mustard, Worcestershire, tomato soup, and sour cream. Blend well. Add salt to taste, if necessary. Heat to serving temperature. Serve topped with grated cheese. Makes 4 servings.
Your Time: 10 minutes
Cooking Time: 16 minutes

## TANGY MUSHROOM-BAKED MEATBALLS

2 *pounds mixed ground meat*
  *(1 pound ground beef, ½*
  *pound ground pork, ½*
  *pound ground veal)*
1 *cup packaged corn flake*
  *crumbs*
1 *egg*
¾ *cup milk*

½ *teaspoon salt*
1 *1¼-ounce package spaghetti*
  *sauce mix with*
  *mushrooms*
2 *10¾-ounce cans mushroom*
  *gravy*
*Hot cooked rice or noodles*
  *(optional)*

Heat oven to 350° F. In a large bowl combine ground meats, corn flake crumbs, egg, milk, salt, and ½ the package of spaghetti sauce mix; blend well. Gently shape into 1½-inch balls. Place meat balls in an ungreased shallow 3-quart baking dish. In a medium-sized bowl combine mushroom gravy and the remaining ½ package spaghetti sauce mix and stir to blend. Pour sauce over meat balls. Bake, uncovered, 45 minutes. If desired, serve over hot cooked rice or noodles. Makes 24 1½-inch meat balls, or 6 to 8 servings.
Your Time: 6 minutes
Baking Time: 45 minutes

## SKILLET TOMATO-RICE

2 *tablespoons butter or*
  *margarine*
1 *pound ground beef chuck*
1 *1½-ounce envelope*
  *spaghetti sauce mix*

1⅓ *cups packaged precooked*
  *rice*
1½ *cups boiling water*
2 *8-ounce cans tomato sauce*
*Grated Parmesan cheese*

Melt butter in a large skillet over moderately low heat (about 225° F.). Add beef and cook over moderately high heat (about

275° F.), stirring occasionally, until beef is brown and crumbly. Add spaghetti sauce mix, rice, water, and tomato sauce. Bring mixture to a boil; reduce heat to moderately low (about 225° F.) and simmer, covered, 5 minutes. Serve sprinkled with cheese. Makes 6 servings.
Your Time: 6 minutes
Cooking Time: 12 minutes

## CHEESE MEAT LOAF

| | |
|---|---|
| *1 pound ground beef* | *3 tablespoons crumbled blue* |
| *2 envelopes instant beef broth* | *cheese* |
| *1 egg* | *¼ cup fine dry bread crumbs* |
| *¼ cup tomato juice* | |

Heat oven to 425° F. In a bowl mix together beef, 1 envelope of the beef broth, egg, tomato juice, cheese, and bread crumbs. Shape into loaf 3 inches in diameter. Sprinkle the remaining beef broth over outside of loaf. Place in an ungreased shallow baking pan. Bake, uncovered, 50 to 55 minutes. Makes 4 servings.
Your Time: 6 minutes
Cooking Time: 50 to 55 minutes

## QUICK-AND-EASY MEAT LOAF

| | |
|---|---|
| *1½ pounds ground beef round* | *⅔ cup evaporated milk,* |
| *1 envelope onion soup mix* | *undiluted* |

Heat oven to 350° F. In a bowl lightly combine ground beef, onion soup mix, and milk with a fork. Place in an ungreased shallow baking dish or pie plate. Moisten hands with water and shape meat into a loaf. Bake, uncovered, 50 minutes. Makes 4 to 6 servings.
Your Time: 2 minutes
Cooking Time: 50 minutes

## GLAZED SKILLET MEAT LOAF

1 ½ *pounds ground beef*
⅔ *cup seasoned fine dry*
  *bread crumbs*
1  *5 ⅓ -fluid-ounce can*
  *evaporated milk,*
  *undiluted*
¼ *cup frozen chopped onion*
1 *teaspoon salt*
⅛ *teaspoon ground pepper*

½ *cup bottled sweet Russian*
  *dressing*
2 *tablespoons shortening*
1 *16-ounce can tiny whole*
  *carrots, drained*
2 *16-ounce cans*
  *French-style green beans,*
  *drained*

Break up meat with a fork in a mixing bowl. Add bread crumbs, milk, onion, salt, pepper, and 2 tablespoons of the bottled dressing. Shape mixture into 2 loaves. Melt shortening in a skillet over moderately high heat (about 325° F.); brown loaves on all sides. Reduce heat to moderately high (about 275° F.); cover and cook about 25 minutes. Spoon off excess fat. Arrange carrots and beans around meat loaves. Combine enough of the dressing with the vegetables to coat them evenly; spoon remainder of dressing over meat loaves. Continue cooking about 5 minutes, or until vegetables are heated. Makes 6 servings.
Your Time: 13 minutes
Cooking Time: About 40 minutes

## VEGETABLE MEAT LOAF

1 *10-ounce package frozen*
  *mixed vegetables*
1 *egg*
½ *cup milk*
1 ½ *teaspoons salt*
⅛ *teaspoon pepper*
¼ *teaspoon rubbed sage*
1 *cup soft bread crumbs*

1 *tablespoon butter or*
  *margarine*
⅓ *cup finely chopped peeled*
  *onion*
1 ½ *pounds ground beef chuck*
1 *10¾-ounce can brown*
  *gravy with onion, heated*
  *to serving temperature*

Heat oven to 375° F. Lightly butter a shallow rectangular 1½-quart baking dish. Prepare vegetables according to package directions; drain and set aside to cool. In a large bowl slightly beat together egg, milk, salt, pepper, and sage. Stir in crumbs and set aside. In a small saucepan over moderate heat (about 250° F.) melt butter. Add onion and cook until lightly browned. Add onion-butter mixture, cooked mixed vegetables, and ground beef to egg mixture. Mix together well, using hands if necessary. Turn meat mixture into prepared baking dish. Shape meat mixture into an 8-x-5-inch oblong loaf. Bake, uncovered, 55 to 60 minutes, or until no red juices run out when a two-tined fork is inserted in the thickest part of the loaf and the top is richly browned. Slice loaf and serve with gravy. Makes 4 to 6 servings.

Your Time: 19 minutes
Cooking and Baking Time: 62 to 67 minutes

### SHEPHERD'S PIE

| | |
|---|---|
| 1  *pound ground beef* | *½ teaspoon dried basil leaves* |
| *¼ cup frozen chopped onion* | *¼ cup packaged shredded* |
| *½ teaspoon salt* | *Cheddar cheese* |
| 1  *package brown gravy mix* | *1½ cups warm seasoned* |
| *(makes 1 cup)* | *mashed potatoes* |
| 1  *cup water* | |
| 1  *10-ounce package frozen* | |
| *peas and carrots* | |

Heat oven to 450° F. Place ground beef and onion in a skillet over moderately high heat (about 375° F.) and cook, breaking meat up with the back of a spoon, until meat is browned and onion is tender. Sprinkle with salt. Blend in gravy mix and water, stirring until thickened. Add vegetables and basil; cover and simmer 5 minutes. Pour into an ungreased 1½-quart casserole. Fold cheese into mashed potatoes; spoon potatoes into a ring on top of meat mixture. Bake, uncovered, 15 minutes, or until potatoes are lightly browned on top. Makes 4 to 6 servings.

Your Time: 12 minutes
Cooking and Baking Time: 25 minutes

## SPICY TACO BURGETTES

*1 pound ground beef*
*⅓ cup chopped celery*
*¼ cup frozen chopped onion*
*½ cup catsup*
*½ cup water*
*1 1¼-ounce package taco*
　*seasoning mix*

*⅓ cup coarsely chopped ripe*
　*pitted olives*
*2 8-ounce container*
　*refrigerated crescent*
　*dinner rolls*
*1 4-ounce package shredded*
　*Cheddar cheese*

Heat oven to 450° F. In a large skillet brown beef over moderately low heat (about 225° F.), stirring occasionally. Drain off excess fat. Add celery, onion, catsup, water, taco seasoning, and ripe olives; stir to blend well. Simmer 10 minutes. Cool slightly. Open roll containers according to label directions and separate dough into 8 rectangles. (Do not separate into triangles.) With a rolling pin lightly roll each rectangle into a square. Place 4 squares on each of 2 ungreased cookie sheets. Place equal amounts of cooled meat mixture in the center of each square. Sprinkle each with some of the shredded cheese. Fold corners of squares toward centers and pinch together. Bake, uncovered, 10 to 12 minutes, or until golden brown. Serve hot. Makes 8 servings.
Your Time: 7 minutes
Cooking and Baking Time: 20 to 22 minutes

## FIFTEEN-MINUTE STEW

*1½ pounds cube or minute*
　*steaks*
*1 16-ounce can whole*
　*carrots*
*1 tablespoon butter or*
　*margarine*

*1 envelope mushroom gravy*
　*mix (makes 1 cup)*
*1 16-ounce can small whole*
　*onions, drained*
*1 16-ounce can whole*
　*potatoes, drained*

Cut steaks into 1½-inch-square pieces. Drain carrots, reserving ¾ cup liquid. Melt butter in a large skillet over moderately low heat (about 225° F.). Increase temperature to moderately high (about 275° F.); add meat and brown quickly on all sides. Remove skillet from heat

and remove browned meat to a plate. Add mushroom gravy mix and the ¾ cup carrot liquid to the skillet; blend well. Place over moderately low heat (about 225° F.) and bring to a boil. Return meat to the skillet and add the vegetables. Simmer, covered, 10 to 15 minutes, or until meat is tender and vegetables are thoroughly heated. Makes 4 servings.
Your Time: 12 minutes
Cooking Time: 15 to 20 minutes

## OVEN-BAKED STEW

1 10½-ounce can condensed beef consommé, undiluted
¾ cup water
¼ cup catsup
⅓ cup all-purpose flour
1 teaspoon salt
⅛ teaspoon pepper
1½ pounds boneless stew beef, cut into 1-inch cubes

1 4-ounce can sliced mushrooms, drained
1 16-ounce can whole carrots, drained
1 16-ounce can white potatoes, drained
1 16-ounce can onions, drained

Heat oven to 350° F. Place beef consommé, water, catsup, flour, salt, and pepper in a jar and shake until blended. Pour into an ungreased deep 2½-quart casserole. Add meat pieces. Cover and bake 30 minutes. Stir gravy and bake 1½ hours longer. Add drained vegetables. Cover and bake 30 minutes, or until meat is fork-tender. If gravy gets too thick during last hour of cooking, stir in a little water. Serves 6.
Your Time: 8 minutes
Baking Time: 2½ hours

## ORIENTAL BEEF

2 tablespoons butter or margarine
1 12-ounce package frozen sandwich steaks, thawed
1 5-ounce can slivered blanched almonds

1 4-ounce can sliced mushrooms, undrained
1 16-ounce can bean sprouts, drained
3 tablespoons soy sauce

Melt butter in large skillet over moderately low heat (about 225° F.). Increase temperature to moderately high (about 350° F.). Add sandwich steaks and brown lightly on both sides. Add remaining ingredients; simmer gently over moderately low heat (about 225° F.) 5 minutes, or until hot. Makes 4 servings.
Your Time: 5 minutes
Cooking Time: 10 minutes

### SKILLET LIVER DINNER

| | |
|---|---|
| *¼ cup vegetable oil* | *1 teaspoon salt* |
| *1 cup sliced peeled onion* | *¼ teaspoon pepper* |
| *1 pound beef liver, cubed* | *1 tablespoon lemon juice* |
| *1 4-ounce jar pimientos,* | *1 16-ounce can lima beans* |
| *drained and sliced* | *Hot cooked rice or noodles* |
| *2 teaspoons cornstarch* | *(optional)* |

Heat oil in heavy skillet over moderate heat (about 250° F.). Add onions and cook until tender but not brown. Add liver and pimientos and brown lightly. Combine cornstarch, salt, pepper, lemon juice, and 1 cup liquid drained from lima beans in a small bowl. Add to meat; cover and simmer gently over moderately low heat (about 225° F.) for 10 minutes. Add lima beans; cook another 5 minutes. Serve on rice or on noodles, if desired. Makes 4 servings.
Your Time: 10 minutes
Cooking Time: 20 minutes

## *Pork and Ham*

### GLAZED APPLES AND PORK

| | |
|---|---|
| *2 tablespoons butter or* | *¼ cup honey* |
| *margarine* | *¼ cup jarred cranberry-orange* |
| *2 packages smoked boneless* | *relish* |
| *pork chops (4 to a* | *1 20-ounce can sliced apples* |
| *package)* | |

Melt butter in a large skillet over moderate heat (about 250° F.). Add pork chops and brown about 5 minutes on each side. Push chops to one side of skillet. Combine honey and cranberry-orange

relish in the skillet; add apples and toss to coat with mixture. Cook about 5 minutes longer to heat apple mixture. Makes 4 servings.
Your Time: 9 minutes
Cooking Time: 16 minutes

### BAKED RICE AND PORK CHOPS

*6 pork chops, about ½ inch thick*
*6 tablespoons bottled Italian salad dressing*
*1 10½-ounce can condensed onion soup*
*1 cup uncooked rice*
*2 canned pimientos, finely chopped*
*Salt*
*Paprika*

Place pork chops in a single layer in an ungreased shallow 3-quart baking dish. Pour dressing over pork chops and turn to coat with the dressing. Cover and marinate in the refrigerator 3 hours or longer. Turn chops once. Heat oven to 400° F. Remove pork chops from baking dish and discard any dressing remaining in the pan. Add enough water to onion soup to make 1½ cups; combine onion soup, rice, and pimiento in the bottom of the shallow baking dish. Arrange pork chops in a single layer on top of the rice mixture; sprinkle chops with salt. Cover and bake 45 minutes. Remove cover and sprinkle pork chops with paprika. Increase oven temperature to 450° F. and bake an additional 15 minutes to brown chops. Makes 4 to 6 servings.
Your Time: 6 minutes
Marinating Time: 3 hours
Baking Time: 1 hour

### PORK CHOPS WITH AMBER RICE

*1 tablespoon vegetable oil*
*8 pork chops, about ½ inch thick*
*1⅓ cups packaged precooked rice*
*1 cup orange juice*
*Salt and pepper*
*1 10½-ounce can condensed chicken with rice soup, undiluted*

Heat oven to 350° F. Heat oil in a large skillet over moderately high heat (about 375° F.). Add pork chops and brown quickly on both sides. Spread rice over the bottom of an ungreased shallow 3-quart casserole. Pour orange juice over rice; stir to combine. Sprinkle browned chops on both sides with salt and pepper and arrange on top of the rice. Pour undiluted soup over chops. Cover and bake 45 minutes. Uncover and bake 10 minutes longer, until chops are fork-tender. Makes 4 servings.

Your Time: 9 minutes

Cooking and Baking Time: 65 minutes

## PORK CHOP-GREEN BEAN CASSEROLE

*6 pork chops, cut ¾ inch thick*
*1 teaspoon salt*
*⅛ teaspoon pepper*
*2 10-ounce packages frozen cut green beans, thawed*

*1 10½-ounce can condensed cream of celery soup, undiluted*
*½ teaspoon ground nutmeg*
*⅓ cup milk*
*¼ teaspoon salt*

Heat oven to 350° F. Trim excess fat from chops; use fat to grease a medium-sized skillet. Season the chops with 1 teaspoon salt and the pepper and place in skillet. Brown lightly over moderately high heat (about 300° F.). Mix beans, soup, nutmeg, milk, and the ¼ teaspoon salt in an ungreased shallow 2-quart baking dish. Arrange chops on top of vegetables. Cover and bake 45 minutes, or until meat is fork-tender. Makes 6 servings.

Your Time: 5 minutes

Cooking and Baking Time: 50 minutes

## GLAZED CANADIAN BACON

*1 pound Canadian bacon, cut into ¼-inch-thick slices*
*1 17-ounce can vacuum-packed sweet potatoes*
*¼ cup thawed undiluted frozen orange juice concentrate*

*3 tablespoons light molasses*
*3 tablespoons prepared mustard*
*¼ teaspoon ground cloves*

Heat oven to 350° F. Arrange Canadian bacon slices, slightly overlapping, in an ungreased shallow 1½-quart baking dish. Place sweet potatoes around bacon. Blend orange juice, molasses, mustard, uncovered, and cloves in a small bowl; pour over bacon. Bake, uncovered, 20 to 25 minutes. Makes 4 to 6 servings.

Your Time: 6 minutes

Baking Time: 20 to 25 minutes

## BAKED HAM STEAK

¼ cup peanut butter
1 ham steak, ¾ inch thick
    (about 1 pound)
¼ cup crushed corn flakes

¼ cup firmly packed
    dark-brown sugar
½ teaspoon dry mustard
1 tablespoon vinegar

Heat oven to 375° F. Spread peanut butter evenly over ham steak. In a small bowl mix corn flakes with remaining ingredients and sprinkle over ham. Place in an ungreased shallow baking dish and bake, uncovered, 20 minutes, or until thoroughly heated. Makes 4 servings.
Your Time: 5 minutes
Baking Time: 20 minutes

## CURRIED PEAR-HAM ROLLS

¾ cup water
1 teaspoon butter or
    margarine
¼ teaspoon salt
1½ tablespoons dried parsley
    flakes
¾ cup packaged precooked
    rice
1 16-ounce can sliced pears
    in heavy syrup

½ cup milk
1 package white sauce mix
    (makes 1 cup)
¼ teaspoon curry powder
6 boiled ham slices, each
    about ⅛ inch thick
1 teaspoon cornstarch
1 tablespoon maple-flavored
    syrup

Combine water, butter, salt, and parsley flakes in a large skillet and bring to a boil over moderately high heat (about 325° F.). Stir in rice; cover and remove from heat. Let stand 5 minutes; then stir gently with a fork. Meanwhile, drain the sliced pears, reserving ¾ cup of the syrup. In a medium-sized saucepan combine ¼ cup of the pear syrup, the milk, and the white sauce mix; blend well. Cook and stir over moderate heat (about 250° F.) until sauce thickens and boils. Remove from heat. Stir in curry powder and mix well. Add rice to sauce and blend well. Place ¼ cup of the curried rice mixture on each ham slice; roll up ham and filling and secure ham with a toothpick. Place the remaining ½ cup pear syrup in the large skillet and blend in the cornstarch. Cook and stir over moderate heat (about 250° F.) until mixture boils and thickens. Stir in the maple-flavored syrup and the pear slices. Arrange ham rolls in the sauce in skillet; cover and simmer over low heat (about 200° F.) 5 minutes, or until heated thoroughly. Makes 4 to 6 servings.
Your Time: 10 minutes
Cooking Time: 25 minutes

## HAM RELISH BAKE

| | |
|---|---|
| 1 *fresh pear* | 1 *tablespoon lemon juice* |
| 1 *8-ounce can whole-berry* | ¼ *teaspoon ground nutmeg* |
| *cranberry sauce* | 1 *1½-pound center-cut ham* |
| 2 *tablespoons honey* | *steak, cut about 1 inch* |
| 1 *teaspoon grated lemon peel* | *thick* |

Heat oven to 350° F. Peel, core, and finely chop pear. In a bowl combine chopped pear with cranberry sauce, honey, lemon peel, lemon juice, and nutmeg. Place ham steak in an ungreased large shallow baking dish. Spoon sauce over the steak and bake, uncovered, 30 minutes. Makes 4 servings.
Your Time: 9½ minutes
Baking Time: 30 minutes

## HAM-CORN BREAD RING WITH CHEESE SAUCE

| | |
|---|---|
| 1 *12-ounce package corn* | 1½ *cups chopped cooked ham* |
| *muffin mix* | *(about ½ to ¾ pound)* |
| 1 *egg* | ¼ *cup frozen chopped onion* |
| ⅔ *cup milk* | *Cheese Sauce (recipe follows)* |
| 1 *teaspoon celery salt* | |

Heat oven to 400° F. Grease an 8-inch ring mold with unsalted shortening. Combine corn muffin mix, egg, milk, and celery salt in a bowl. Add ham and onion; stir to mix thoroughly. Spoon into prepared mold. Bake 30 minutes, or until golden brown and a toothpick inserted into corn bread comes out clean. Turn ring out onto a platter; pour some of Cheese Sauce into center and over ring. Serve remainder in a small bowl. Makes 4 servings.

### *CHEESE SAUCE*

| | |
|---|---|
| 2 *10¾-ounce cans condensed* | 1 *16-ounce can cut green* |
| *Cheddar cheese soup,* | *beans, drained* |
| *undiluted* | ½ *teaspoon dry mustard* |
| ⅔ *cup milk* | |

Combine soup and milk in a saucepan. Place over moderate heat (about 250° F.). Cook and stir until blended and smooth. Add beans and mustard; cook and stir until heated. Makes 4 cups sauce.
Your Time: 4 minutes
Cooking and Baking Time: 35 minutes

## CREAMY HAM SKILLET

2 tablespoons butter or
   margarine
½ pound boiled ham, cut in
   ½-inch-wide strips
1 10½-ounce can condensed
   cream of celery soup,
   undiluted
½ cup water
¼ cup mayonnaise

1 11-ounce can small peas and
   onions, drained
2 16-ounce cans sliced
   potatoes, drained
1 teaspoon dried parsley
   flakes
2 teaspoons prepared mustard
⅛ teaspoon pepper

Melt butter in a large skillet over moderate heat (about 250° F.). Add ham strips and cook until slightly brown. Stir in remaining ingredients and blend well. Cook, uncovered, until mixture is heated through, stirring occasionally. Makes 6 servings.
Your Time: 7 minutes
Cooking Time: 20 minutes

## LUNCHEON-HAM CORN BREAD

1 package corn muffin mix
½ pound sliced boiled ham,
   diced
⅔ cup chopped salted peanuts

1 package cheese-sauce mix
   (makes 1 cup)
1 8-ounce can mixed
   vegetables, drained

Heat oven to 400° F. Grease an 8-inch-square pan with unsalted shortening. Prepare corn muffin mix according to package directions. Stir in ham and peanuts. Pour into prepared pan. Bake, uncovered, 20 to 25 minutes. While bread is baking, prepare cheese sauce following the package directions. Add vegetables to cheese sauce and heat. Cut bread into squares. Serve with sauce. Makes 6 servings.
Your Time: 12 minutes
Cooking and Baking Time: 20 to 25 minutes

## HAM ROLLS WITH HOLLANDAISE

1  *12-ounce package frozen
rice with bell peppers and
parsley in cooking pouch*
1  *4-ounce can sliced
mushrooms, drained*
8  *slices boiled ham, thick
enough to roll (about ⅛
inch)*

1  *5-ounce jar Hollandaise
sauce*
¼  *cup diced toasted almonds*

Heat oven to 350° F. Cook rice according to package directions and place in a medium-sized bowl. Add mushrooms and blend well, fluffing mixture with a fork. Place about ¼ cup of the rice mixture on each ham slice. Roll up slices and place rolls seam side down in an ungreased shallow 2-quart baking dish. Bake, uncovered, 20 minutes. Spoon sauce over top. Bake 5 minutes longer, or until heated through. Sprinkle top with almonds. Makes 4 servings.
Your Time: 8 minutes
Cooking and Baking Time: 45 minutes

## PINEAPPLE-HAM BAKE

1  *10-ounce package frozen
broccoli spears*
4  *1-ounce slices precooked
ham*
1  *8½-ounce can pineapple
slices*

1  *10¾-ounce can condensed
Cheddar cheese soup,
undiluted*
*Paprika*

Cook broccoli according to package directions. Grease a 1½-quart shallow baking dish with unsalted shortening and arrange broccoli spears in dish. Arrange ham slices over broccoli. Drain pineapple and reserve syrup. Combine soup and pineapple syrup in a small bowl and pour mixture over ham slices. Arrange pineapple slices on top of ham. Sprinkle with paprika. Bake, uncovered, 25 minutes, or until sauce is bubbly. Makes 4 servings.
Your Time: 7 minutes
Cooking Time: 40 minutes

## POLYNESIAN BEANS

2 tablespoons butter or
  margarine
½ medium-sized green pepper,
  cut into strips
1 16-ounce can pork and
  beans with tomato sauce

1 cup diced ready-to-eat ham
2 tablespoons instant minced
  onion
1 teaspoon curry powder
½ cup sliced peeled banana

Heat butter in a skillet over moderately low heat (about 225° F.); add green pepper and cook until tender. Remove skillet from heat. Add beans, ham, onion, and curry powder; mix well. Return mixture to moderately low heat (about 225° F.) and cook about 10 minutes, or until hot, stirring occasionally. Fold in banana. Makes 2 to 3 servings.
Your Time: 9 minutes
Cooking Time: 15 minutes

## HAM AND SWEET POTATO CASSEROLE

1 17-ounce can sweet
  potatoes, drained
1 13¼-ounce can crushed
  pineapple, undrained
3 tablespoons light-brown
  sugar

2 teaspoons prepared mustard
1 pound boiled ham, cut into
  4 ½-inch-thick slices
3 tablespoons packaged
  seasoned coating mix for
  chicken

Heat oven to 400° F. Arrange sweet potatoes around the edges of an ungreased shallow 3-quart baking dish. Pour crushed pineapple into center of dish, spooning some of the pineapple syrup over potatoes. Sprinkle sugar over potatoes and pineapple. Spread mustard on one side of each ham slice and arrange ham over pineapple, mustard side up. Sprinkle seasoned coating mix over mustard. Bake, uncovered, 20 minutes, or until thoroughly heated. Makes 4 servings.
Your Time: 4 minutes
Baking Time: 20 minutes

## RAVIOLI CASSEROLE

3 tablespoons butter or
 margarine
1 4-ounce can sliced
 mushrooms, drained
2 cups diced cooked ham

¾ cup cooked peas
⅛ teaspoon pepper
2 15-ounce cans cheese ravioli
2 tablespoons grated
 Parmesan cheese

Heat oven to 375° F. Melt butter in skillet over moderate heat (about 250° F.); add mushrooms and cook until lightly browned. Stir in ham, peas, and pepper. Pour 1 can of ravioli into the bottom of an ungreased shallow 1½-quart baking dish. Pour ham mixture into center of dish; spoon remaining can of ravioli around ham. Top with cheese. Bake, uncovered, 25 minutes. Makes 4 servings.
Your Time: 8 minutes
Baking Time: 25 minutes

# *Veal*

## ITALIAN VEAL CUTLETS

½ cup fine dry bread crumbs
¼ cup grated Parmesan
 cheese
4 teaspoons paprika
1¼ pounds veal, cut for
 scaloppine

3 tablespoons butter or
 margarine
Tomato-Mushroom Sauce
 (recipe follows)

Combine bread crumbs, grated cheese, and paprika in a pie plate; mix thoroughly. Coat veal cutlets lightly with the bread mixture. Melt butter in a 10-inch skillet over moderately high heat (about 275° F.). Add cutlets and brown 4 to 5 minutes on each side, until meat is fork-tender. Serve immediately with the tomato sauce. Makes 4 to 5 servings.

## TOMATO-MUSHROOM SAUCE

*2  8-ounce cans tomato sauce        1  teaspoon sugar
      with mushrooms
½  teaspoon dried oregano
      leaves*

Combine all ingredients in a saucepan; heat over moderately low heat (about 225° F.), stirring occasionally, until heated through. Serve with veal. Makes 2 cups.
Your Time: 4 minutes
Cooking Time: 20 minutes

## VEAL AU GRATIN

*8  veal cutlets cut for               4  slices Swiss cheese
      scaloppine                        4  thin slices boiled ham
1  egg, slightly beaten               3  tablespoons butter or
1  cup fine dry bread crumbs            margarine*

Dip veal cutlets first in egg and then in crumbs. Place a slice of cheese and a slice of ham on half the cutlets. Top with rest of cutlets. Melt butter in a skillet over moderate heat (about 250° F.). Brown meat stacks about 5 minutes on each side or until meat is fork-tender and cheese is melted. Makes 4 servings.
Your Time: 10 minutes
Cooking Time: 10 minutes

## VEAL WITH HERB SAUCE

*1½  pounds veal, cut for            2  tablespoons instant
      scaloppine                         minced onion
3  tablespoons bottled Italian     ¼  teaspoon salt
      dressing                        1  package chicken-gravy mix
1  cup hot water                        (makes 1 cup)*

Cut meat into 1½-inch strips. Heat dressing in skillet over moderately high heat (about 375° F.); cook veal until lightly browned on both sides. Reduce heat to moderately low (about 225° F.); add water, onion, and salt and cook 45 to 50 minutes, or until fork-tender. Remove meat to a warm platter. Pour meat juices into a 1-cup measuring cup and add enough water to make 1 cup liquid. Pour

gravy mix into a bowl and blend in meat juices. Pour mixture into skillet and cook over moderately low heat (about 225° F.) until thickened. Serve sauce over the veal. Makes 4 to 6 servings.
Your Time: 9 minutes
Cooking Time: 55 to 60 minutes

## VEAL STROGANOFF

1  10½-ounce can condensed golden mushroom soup, undiluted
½ cup water

1  pound boneless veal, cut for scaloppine
¼ cup commercial sour cream

Combine soup and water in a medium-sized skillet. Add veal pieces. Place over moderate heat (about 250° F.) and simmer, covered, about 35 minutes, or until veal is fork-tender. Remove from heat and stir in sour cream. Makes 4 servings.
Your Time: 4 minutes
Cooking Time: 35 minutes

## VEAL AND ZUCCHINI PARMIGIANA

2  tablespoons vegetable oil
4  frozen breaded veal cutlets
2  16-ounce cans zucchini in tomato sauce
⅛ teaspoon dried oregano leaves

⅛ teaspoon dried basil leaves
Pinch of garlic powder
1  8-ounce package mozzarella cheese, thinly sliced
Dried parsley flakes

Heat oil in a large skillet over moderately high heat (about 325° F.). Place 2 of the veal cutlets in skillet and cook about 5 minutes, turning to brown both sides. Remove from skillet and repeat with the remaining 2 cutlets, adding additional oil if necessary. Remove veal and reserve. Combine zucchini, oregano, basil, and garlic powder in the skillet. Place over moderately low heat (about 225° F.) and simmer about 5 minutes. Arrange browned veal pieces on top of zucchini mixture and place cheese slices on top of veal. Cover and cook an additional 5 minutes, or until cheese melts. Sprinkle with parsley flakes. Makes 4 servings.
Your Time: 10 minutes
Cooking Time: 22 minutes

# *Sausages and Frankfurters*

## LIMA BEANS AND SAUSAGE

1  10¾-ounce can condensed
   tomato soup, undiluted
¼  cup catsup
½  teaspoon salt
¼  teaspoon pepper
3  tablespoons instant minced
   onion

¼  cup chopped green pepper
2  16-ounce cans lima beans,
   drained
1  8-ounce package
   brown-and-serve sausage
   links

Mix soup, catsup, salt, pepper, onion, and green pepper in large skillet; fold in lima beans. Cover and simmer over moderately low heat (about 225° F.) 10 to 15 minutes, stirring occasionally, until green pepper is tender. Arrange sausage links over the lima beans. Cover and simmer 10 minutes, stirring occasionally. Makes 4 servings.
Your Time: 8 minutes
Cooking Time: 20 to 25 minutes

## SAUSAGE-CORN ESCALLOP

2  tablespoons butter or
   margarine
½  cup finely chopped green
   pepper
⅓  cup frozen chopped onion
2  4-ounce cans cocktail
   sausages, drained and
   sliced thick
1  17-ounce can cream-style
   corn, undrained
1  12-ounce can whole-kernel
   corn, drained

½  teaspoon salt
¼  teaspoon Worcestershire
   sauce
Few grains pepper
1  4-ounce package shredded
   Cheddar cheese
½  cup crushed cheese crackers
1  tablespoon melted butter or
   margarine

Heat oven to 375° F. Melt butter in a skillet over moderately low heat (about 225° F.). Add green pepper, onion, and sausage and cook until pepper and onion are tender. Combine cooked mixture, cream-style corn, whole-kernel corn, salt, Worcestershire, and pepper in a medium-sized bowl. Pour half the mixture into an ungreased deep 1½-quart casserole. Sprinkle with half the cheese. Add remaining corn mixture and cheese. Toss the cracker crums with

the 1 tablespoon melted butter and sprinkle over cheese. Bake, uncovered, 25 to 30 minutes, or until mixture bubbles around the edges. Serve as a luncheon or supper dish. Makes 4 to 6 servings.
Your Time: 13 minutes
Baking Time: 25 to 30 minutes

## SAUSAGE WITH HOT MACARONI

1  *1½-to-1¾-pound Polish sausage ring (kielbasa)*
1  *8-ounce package elbow macaroni*
¾  *cup bottled Caesar salad dressing*

½  *cup packaged frozen chopped green pepper*
¼  *cup packaged frozen chopped onion*

Place sausage in a large pot of boiling water; cover and cook over low heat (about 200° F.) for 20 minutes. While sausage is cooking, cook macaroni in a medium-sized saucepan according to package directions; drain and return to saucepan. In a small saucepan combine salad dressing, green pepper, and onion; cook over moderate heat (about 250° F.), stirring constantly, until vegetables are tender. Pour dressing mixture over macaroni in saucepan; blend well and cook over moderately low heat (about 225° F.), stirring frequently, until heated. Arrange macaroni on a platter and top with the sausage. Makes 4 servings.
Your Time: 7 minutes
Cooking Time: 40 minutes

## SAUSAGE AND NOODLE CASSEROLE

1  *5.5-ounce package noodles with sour cream and cheese sauce*
2  *tablespoons butter or margarine*
½  *cup milk*
1  *teaspoon Worcestershire sauce*

⅛  *teaspoon garlic powder*
1  *tablespoon freeze-dried chopped chives*
2  *5-ounce packages miniature smoky link sausages*

Heat oven to 350° F. Prepare noodles as directed on package. When noodles are cooked, drain well, and place in an ungreased 1½-quart casserole. Add sauce mix from the package, the butter, and milk;

blend thoroughly. Stir in Worcestershire, garlic powder, and chopped chives. Add sausage links and mix well. Cover and bake 20 to 25 minutes, or until thoroughly heated. Makes 4 servings.
Your Time: 6 minutes
Cooking and Baking Time: 40 to 45 minutes

## SWEET POTATO AND SAUSAGE CASSEROLE

| | |
|---|---|
| 2  17-ounce cans vacuum-packed sweet potatoes | 2  tablespoons dark-brown sugar |
| 1  pound bulk sausage meat | 2  tablespoons melted butter or margarine |
| Salt | 2  tablespoons light cream |
| 1  8¼-ounce can sliced pineapple, drained, slices cut in half | ¼  cup firmly packed dark-brown sugar |

Slice potatoes into ½-inch crosswise slices. Heat oven to 350° F. Cook sausage meat in a skillet over moderate heat (about 250° F.), until lightly browned, stirring with a fork to break up pieces. Place half of the potato in a layer in bottom of an ungreased shallow 2-quart baking dish; sprinkle lightly with salt. Sprinkle sausage meat over potatoes for second layer. Place pineapple over sausage. Sprinkle lightly with salt and the 2 tablespoons brown sugar. Top with remaining potato slices. Brush with melted butter and cream. Sprinkle with the remaining ¼ cup brown sugar. Bake, uncovered, 45 minutes. Makes 4 servings.
Your Time: 11 minutes
Cooking and Baking Time: 1 hour

## BEAN POT CASSEROLE

| | |
|---|---|
| 2  tablespoons butter or margarine | ½  cup Burgundy wine |
| ½  cup frozen chopped onion | 8  frankfurters |
| 2  16-ounce cans barbecue beans | 8  strips process American cheese about ⅜ inch thick and 3½ inches long |
| ½  cup chili sauce | |

Heat oven to 350° F. Melt butter in skillet over moderate heat (about 250° F.); add onions and cook until tender, or about 5 minutes. Add beans, chili sauce, and wine. Pour into an ungreased

shallow 2-quart baking dish. Split frankfurters almost in half and arrange over beans. Bake, uncovered, 25 minutes. Place a strip of cheese in each frankfurter. Bake 15 minutes longer, until cheese is melted. Makes 4 to 6 servings.
Your Time: 6½ minutes
Cooking and Baking Time: 45 minutes

## BAKED FRANKFURTER BOATS

8 *frankfurter buns, split*
¼ *cup melted butter or*
  *margarine*
2 *teaspoons prepared mustard*
2 *teaspoons bottled*
  *horseradish*

¾ *cup packaged shredded*
  *Cheddar cheese*
½ *cup bottled India relish*
8 *frankfurters*

Heat oven to 400° F. Brush the insides of the buns with the melted butter. Combine mustard and horseradish; spread over butter. Combine cheese and relish. Split frankfurters almost through lengthwise; spoon cheese-relish mixture into the center of each frankfurter. Place a frankfurter, cut side up, on each bun. Arrange on a cookie sheet and bake, uncovered, 10 minutes, or until buns are lightly browned and cheese is melted. Makes 8 sandwiches.
Your Time: 7 minutes
Baking Time: 10 minutes

## BARBECUED FRANKFURTERS

2 *tablespoons butter or*
  *margarine*
1 *pound frankfurters*
1 *small onion, peeled and*
  *sliced*

1 *10¾-ounce can beef gravy*
2 *tablespoons vinegar*
2 *tablespoons brown sugar*
2 *tablespoons mincemeat or*
  *raisins*

Melt butter in a medium-sized skillet over moderate heat (about 250° F.). Add frankfurters and onion and cook until frankfurters are lightly browned. Add beef gravy, vinegar, brown sugar, and mincemeat or raisins. Stir until sauce is smooth. Cover and simmer gently over low heat (about 200° F.) about 5 minutes. Makes 4 to 5 servings.
Your Time: 6 minutes
Cooking Time: 10 minutes

## FRANKFURTER-BEAN SKILLET

1  16-ounce can beans with         ½ teaspoon dry mustard
   pork and molasses sauce         6 frankfurters, cut in half
2  tablespoons dark molasses          lengthwise
1  teaspoon instant minced        1 20-ounce can pineapple
   onion                             slices, drained

Combine beans, molasses, onions, and mustard in a medium-sized
skillet. Insert a frankfurter halfway through the hole in each
pineapple slice and arrange on top of beans. Place skillet over
moderately low heat (about 225° F.) and simmer, covered, about 10
minutes, or until mixture is thoroughly heated. Makes 4 servings.
Your Time: 7 minutes
Cooking Time: 10 minutes

## BROCCOLI-BOLOGNA CASSEROLE

1  tablespoon butter or           4 slices ham bologna, cut
   margarine                        ¼-inch thick (about 1
¼  cup thinly sliced celery         pound)
1  10¾-ounce can beef gravy       ¾ cup herb-seasoned dry
2  10-ounce packages frozen          stuffing mix
   broccoli spears, cooked
   and drained

Heat oven to 450° F. Melt butter in saucepan over moderately low
heat (about 225° F.); add celery and cook until tender. Remove
from heat and stir in gravy. Arrange broccoli in the bottom of an
ungreased shallow 2-quart baking dish. Arrange bologna over
broccoli. Top with gravy and sprinkle with stuffing mix. Bake,
uncovered, 15 minutes. Makes 4 servings.
Your Time: 11 minutes
Cooking and Baking Time: 25 minutes

## SPICED CABBAGE WITH KNACKWURST

2 tablespoons butter or
    margarine
½ cup frozen chopped onion
2 16-ounce jars red cabbage,
    undrained
1 22-ounce can apple pie
    filling
¼ cup red wine vinegar
1 teaspoon bottled lemon
    juice

½ teaspoon salt
½ teaspoon caraway seeds
¼ teaspoon ground nutmeg
¼ teaspoon dried thyme
    leaves
2 1-pound packages
    knackwurst (8)

Melt butter in a large skillet over moderately low heat (about 225° F.). Add onion and cook until tender, about 5 minutes. Add cabbage and cook until heated through. Add pie filling, vinegar, lemon juice, salt, caraway seeds, nutmeg, and thyme. Stir to blend well. Cook until mixture is thoroughly heated. Meanwhile cook knackwurst according to package directions. Arrange the cabbage in a serving dish and top with the hot knackwurst. Makes 6 to 8 servings.
Your Time: 10 minutes
Cooking Time: 20 minutes

## QUICK CHOUCROUTE

1 27-ounce can sauerkraut,
    undrained
1 8-ounce jar applesauce
1 cup dry white wine
1 teaspoon caraway seeds
    (optional)

1 pound knackwurst (about
    4)
Hot mashed potatoes or
    cooked noodles (optional)

In a large skillet combine sauerkraut, applesauce, wine, and caraway seeds; blend well. Top sauerkraut with the knackwurst. Cover skillet and simmer over moderate heat (about 250° F.) 5 minutes. Remove cover and continue to cook until most of liquid is absorbed, about 15 minutes. Serve with mashed potatoes or noodles, if desired. Makes 4 servings.
Your Time: 8 minutes
Cooking Time: 20 minutes

## FRANKFURTER-CHEESE SOUFFLÉ

*8 frankfurters (about 1     2 12-ounce packages frozen*
*   pound)                          cheese soufflé*

Heat oven to 325° F. Slit frankfurters lengthwise three-quarters through. Open cut frankfurters flat. Arrange frankfurters around edges of an ungreased shallow 2-quart (11¾-x-7³₈-x-1¾-inch) baking dish so that part of the cut frankfurter is on the side of the dish and part is on the bottom. Allow 2 frankfurters for each long side and 1 for each short side of dish. (Sides of dish will be partly lined with 6 cut frankfurters.) Lay the remaining 2 frankfurters flat on the bottom of the dish, cut side down. Remove the 2 cheese soufflés from their containers and place side by side on top of frankfurters in the dish. Bake, uncovered, 60 to 70 minutes, or until knife inserted in side of soufflé comes out clean. Serve immediately. Makes 6 servings.
Your Time: 5 minutes
Baking Time: 60 to 70 minutes

## FANCY FRANKFURTERS

*5 frankfurters*                          *¾ teaspoon salt*
*1 3½-ounce can French fried*      *⅛ teaspoon pepper*
*   onions*                              *1 10½-ounce can condensed*
*1 16-ounce package frozen*            *cream of celery soup,*
*   shredded potatoes for*               *undiluted*
*   hashed browns, thawed*           *⅓ cup milk*
*2 tablespoons melted butter*
*   or margarine*

Heat oven to 375° F. Slice each frankfurter in half lengthwise. In a small bowl crumble French fried onions with your fingers. Reserve 2 tablespoons for topping. Combine potatoes, butter, crumbled onions, salt, and pepper in an ungreased shallow 1½-quart baking dish and blend well. Combine celery soup and milk in a small bowl. Pour about ¾ of the soup mixture over potato mixture and blend well. Arrange frankfurters, cut side down, on top of potatoes. Sprinkle the reserved 2 tablespoons crumbled onions on top. Pour remaining soup mixture over onions. Bake, uncovered, 25 minutes, or until heated through. Makes 3 to 4 servings.
Your Time: 8 minutes
Baking Time: 25 minutes

## FRANKFURTER-NOODLE CASSEROLE

3 cups uncooked broad egg
 noodles
1 envelope green pea soup
 mix
3 cups hot water
1 4-ounce package shredded
 process American cheese

6 frankfurters, cut into 1-inch
 pieces
¼ cup sliced stuffed olives
¼ cup finely chopped onion
⅛ teaspoon pepper

Heat oven to 350° F. Cook noodles as directed on package. Drain well. While noodles are cooking, pour soup mix into a saucepan; add the 3 cups hot water and cheese. Cook over moderate heat (about 250° F.), stirring constantly, until cheese is melted. Add frankfurters, olives, onion, and pepper; mix well. Pour half the noodles into an ungreased 8-x-8-x-2-inch baking dish. Pour in half the soup mixture. Repeat the noodle and soup layers. Bake, uncovered, 20 minutes. Makes 4 to 6 servings.
Your Time: 11½ minutes
Cooking and Baking Time: 40 minutes

## POTATO-FRANKFURTER CASSEROLE

1 17-ounce can peas and
 onions
1 10¾-ounce can condensed
 Cheddar cheese soup,
 undiluted

¼ teaspoon dry mustard
1 16-ounce package frozen
 French fried potatoes,
 unthawed
6 frankfurters, thinly sliced

Heat oven to 350° F. Grease a deep 2-quart casserole with unsalted shortening. Drain peas and measure out ½ cup of the liquid to use in recipe; discard remaining liquid. Combine the ½ cup liquid, soup, and mustard in a small bowl. Mix cheese sauce, potatoes, frankfurters, and peas together; pour into prepared casserole. Bake 30 minutes; remove from oven and gently stir edges of mixture into the center so it will heat thoroughly. Return to oven and bake, uncovered, 30 minutes longer. Makes 6 servings.
Your Time: 6 minutes
Baking Time: 1 hour

## FRANKFURTER AND RICE CASSEROLE

1½ cups packaged precooked
 rice
1 tablespoon vegetable oil
1 pound frankfurters, cut
 into 2-inch slices
2 8-ounce cans tomato sauce
½ cup water
2 tablespoons instant
 minced onion

10 pitted ripe olives, halved
1 10-ounce package frozen
 peas
½ teaspoon salt
Few grains pepper
½ cup packaged shredded
 Cheddar cheese

Heat oven to 350° F. Grease a deep 2½-quart casserole with unsalted shortening. Prepare rice, following directions on package. Heat oil in a skillet over moderately high heat (about 350° F.); add frankfurters and cook until lightly browned on all sides, stirring occasionally. Add tomato sauce, water, and onion; cook over moderate heat (about 250° F.) for 5 minutes. Remove from heat. Add rice, olives, peas, salt, and pepper to skillet; mix well. Pour into prepared casserole and sprinkle with cheese. Bake, uncovered, 30 minutes. Makes 6 servings.
Your Time: 14 minutes
Cooking and Baking Time: 50 minutes

## SUPPER IN A SKILLET

2 tablespoons butter or
 margarine
½ cup frozen chopped onion
½ cup frozen chopped green
 pepper
1 16-ounce can tomatoes in
 tomato purée
1 cup tomato juice
1 teaspoon salt

⅛ teaspoon pepper
⅛ teaspoon garlic powder
¼ teaspoon dried oregano
 leaves
¼ teaspoon dried basil leaves
1 pound frankfurters, cut into
 ½-inch slices
2 cups uncooked medium egg
 noodles

Melt butter in a large skillet over moderate heat (about 250° F.). Add onion and green pepper and cook until fork-tender, about 5 minutes. Add tomatoes, tomato juice, salt, pepper, garlic powder, oregano, basil, and sliced frankfurters. Cover skillet and bring mixture to a boil. Add noodles and stir to blend well. Cover and cook over moderately low heat (about 225° F.) 10 minutes, or until noodles are tender; stir occasionally. Makes 6 servings.
Your Time: 8 minutes
Cooking Time: 20 minutes

# Canned Meats

## TORTILLA CASSEROLE

2 15½-ounce cans barbecue
  sauce and beef
2 teaspoons chili powder
1 20-ounce can red kidney
  beans, undrained

1 4-ounce package shredded
  Cheddar cheese
1 11-ounce can tortillas (17
  tortillas)

Heat oven to 400° F. In a medium-sized bowl combine barbecue sauce and beef, chili powder, kidney beans, and half the cheese; blend well. Using ²⁄₃ of the mixture, spread some of it on each tortilla. Fold tortillas in half and arrange, overlapping, in an ungreased shallow 3-quart baking dish, folded edges down. Pour remaining meat mixture around tortillas and sprinkle top with the remaining cheese. Bake, uncovered, about 15 minutes, or until cheese is melted and sauce bubbles. Makes 8 servings.
Your Time: 12 minutes
Baking Time: 15 minutes

## SAUERBRATEN STEW

2 12-ounce cans meatballs in
  gravy
1 8-ounce can sliced carrots,
  undrained
⅓ cup frozen chopped onion
2 tablespoons wine vinegar

1 tablespoon dark-brown
  sugar
1 bay leaf
Few grains ground cloves
⅛ teaspoon pepper
6 or 7 1¾-inch gingersnaps

Combine the 2 cans of meatballs in a large saucepan; stir in carrots (including liquid), chopped onion, vinegar, brown sugar, bay leaf, cloves, and pepper. Cook over moderately low heat (about 225° F.) about 10 minutes, stirring occasionally, until heated through. While stew is cooking, place the gingersnaps in a plastic bag and crush finely by rolling a rolling pin over the bag. Measure out ¹⁄₃ cup crumbs. When stew is heated, add gingersnap crumbs and stir well. Cook 1 minute longer. Makes 4 servings.
Your Time: 6 minutes
Cooking Time: 11 minutes

## QUICK SWEDISH MEATBALLS

*1 15-ounce can meatballs in        ¼ teaspoon ground allspice*
*   spaghetti sauce               ¼ cup heavy cream*
*½ teaspoon bottled brown*
*   sauce*

Combine meatballs in spaghetti sauce, brown sauce, and allspice in a saucepan. Place over moderately low heat (about 225° F.) and simmer 5 or 6 minutes. Add heavy cream, heat another minute, and serve. Makes 2 or 3 servings.
Your Time: 3 minutes
Cooking Time: 6 or 7 minutes

## CONTINENTAL STEW

*1 24-ounce can beef stew        2 tablespoons tomato paste*
*1 16-ounce can peas with        2 tablespoons dry sherry*
*   onions, undrained*

Combine ingredients in a medium-sized saucepan. Place over moderately low heat (about 225° F.) and cook until liquid bubbles and meat is hot, or about 6 minutes. Makes 3 servings.
Your Time: 3 minutes
Cooking Time: 6 minutes

## BURGER BAKE WITH BISCUITS

*2 9-ounce packages frozen       ⅛ teaspoon Tabasco*
*   whole green beans            1 8-ounce container*
*1 15-ounce can meatballs           refrigerated biscuits (10*
*   with gravy                      biscuits)*
*1 10¾-ounce can condensed       1 tablespoon melted butter or*
*   tomato soup, undiluted          margarine*
*½ teaspoon dry mustard          1 teaspoon poppy seeds*

Heat oven to 425° F. Cook beans according to package directions. Drain. In a saucepan combine meatballs with gravy, tomato soup, mustard, and Tabasco. Place over moderately high heat (about 350° F.) and heat, stirring frequently, until mixture is bubbling. Stir in drained cooked beans. Spoon into an ungreased shallow 1½-quart casserole. Open biscuit container according to label directions.

Arrange biscuits around the edge of casserole. Brush tops of biscuits with melted butter and sprinkle with poppy seeds. Bake, uncovered, 20 minutes, or until biscuits are thoroughly baked. Makes 6 servings.
Your Time: 10 minutes
Cooking and Baking Time: 35 minutes

## CREAMED CORNED BEEF

1  3-ounce can sliced broiled
   mushrooms
Milk
2  packages white sauce mix
   (each making 1 cup)
½  cup dry white wine
½  cup grated Parmesan cheese

⅛  teaspoon paprika
1  12-ounce can corned beef,
   chopped
½  cup cooked and drained
   peas
1  7-ounce package toaster
   corn cakes

Drain mushrooms, reserving the liquid. Measure liquid and add enough milk to make 1½ cups. Prepare the 2 packages white sauce mix according to package directions, using the 1½ cups mushroom-milk liquid and the ½ cup wine. When sauce is thickened, stir in cheese and paprika. Cook and stir until cheese is melted. Stir in corned beef, mushrooms, and peas. Heat the mixture thoroughly. Toast the corn cakes. Serve the creamed corned beef mixture over the corn cakes. Makes 6 servings.
Your Time: 15 minutes
Cooking Time: 15 minutes

## QUICK CORNED-BEEF DINNER

2  tablespoons butter or
   margarine
1  16-ounce can potatoes,
   drained
½  small head cabbage, cut
   into 4 wedges
Salt
1  12-ounce can corned beef
1  15-ounce can whole
   carrots, drained

1  package white sauce mix
   (makes 1 cup)
1½  teaspoons prepared
   horseradish
1  teaspoon prepared
   mustard
½  teaspoon vinegar

Melt butter in a 10-inch skillet over moderately low heat (about 225° F.). Add potatoes and cook over moderately high heat (about

275° F.), stirring frequently, for about 5 minutes, or until potatoes are glazed and are starting to brown. Remove from heat. Arrange cabbage wedges in a layer in skillet with the potatoes; sprinkle with salt and add ½ cup water. Cover and cook over moderately low heat (about 225° F.) for 15 minutes, or until cabbage is almost tender. Remove skillet from heat. Cut corned beef into 4 slices. Arrange cabbage and corned beef to one side of skillet. Place potatoes and carrots in separate groups at other side of skillet. Cover and return to heat; cook 10 minutes. Remove vegetables and meat to a warm platter and keep warm in a 200° F. oven. Place white sauce mix in saucepan. Pour drippings from skillet into a 1-cup measuring cup and add enough water to make 1 cup liquid. Blend liquid into mix in saucepan. Add horseradish, mustard, and vinegar. Cook over moderate heat (about 250° F.) about 5 minutes, or until sauce is thickened. Serve with meat and vegetables. Makes 4 servings.
Your Time: 19 minutes
Cooking Time: 30 minutes

## CORNED BEEF AND MACARONI DINNER

1½ cups uncooked elbow
   macaroni
1 12-ounce can corned beef,
   coarsely chopped
1 10½-ounce can condensed
   cream of chicken soup,
   undiluted
1 cup milk

¼ pound process American
   cheese, cubed
½ cup finely chopped peeled
   onion
¾ cup packaged fine dry
   bread crumbs
3 tablespoons melted butter
   or margarine

Heat oven to 350° F. Cook macaroni according to package directions; drain. Combine corned beef, chicken soup, milk, cheese, and onion in a medium-sized bowl. Alternate layers of cooked macaroni and meat mixture in an ungreased deep 2-quart casserole. Toss bread crumbs and butter with a fork to combine; sprinkle over top. Bake, uncovered, 1 hour. Makes 4 to 6 servings.
Your Time: 5 minutes
Cooking Time: 1 hour and 12 minutes

## CORNED BEEF SUPPER CASSEROLE

1  10½-ounce can condensed
   cream of celery soup,
   undiluted
1¾ cups hot water
1  cup cooked or canned
   green beans, drained

1  12-ounce can corned beef,
   coarsely chopped
1⅓ cups packaged precooked
   rice
½  cup canned French fried
   onion rings

Heat oven to 375° F. Mix soup and hot water in a bowl; add green beans. Pour half of the soup mixture into an ungreased deep 1½-quart casserole. Arrange corned beef over soup. Sprinkle with rice. Pour in remaining soup mixture. Cover and bake 10 minutes. Stir mixture gently and sprinkle with onions. Return to oven and bake uncovered 30 minutes longer. Makes 4 to 6 servings.
Your Time: 7 minutes
Cooking Time: 40 minutes

## CHILI CASSEROLE

1  12-ounce can corned beef,
   finely diced
1  package chili mix
½  cup water
1  16-ounce can whole
   tomatoes, undrained
1  16-ounce can kidney beans,
   undrained

1  8-ounce container
   refrigerated biscuits (10
   biscuits)
1  tablespoon melted butter or
   margarine
½  cup chopped peanuts

Heat oven to 450° F. Mix together corned beef, chili mix, water, tomatoes, and kidney beans in a medium-sized bowl; pour mixture into an ungreased shallow 2-quart casserole. Bake, uncovered, 15 minutes. Remove from oven. Open biscuit container according to label directions. Arrange biscuits over chili mixture; brush biscuits with butter and sprinkle with peanuts. Return to oven and bake, uncovered, 8 to 10 minutes. Makes 6 to 8 servings.
Your Time: 10 minutes
Cooking Time: 23 to 25 minutes

## SPINACH-HASH PIE

| | |
|---|---|
| 2 teaspoons instant minced onion | 4 eggs |
| ¼ cup milk | ½ teaspoon salt |
| 1 15-ounce can corned beef hash | ¼ teaspoon pepper |
| | ¼ teaspoon ground nutmeg |
| 1 16-ounce can spinach, well drained | 1 tablespoon grated Parmesan cheese |

Heat oven to 350° F. Grease a 9-inch pie plate with unsalted shortening. Mix onion and milk in a small bowl and let stand 3 minutes. Spoon corned beef hash into prepared pie plate and spread evenly over bottom and sides to form a pie shell. Spoon spinach over hash. Beat together eggs, milk mixture, salt, pepper, and nutmeg in a small bowl. Pour over spinach and mix together lightly. Bake, uncovered, 40 to 45 minutes, or until custard is set. Sprinkle with Parmesan cheese before serving. Makes 6 servings.
Your Time: 8 minutes
Baking Time: 40 to 45 minutes

## CRANBERRY-GLAZED BAKED HAM

| | |
|---|---|
| 1 6 to 7-pound canned ham | ⅛ teaspoon ground cinnamon |
| 1 14-ounce jar cranberry-orange relish | ⅛ teaspoon ground cloves |
| | Orange slices (optional) |
| 1 tablespoon dark-brown sugar | Parsley sprigs (optional) |

If possible, have butcher remove ham from the can, cut it into ¼-inch-thick slices. Then tie the slices securely into the original shape, about 1 inch from the top and 1 inch from the bottom. (If more convenient, the ham can be sliced and tied at home.) Heat oven to 325° F. Place tied ham on a rack in a shallow roasting pan. Bake 15 minutes per pound, or about 1½ to 1¾ hours. Meanwhile combine remaining ingredients. Spoon over top of ham at 10-minute intervals during the final ½ hour of baking time. Place ham on serving platter and remove twine. Garnish the platter with orange slices and parsley sprigs, if desired. Ham is ready to serve without carving. Makes 18 to 20 servings.
Your Time: 5 minutes (Add 12 minutes if you slice the ham yourself)
Baking Time: 1½ to 1¾ hours

## DEVILED HAM TETRAZZINI

2 cups uncooked spaghetti
broken into 2-inch pieces
1½ teaspoons instant minced
onion
1 10½-ounce can condensed
cream of chicken soup,
undiluted

⅔ cup milk
1 4-ounce package shredded
Cheddar cheese
1 teaspoon Worcestershire
sauce
1 4½-ounce can deviled ham

Heat oven to 350° F. Cook and drain spaghetti as package directs. Combine spaghetti and remaining ingredients in an ungreased deep 3-quart casserole. Stir well to blend. Bake, covered, 20 minutes. Makes 4 to 6 servings.
Your Time: 15 minutes
Cooking and Baking Time: 30 minutes

## HAM-AND-TURKEY MUFFIN BROIL

4 English muffins
1 4½-ounce can deviled ham
¼ teaspoon prepared
horseradish
1 3-ounce package pressed
turkey or chicken

2 medium-sized tomatoes, cut
into ¼-inch slices
1 8-ounce jar pasteurized
process cheese spread

Preheat broiler. Split muffins and place halves on a cookie sheet. Broil 6 inches from source of heat about 1 minute, or until lightly browned. In a small bowl combine deviled ham and horseradish. Spread a layer of the ham mixture on toasted surface of each muffin half. Divide turkey among the muffin halves over ham mixture. Place a tomato slice on top of each. Spoon about 2 tablespoons of the cheese spread on top of each. (Refrigerate remaining spread and serve over vegetables at another time.) Broil sandwiches about 6 inches from heat about 2½ minutes, or until cheese spread melts and begins to brown. Serve hot. Makes 4 servings.
Your Time: 7 minutes
Broiling Time: 3½ minutes

## BEANS AND TOMATO GRILL

2 13-ounce cans baked beans          ½ cup packaged shredded
  in molasses sauce                    process American cheese
1 12-ounce can luncheon              2 tablespoons fine dry
  meat, cut into ½-inch                seasoned bread crumbs
  cubes                              2 tablespoons melted butter
3 small tomatoes, cut into             or margarine
  halves crosswise

Heat oven to 375° F. Combine baked beans and luncheon meat in a medium-sized bowl; pour into an ungreased shallow 1½-quart baking dish. Arrange tomato halves on top. Toss together cheese, bread crumbs, and butter; mound on top of tomatoes. Bake, uncovered, 30 minutes, or until lightly browned. Makes 4 servings.
Your Time: 8 minutes
Baking Time: 30 minutes

## LUNCHEON MEAT AND BAKED BEANS

2 12-ounce cans luncheon             1 tablespoon red wine vinegar
  meat, each cut into 8 slices       ¼ cup firmly packed brown
2 18-ounce jars New                    sugar
  England-style baked beans          ¼ teaspoon dry mustard
1 16-ounce can sliced cling          ⅛ teaspoon ground cloves
  peaches

Heat oven to 375° F. Lightly butter a shallow rectangular 2-quart baking dish. Arrange luncheon meat slices overlapping across the center of the prepared baking dish. Spoon beans along both sides of the meat slices. Drain the peaches and reserve 2 tablespoons of the syrup. Place 1 peach slice in between 2 slices of luncheon meat. Repeat until peach slices are arranged between all the meat slices. If any peaches are left over, arrange them over the beans. Blend together the reserved 2 tablespoons peach syrup, wine vinegar, brown sugar, mustard, and cloves in a small bowl. Brush mixture over luncheon meat and peach slices. Pour any leftover sauce over beans. Bake, uncovered, 25 to 30 minutes, or until meat slices are lightly browned and beans are bubbling hot. Makes 6 to 8 servings.
Your Time: 13 minutes
Baking Time: 30 minutes

## CHILI BEAN BAKE

1 package chili mix
1 16-ounce can whole
   tomatoes, undrained
½ cup water
1 20-ounce can kidney beans,
   undrained

1 16-ounce can lima beans,
   drained
1 12-ounce can luncheon
   meat, sliced
1 cup crumbled corn chips

Heat oven to 375° F. Combine chili mix, tomatoes, and water in saucepan; heat over moderately low heat (about 225° F.) 15 minutes, stirring occasionally. Add undrained kidney beans and the lima beans to sauce; pour into an ungreased shallow 2½-quart baking dish. Arrange luncheon meat over top. Bake, uncovered, 25 to 30 minutes. Sprinkle with crumbled corn chips. Makes 4 to 6 servings.
Your Time: 4 minutes
Cooking Time: 40 to 45 minutes

## ITALIAN RICE SKILLET

⅓ cup bottled Italian salad
   dressing
1 12-ounce can luncheon
   meat, diced
1 cup frozen chopped onion
1⅔ cups water
1⅓ cups packaged precooked
   rice

1 tablespoon dried parsley
   flakes
3 tablespoons sliced stuffed
   green olives
1 8-ounce can tomato sauce
   with cheese
Grated Parmesan cheese

Heat salad dressing in a large skillet over moderate heat (about 250° F.). Add meat and brown lightly on all sides. Add onion and cook until tender. Add water and bring to a boil. Stir in rice, parsley, and olives. Remove skillet from heat and cover. Let stand about 5 minutes. Stir in tomato sauce. Return to heat for a few minutes, until heated. Serve with Parmesan cheese. Makes 4 servings.
Your Time: 16 minutes
Cooking Time: 22 minutes

## LUNCHEON MEAT À LA MODE

2 *tablespoons instant minced*
   *onion*
¼ *cup water*
1 *12-ounce can luncheon*
   *meat, finely chopped*
1 *cup finely chopped celery*
½ *cup chopped green pepper*
½ *teaspoon dry mustard*
1 *16-ounce can tart red*
   *cherries*
2 *tablespoons cornstarch*

½ *cup firmly packed*
   *light-brown sugar*
*Few grains ground cloves*
3 *tablespoons lemon juice*
*Few drops red food coloring*
1 *8-ounce container*
   *refrigerated biscuits (10*
   *biscuits)*
1 *tablespoon butter or*
   *margarine*

Heat oven to 425° F. Mix onion and water together and let stand 5 minutes. Combine luncheon meat, celery, green pepper, mustard, and onion in a medium-sized bowl; spread over bottom of an ungreased 9-inch-square pan. Drain cherries and reserve juice. Mix cornstarch, brown sugar, and cloves in saucepan; stir in cherry juice, lemon juice, and red food coloring. Cook over moderate heat (about 250° F.), stirring constantly, until thickened. Fold in cherries and pour sauce over meat. Open container of biscuits according to label directions and arrange biscuits over cherries. Dot biscuits with butter. Bake, uncovered, 25 minutes. Makes 6 servings.
Your Time: 18 minutes
Cooking and Baking Time: 30 minutes

## BEAN-SAUSAGE SKILLET DINNER

¼ *cup molasses*
2 *tablespoons catsup*
2 *tablespoons vinegar*
2 *tablespoons prepared*
   *mustard*
1 *21-ounce can pork and*
   *beans, undrained*

1 *20-ounce can red kidney*
   *beans, undrained*
2 *4-ounce cans Vienna*
   *sausage*

Blend molasses, catsup, vinegar, and mustard in a skillet; fold in pork and beans and kidney beans. Arrange Vienna sausages over top. Cover and heat over moderate heat (about 250° F.) about 15 minutes, stirring occasionally, until piping hot. Makes 4 to 6 servings.
Your Time: 6 minutes
Cooking Time: 15 minutes

# Pasta Dishes

### LAZY MAN'S LASAGNA

6 *brown-and-serve sausage links*
1 *14-ounce jar spaghetti sauce*
⅛ *teaspoon salt*
¼ *teaspoon garlic salt*
*Few grains pepper*
3 *cups cooked broad egg noodles*

1 *cup cream-style cottage cheese*
1 *4-ounce package shredded mozzarella cheese*
2 *tablespoons grated Parmesan cheese*

Heat oven to 375° F. In a skillet over moderate heat (about 250° F.) cook sausages until brown on all sides. Remove and cut sausages into slices ½ inch thick. In a small bowl combine sauce, salt, garlic salt, pepper, and sliced sausages. Place half of noodles in the bottom of an ungreased shallow 2-quart casserole. Spread half of sauce over noodles; add remaining noodles and spread cottage cheese evenly over noodles. Top with remaining sauce and mozzarella. Top with Parmesan. Bake, uncovered, 35 minutes. Let stand 5 minutes before serving. Makes 4 servings.
Your Time: 11 minutes
Baking Time: 35 minutes
Standing Time: 5 minutes

### QUICK LASAGNA

2 *cups wide egg noodles, cooked*
1 *cup small-curd creamed cottage cheese*

1 *16-ounce jar spaghetti sauce with meat*
¼ *cup coarsely shredded process American cheese*

Heat oven to 375° F. Grease a shallow 1½-quart baking dish with unsalted shortening. Arrange cooked noodles in prepared baking dish; spread cottage cheese over noodles. Pour on spaghetti sauce; sprinkle shredded American cheese on top. Bake, uncovered, 20 to 25 minutes. Makes 4 servings.
Your Time: 2 minutes
Cooking and Baking Time: 30 to 35 minutes

## MACARONI DINNER

2  tablespoons vegetable oil
⅓ cup frozen chopped onion
1  small clove garlic, peeled
      and minced
1  8-ounce can tomato sauce
3  cups hot water
1½ teaspoons salt

¼ teaspoon pepper
3  cups uncooked elbow
      macaroni
½ pound sliced salami
1  medium-sized green
      pepper, sliced

Heat oil in a large skillet over moderate heat (about 250° F.); add onion and garlic and cook 3 to 4 minutes, or until tender, stirring occasionally. Remove skillet from heat. Mix in tomato sauce, water, salt, and pepper; stir in macaroni. Cut salami slices into halves and place on top. Cover skillet and place over moderate heat (about 250° F.) until mixture comes to a boil. Reduce heat to moderately low (about 225° F.) and cook 15 minutes, stirring occasionally, or until macaroni is tender. Place green pepper slices over macaroni and cook 10 minutes longer. Makes 4 to 6 servings.
Your Time: 10 minutes
Cooking Time: 35 minutes

## STUFFED MACARONI SHELLS

15  macaroni shells for
      stuffing
1½ cups small-curd creamed
      cottage cheese
¼ cup grated Parmesan
      cheese
¼ cup packaged shredded
      Cheddar cheese

1  egg, slightly beaten
2  tablespoons cracker meal
¼ teaspoon salt
2  15½-ounce cans barbecue
      sauce and beef

Cook shells in 3 quarts boiling water with 1 tablespoon salt over moderate heat (about 250° F.) for 20 to 25 minutes. Drain and cool in running cold water. Mix cottage cheese, Parmesan cheese, Cheddar cheese, eggs, cracker meal, and salt in a medium-sized bowl; spoon mixture into macaroni shells. Pour barbecue sauce and beef into a skillet; place over moderately low heat (about 225° F.) and heat 5 minutes. Arrange stuffed shells over sauce; cover and cook 15 minutes, or until well heated. Makes 4 to 6 servings.
Your Time: 12 minutes
Cooking Time: 40 to 45 minutes

## ONE-POT SPAGHETTI

2 tablespoons butter or           1 teaspoon salt
   vegetable oil                1 small can tomato paste
1 pound ground beef chuck    6 cups water
1 1½-ounce envelope            1 8-ounce package spaghetti
   spaghetti sauce mix

Melt butter in a Dutch oven over moderately low heat (about 225° F.). Add meat; cook and stir over moderately high heat (about 275° F.) until brown and crumbly. Add spaghetti sauce mix, salt, and tomato paste and blend well. Add water. Break spaghetti into 3-inch pieces. Bring sauce to a rolling boil over moderate heat (about 250° F.). Add spaghetti, boil gently, uncovered, 10 minutes, or until spaghetti is tender and sauce is thick, stirring occasionally. Let stand 5 minutes before serving. Makes 4 servings.
Your Time: 7 minutes
Cooking Time: 20 minutes
Standing Time: 5 minutes

# CHAPTER

# V

# *Vegetables*

You may be wondering what vegetables are doing in a *Timesaver Cookbook*. What could be easier than opening a can of corn or a package of beans or dropping a boil-in bag of buttered vegetables into hot water?

But vegetables are a little like the secondary colors on an artist's palette. Properly used, they can glamorize a main dish, setting it off so that it looks better than ever. Think of the times when you're faced with serving plain hamburger or leftover roast. That's when a vegetable that has been treated with a little extra care can make the ordinary meal extraordinary.

And treating vegetables with care takes little time when you consider the number of sauce mixes (dehydrated so they store indefinitely on the pantry shelf) and condensed canned soups that make excellent sauces for vegetables. The Green Bean Casserole (page 143), which uses frozen beans, canned soup, and canned French fried onions, has become one of those favorite combinations that scores of people love—a classic example of using soups as sauce. Savory Spinach (page 158), which depends for its exceptionally good flavor on sour cream and packaged salad dressing mix, and Glazed Carrot Slices (page 147), spiked surprisingly with cranberry-orange relish and brandy, can become your individual ways of making a vegetable superb.

It takes very little time to brush frozen potato puffs with herb butter before heating them, but the difference in appearance and taste is notable. It takes very little time to drain canned vegetables of their liquid, cook down the liquid with a pinch of herb, add the vegetables, and heat. They taste like a new food. Leftover roast with potatoes or Leftover Roast with Potatoes Fines Herbes? Even the ear catches the difference.

You'll find it very easy to give vegetables a Timesaver beauty treatment. They take well to special seasonings, and a few minutes with paring knife, dicer, or corer can give them undeniable visual appeal. Get to know your vegetables from A to Z (Asparagus to Zucchini is our lineup here) and introduce them into your timesaving meal plans. They belong there because they bring color, nutrition, and flavor to all meals.

## MARINATED ASPARAGUS SPEARS

2 10-ounce packages frozen jumbo asparagus spears
½ cup water
2 tablespoons lemon juice
1 tablespoon olive oil
1 teaspoon grated lemon peel
½ teaspoon onion salt
Lemon twists (optional)

Place asparagus in a large skillet; add remaining ingredients. Cover and simmer over moderately low heat (about 225° F.) 10 to 12 minutes, or until asparagus is fork-tender. Remove from heat. Pour asparagus and the liquid into a bowl. Let stand until cool; then refrigerate to chill thoroughly or at least 3 hours. When ready to serve, drain and serve asparagus as a vegetable or on lettuce as a salad. Garnish each portion with a lemon twist, if desired. Makes 6 servings.
Your Time: 6 minutes
Cooking Time: 10 to 12 minutes
Chilling Time: 3 hours

## SWEET-SOUR BAKED BEANS

2 13-ounce cans baked beans with pork and molasses sauce
1 teaspoon prepared mustard
¼ cup sweet pickle relish
½ cup dark seedless raisins
½ cup chili sauce
1 20-ounce can apple slices, drained

Place baked beans in a large saucepan; add mustard, pickle relish, raisins, and chili sauce and blend well. Stir in the apple slices. Cover and cook over moderate heat (about 250° F.), stirring occasionally, until mixture is thoroughly heated. Makes 6 servings.
Your Time: 5 minutes
Cooking Time: 10 minutes

## DANISH BEAN BAKE

4  *slices raw bacon, cut into*          2  *teaspoons prepared mustard*
     *1-inch pieces*                            1  *teaspoon Worcestershire*
2  *tablespoons chopped green*                  *sauce*
     *onions or scallions*                 1  *teaspoon vinegar*
1  *1¼-ounce wedge Roquefort*            2  *16-ounce cans pork and*
     *cheese, crumbled*                         *beans*

Heat oven to 350° F. Cook bacon in a skillet over moderately high heat (about 325° F.) until almost crisp. Remove from heat. Add onion and cook until lightly browned. Remove from heat. Add cheese, mustard, Worcestershire, and vinegar; stir until blended. Stir in pork and beans; pour into an ungreased deep 1-quart casserole. Bake, uncovered, 25 to 30 minutes, or until piping hot. Makes 6 servings.
Your Time: 10 minutes
Cooking and Baking Time: 35 minutes

## CREAMY DILLED GREEN BEANS

2  *9-ounce packages frozen*            2  *tablespoons milk or light*
     *whole green beans*                       *cream*
1  *4-ounce container whipped*          1  *teaspoon dried dillweed*
     *cream cheese*                        ¼  *teaspoon salt*

Cook beans according to package directions. Drain thoroughly. Add cream cheese, milk, dillweed, and salt to hot green beans. Toss together lightly to mix. Makes 6 servings.
Your Time: 4 minutes
Cooking Time: 10 minutes

## CREOLE GREEN BEANS

2 tablespoons butter or
    margarine
⅓ cup frozen chopped onion
⅓ cup frozen chopped green
    pepper
2 16-ounce cans cut green
    beans, drained
1 11-ounce can condensed
    tomato bisque soup,
    undiluted

½ cup milk
Few grains pepper
1 cup soft bread crumbs
1 4-ounce package shredded
    Cheddar cheese

Heat oven to 400° F. Heat butter in skillet over moderately low heat (about 225° F.); add onion and green pepper and cook about 5 minutes, or until tender. Mix green beans, cooked vegetables, soup, milk, and pepper in a medium-sized bowl. Pour into an ungreased shallow 1½-quart baking dish. Mix bread crumbs and cheese; sprinkle over top of vegetable mixture. Bake, uncovered, 20 minutes. Makes 6 servings.
Your Time: 8 minutes
Cooking and Baking Time: 26 minutes

## GREEN BEAN CASSEROLE

2 9-ounce packages frozen
    French-style green beans
1 10½-ounce can condensed
    cream of mushroom soup,
    undiluted

½ cup milk
1 3½-ounce can French fried
    onions

Heat oven to 375° F. Cook beans according to package directions. Blend together mushroom soup and milk in a medium-sized bowl. Drain cooked beans and add to soup mixture. Reserve ⅓ cup of the onions for topping; add remaining onions to green bean mixture. Pour into an ungreased deep 1-quart casserole. Sprinkle reserved onions on top. Bake, uncovered, 25 minutes, or until hot and lightly browned. Makes 6 servings.
Your Time: 3 minutes
Cooking and Baking Time: 35 minutes

## FESTIVE GREEN BEANS

¼ cup butter or margarine
½ cup thinly sliced peeled
  onion
2 9-ounce packages
  French-style green beans,
  partially thawed

2 tablespoons chopped
  canned pimiento
1 teaspoon salt
¼ teaspoon dried basil leaves
Few grains pepper

Melt butter in a large skillet over moderate heat (about 250° F.). Add onion and cook until lightly browned. Add remaining ingredients and cook, covered, 5 minutes, stirring occasionally. Uncover and cook, stirring frequently, until most of the liquid has evaporated, about 2 minutes longer. Makes 6 to 8 servings.
Your Time: 5 minutes
Cooking Time: 10 minutes

## BEETS IN PORT

1 16-ounce can whole beets,
  drained
½ cup beet liquid
½ cup port wine

2 teaspoons cornstarch
1 teaspoon butter or
  margarine
½ teaspoon salt

Combine beet liquid and all but 1 tablespoon of the port in a saucepan. Thoroughly blend the 1 tablespoon port and the cornstarch. Add to beet-liquid mixture. Cook over moderate heat (about 250° F.), stirring constantly, until mixture is thick and transparent. Add beets and remaining ingredients. Heat. Makes 4 servings.
Your Time: 6 minutes
Cooking Time: 3 minutes

## BROCCOLI SUPREME

1 10-ounce package frozen
  broccoli spears
1 10½-ounce can condensed
  cream of mushroom soup,
  undiluted

1 cup commercial sour cream
3 tablespoons grated
  Parmesan cheese
2 tablespoons butter or
  margarine

Heat oven to 350° F. Slightly thaw broccoli by placing package in pan of warm water. Put separated pieces in an ungreased deep 1½-quart casserole. Combine soup and cream; pour over broccoli. Sprinkle top with cheese and dot with butter. Bake, uncovered, 30 to 35 minutes. Makes 4 servings.
Your Time: 5 minutes
Baking Time: 30 to 35 minutes

## BROCCOLI-CHEESE CUSTARD

| | |
|---|---|
| 1  10-ounce package frozen chopped broccoli | ⅛ teaspoon ground nutmeg |
| 1½ tablespoons flour | 1  10¾-ounce can condensed Cheddar cheese soup |
| ½ cup milk | 3  eggs, slightly beaten |
| 1  teaspoon instant minced onion | |

Heat oven to 350° F. Cook broccoli according to package directions; drain thoroughly. Arrange broccoli in the bottom of an ungreased shallow 1½-quart baking dish. In a medium-sized bowl combine flour and about 2 tablespoons of the milk and blend until smooth. Add remaining milk, onion, nutmeg, and soup and beat with a rotary beater until mixture is smooth. Add eggs and beat with rotary beater to blend well. Pour mixture over broccoli. Place baking dish in a 12¾-x-9-x-2-inch baking pan. Pour boiling water into the larger pan to a depth of 1½ inches. Bake, uncovered, 45 to 50 minutes, or until a knife inserted about 1 inch from the center of the custard comes out clean. Serve immediately. Makes 4 servings.
Your Time: 8 minutes
Cooking and Baking Time: 53 to 58 minutes

## CREAMED BROCCOLI

| | |
|---|---|
| 2  10-ounce packages frozen broccoli spears | ¼ teaspoon onion salt |
| 1  10½-ounce can condensed cream of mushroom soup, undiluted | ¼ cup fine dry seasoned bread crumbs |
| 1  cup commercial sour cream | 1  tablespoon melted butter or margarine |
| ¼ teaspoon dried savory leaves | |

Heat oven to 350° F. Cut larger broccoli spears in half lengthwise and arrange in an ungreased shallow 1½-quart casserole. Blend together soup, sour cream, savory, and onion salt in a small bowl. (Mixture will be a little thick.) Pour evenly over broccoli, separating pieces of broccoli if necessary to allow sauce to run down. Mix together crumbs and butter and sprinkle over top. Bake, uncovered, 35 to 40 minutes, or until broccoli is tender. Makes 6 to 8 servings.
Your Time: 10 minutes
Baking Time: 35 to 40 minutes

### COMPANY BRUSSELS SPROUTS

2 10-ounce packages frozen Brussels sprouts
2 tablespoons butter or margarine
1 5-ounce can water chestnuts, drained and sliced

¼ teaspoon crushed dried rosemary leaves
1 10½-ounce can condensed cream of chicken soup, undiluted
1 tablespoon dry sherry

Cook Brussels sprouts according to package directions. Heat butter in saucepan over moderate heat (about 250° F.); add water chestnuts and rosemary and cook until lightly browned. Stir in soup and sherry. Heat, stirring occasionally. Drain cooked Brussels sprouts and add to sauce. Heat for a few minutes. Makes 4 to 6 servings.
Your Time: 8½ minutes
Cooking Time: 15 minutes

### CABBAGE IN CHEESE SAUCE

1¼ cups milk
4 cups coarsely shredded cabbage
½ cup finely chopped green pepper

1 package cheese sauce mix (making 1 cup)

Heat the milk in a large saucepan over moderately low heat (about 225° F.) until milk just bubbles around the edges. Add cabbage and green pepper; cover loosely and cook over low heat (about 200° F.) about 5 minutes, or until cabbage is just tender. Stir occasionally. Remove from heat; do not drain cabbage. Sprinkle dry cheese sauce mix over cabbage and stir to combine. Return to heat and cook,

stirring constantly, until thickened. Makes 4 to 6 servings.
Your Time: 5 minutes
Cooking Time: 8 minutes

## CHILI CABBAGE

*7 cups shredded cabbage*
*Boiling salted water*
*⅓ cup mayonnaise or salad*
*    dressing*

*⅓ cup chili sauce*
*¼ teaspoon ground dillseed*

Cook cabbage in boiling salted water over moderately low heat
(about 225° F.) and covered with a lid for 8 minutes, or until tender.
Drain well. Mix mayonnaise, chili sauce, and dillseed in a small bowl;
fold into cabbage. Serve immediately. Makes 6 servings.
Your Time: 7 minutes
Cooking Time: 8 minutes

## GLAZED CARROT SLICES

*¼ cup butter or margarine*
*½ cup firmly packed*
*    light-brown sugar*
*½ cup jarred cranberry-orange*
*    relish*

*2 tablespoons brandy*
*3 16-ounce cans sliced*
*    carrots, very well drained*
*Parsley sprigs*

Melt butter in a large skillet over moderate heat (about 250° F.).
Add sugar, relish, and brandy and stir to blend. Add carrots and cook
about 10 minutes, or until carrots are well coated with glaze, turning
them frequently. Garnish with parsley sprigs. Makes 8 servings.
Your Time: 7 minutes
Cooking Time: 15 minutes

## GOLDEN CAULIFLOWER

*2 10-ounce packages frozen*
*    cauliflower*
*1 package cheese sauce mix*
*    (makes 1 cup)*
*1 cup milk*

*1 tablespoon prepared*
*    mustard*
*2 tablespoons diced toasted*
*    almonds*

Cook cauliflower according to package directions; drain thoroughly. Meanwhile place cheese sauce mix in a medium-sized saucepan. Gradually add milk, stirring constantly until smooth. Cook over moderate heat (about 250° F.), stirring constantly, until sauce comes to a boil and is smooth and thickened. Blend in mustard. Arrange drained cauliflower in a serving dish. Pour sauce over top. Sprinkle with diced almonds. Makes 6 servings.
Your Time: 8 minutes
Cooking Time: 9 minutes

## CELERY HEARTS EN CASSEROLE

2  16-ounce cans celery hearts,
    drained
1  10½-ounce can condensed
    golden mushroom soup,
    undiluted
½  cup milk

½  cup chopped peanuts
½  cup crushed round buttery
    crackers
3  tablespoons butter or
    margarine

Heat oven to 350° F. Grease a shallow 1½-quart casserole with unsalted shortening. Drain celery hearts and arrange in prepared casserole. Combine soup, milk, and peanuts. Pour over celery hearts in casserole. Sprinkle evenly with cracker crumbs and dot with butter. Bake, uncovered, about 30 minutes, or until bubbling. Makes 6 servings.
Your Time: 10 minutes
Baking Time: 30 minutes

## BAKED CORN ON THE COB

5  tablespoons softened butter
    or margarine
½  teaspoon dried chives
¼  teaspoon prepared mustard

¼  teaspoon salt
Few grains pepper
4  ears frozen corn, defrosted

Heat oven to 400° F. In a small bowl combine butter, chives, mustard, salt, and pepper. Spread each ear of corn generously with butter mixture and wrap each securely in a piece of aluminum foil. Place corn on a cookie sheet. Bake 45 minutes. Makes 4 servings.
Your Time: 4 minutes
Baking Time: 45 minutes

## QUICK CREAMED CORN

1  10-ounce package frozen
   corn
1  4-ounce container whipped
   cream cheese

2  tablespoons milk
¼  teaspoon salt
Few grains pepper

Cook corn according to directions on package; drain. Add cream cheese, milk, salt, and pepper; combine thoroughly. Heat and gently stir over low heat (about 200° F.) just until cheese melts and mixture is piping hot. Makes 3 to 4 servings.
Your Time: 3 minutes
Cooking Time: 10 minutes

## DOUBLE ONION CASSEROLE

2  10-ounce packages frozen
   creamed small onions in
   cooking pouch
½  cup packaged shredded
   Cheddar cheese

⅓  cup toasted diced almonds
1½  teaspoons dried parsley
   flakes
1  cup canned French fried
   onion rings

Heat oven to 350° F. Heat creamed onions according to package directions. Pour contents of packages into an ungreased deep 1-quart casserole. Stir in cheese, almonds, and parsley flakes. Bake, uncovered, 15 minutes. Sprinkle onion rings over top of casserole. Bake, uncovered, an additional 3 to 5 minutes, or until onion rings are heated and crisp. Makes 6 servings.
Your Time: 5 minutes
Cooking and Baking Time: 35 minutes

## CREAMED ONIONS AU GRATIN

2  16-ounce cans onions,
   drained
1  10½-ounce can condensed
   cream of celery soup,
   undiluted

½  cup packaged shredded
   Cheddar cheese
¼  cup chopped almonds

Heat oven to 375° F. Place onions in an ungreased deep 1-quart casserole; gently stir in soup. Sprinkle top with cheese and nuts. Bake, uncovered, 20 to 25 minutes, until hot. Makes 4 to 6 servings.
Your Time: 5 minutes
Baking Time: 20 to 25 minutes

### CREAMED ONIONS WITH SHERRY

2 16-ounce cans whole boiled       3 tablespoons dry sherry
  onions                            1 1¾-ounce can French fried
1 cup milk                             onions
2 packages white sauce mix        Paprika
  (making 1 cup each)

Heat oven to 400° F. Drain onions and measure ¾ cup of the liquid; pour into a saucepan. Add milk and blend in white sauce mix; cook over moderately low heat (about 225° F.), stirring constantly, until sauce comes to a boil. Continue cooking for 1 minute longer. Remove from heat. Stir in sherry and whole onions. Pour into an ungreased deep 1½-quart casserole. Bake, uncovered, 25 minutes. Remove from oven and sprinkle top with French fried onions and paprika. Continue baking, uncovered, for 5 minutes. Makes 6 servings.
Your Time: 8 minutes
Cooking and Baking Time: 35 minutes

### SUPER ONIONS

2 16-ounce cans onions,            ½ cup packaged shredded
  drained                             Cheddar cheese
1 10½-ounce can condensed        ¼ cup chopped almonds
  cream of celery soup,
  undiluted

Heat oven to 375° F. Place onions in an ungreased deep 1-quart casserole; gently stir in soup. Sprinkle with cheese and nuts. Bake, uncovered, 20 to 25 minutes, until hot. Makes 6 servings.
Your Time: 5 minutes
Baking Time: 20 to 25 minutes

## COMPANY CREAMED PEAS

1 16-ounce can peas,
   undrained
1 10½-ounce can condensed
   cream of mushroom soup,
   undiluted

2 slices crisp-cooked bacon,
   crumbled

Combine peas and soup in a saucepan. Cook over moderately low heat (about 225° F.) until hot and bubbly. Serve topped with crumbled bacon. Makes 4 servings.
Your Time: 5 minutes
Cooking Time: 5 minutes

## PEAS AND MUSHROOMS

1 10-ounce package frozen
   green peas with sautéed
   mushrooms
2 tablespoons butter or
   margarine

¼ teaspoon dried basil leaves
⅛ teaspoon salt
Few grains pepper

Prepare peas according to package directions. Add butter, basil, salt, and pepper to peas and mix well. Makes 4 servings.
Your Time: 1 minute
Cooking Time: 8 minutes

## BAKED POTATOES PARMESAN

6 medium-sized baking
   potatoes
6 tablespoons softened butter
   or margarine

Salt and pepper
3 tablespoons grated
   Parmesan cheese

Heat oven to 350° F. Scrub potatoes thoroughly and cut in half lengthwise. Score cut side of each half lengthwise with the tines of a fork. Spread softened butter over cut side and sprinkle with salt and pepper. Place potatoes on a cookie sheet, cut side up, and bake about 55 minutes. Potatoes should be fork-tender. Sprinkle potatoes with Parmesan cheese 25 minutes before end of baking time. Makes 6 servings.
Your Time: 10 minutes
Baking Time: About 55 minutes

## CHEESE-POTATO BALLS

1 16-ounce can tiny white     ¼ cup grated Parmesan cheese
   potatoes, drained         1 tablespoon dried parsley
2 tablespoons shortening          flakes

Dry potatoes on paper towels. Melt shortening in skillet over
moderately high heat (about 275° F.); add potatoes and cook until
lightly browned, turning frequently. Mix cheese and parsley together
and roll potatoes in mixture before serving. Makes 4 servings.
Your Time: 4 minutes
Cooking Time: 20 minutes


## POTATOES DAUPHINE

½ clove garlic, peeled          ½ cup grated Swiss or
Salt                                        Gruyère cheese
1 9-ounce package frozen     ½ teaspoon salt
   French fried potatoes       ¼ teaspoon pepper
3 tablespoons butter or        ¼ teaspoon onion salt
   margarine, softened          ½ cup milk
1 tablespoon flour

Heat oven to 325° F. Rub surface of shallow baking dish with cut
side of garlic. Sprinkle salt on bottom of baking dish. Arrange half
the frozen potatoes in bottom of baking dish. Combine softened
butter, flour, cheese, and seasonings in a small bowl. Heat milk and
pour into cheese mixture, stirring constantly. Pour half this mixture
over potatoes in dish. Repeat layers. Bake, uncovered, 30 minutes, or
until bubbly and lightly browned. Makes 4 servings.
Your Time: 8 minutes
Cooking and Baking Time: 35 minutes


## CURRIED SCALLOPED POTATOES

1 5⅝-ounce package            ½ teaspoon curry powder
   scalloped potato mix        ½ cup shredded Swiss cheese
½ cup frozen chopped onion

Heat oven to 400° F. Prepare scalloped potato mix in a 1½-quart
casserole as directed on package. Stir in onion and curry powder;
bake, uncovered, for 15 minutes. Remove from oven and sprinkle

shredded Swiss cheese on top. Return to oven and bake, uncovered, 20 to 25 minutes longer. Makes 4 servings.
Your Time: 4 minutes
Baking Time: 35 to 40 minutes

## PARSLEY POTATO PUFFS

1 8-ounce package frozen
  French fried potato puffs,
  defrosted
3 tablespoons melted butter
  or margarine

½ teaspoon dried parsley
  flakes
¼ teaspoon salt

Heat oven to 375° F. Place potato puffs on a cookie sheet. In a small bowl combine melted butter, parsley, and salt. Brush mixture evenly over potatoes with a pastry brush. Bake, uncovered, 15 minutes. Makes 4 servings.
Your Time: 2 minutes
Baking Time: 15 minutes

## QUICKIE STUFFED POTATOES

2 cups prepared instant
  mashed potatoes
½ cup cream-style cottage
  cheese
2 tablespoons chopped
  stuffed green olives

1 tablespoon snipped chives
5 tablespoons packaged
  shredded Cheddar cheese

Combine mashed potatoes, cottage cheese, olives, and chives. Fashion 5 small boats from aluminum foil by folding 15-x-6-inch pieces of foil in half lengthwise. Bring sides up, making a boat shape; pinch ends closed. Spoon potato mixture into boats. Sprinkle tops with cheese. Place in preheated broiler about 3 inches from heat for about 5 minutes, or until cheese melts and tops are slightly browned. Makes 4 servings.
Your Time: 12 minutes
Broiling Time: 5 minutes

## CINNAMON-LEMON YAMS

2 17-ounce cans
   vacuum-packed yams
¼ cup melted butter or
   margarine
2 tablespoons bottled lemon
   juice

1 teaspoon ground cinnamon
¼ cup packaged corn flake
   crumbs

Heat oven to 350° F. Arrange yams in an ungreased shallow 2-quart
baking dish. Combine butter, lemon juice, and cinnamon; pour over
yams. Sprinkle with crumbs. Bake, uncovered, 30 minutes. Makes 6
servings.
Your Time: 3 minutes
Baking Time: 30 minutes

## PINEAPPLE-PECAN SWEET POTATOES

2 17-ounce cans
   vacuum-packed sweet
   potatoes
2 tablespoons melted butter
   or margarine
2 tablespoons lemon juice
1 8¼-ounce can crushed
   pineapple, well drained

¼ cup chopped pecans
3 tablespoons dark-brown
   sugar
2 tablespoons imitation bacon
   pieces (optional)
½ teaspoon salt
¼ teaspoon ground cinnamon

Heat oven to 375° F. In the large bowl of an electric mixer place
sweet potatoes, butter, and lemon juice; beat at low speed until well
blended. Stir in remaining ingredients and turn into an ungreased
deep 1½-quart casserole or baking dish. Bake, uncovered, 25 minutes,
or until heated thoroughly and top is lightly browned. Makes 6 to 8
servings.
Your Time: 10 minutes
Baking Time: 25 minutes

## ORANGE-GLAZED SWEET POTATOES

1 cup water
1 3-ounce package
   orange-flavored gelatin
¼ cup firmly packed
   light-brown sugar
Few grains salt

1 tablespoon butter or
   margarine
1 17-ounce can
   vacuum-packed sweet
   potatoes

Heat water to boiling in a large skillet over moderately low heat (about 225° F.); add gelatin, sugar, and salt and stir until dissolved. Add butter and simmer 5 minutes. Carefully remove potatoes from can and place them in the gelatin mixture. Cook, uncovered, over moderate heat (about 250° F.) for 10 minutes, basting frequently, until syrup thickens and potatoes are glazed. Makes 4 servings.
Your Time: 5 minutes
Cooking Time: 15 minutes


### CURRIED RICE

*1⅓ cups water*
*1 chicken bouillon cube*
*¼ to ½ teaspoon curry*
  *powder*

*1⅓ cups packaged precooked*
  *rice*

In saucepan bring water, bouillon cube, and curry powder to a boil over high heat (about 300° F.). Stir in rice. Remove from heat. Cover and let stand 5 minutes. Stir lightly with a fork before serving. Makes 4 servings.
Your Time: 3 minutes
Cooking and Standing Time: 10 minutes


### CURRIED RICE AND APPLESAUCE

*1 6-ounce package curry rice*
  *mix*
*¾ cup sweetened applesauce*

*¼ cup toasted slivered*
  *almonds*

Prepare curry rice according to top-of-range directions on package. Be sure all the liquid is absorbed and the rice is tender. Remove from heat and stir in applesauce. Sprinkle with toasted almonds. Makes 6 servings.
Your Time: 5 minutes
Cooking Time: 25 to 30 minutes


### FRUITED RICE

*1 8½-ounce can pineapple*
  *tidbits*
*1 7-ounce package precooked*
  *chicken-flavored rice mix*
*2 tablespoons butter or*
  *margarine*

*¼ cup dark seedless raisins*
*2 tablespoons diced canned*
  *pimiento*

Drain pineapple tidbits, measuring the syrup. Add enough cold water to make 1¾ cups liquid. In a medium-sized saucepan combine measured liquid, contents of the seasoning packet in rice mix and the butter. Bring to a full boil over moderate heat (about 250° F.). Stir in rice mixture and blend well. Add raisins, pimiento, and pineapple tidbits and stir to blend. Cover and remove from heat. Let stand until most of the liquid has been absorbed, about 8 minutes. Stir well before serving. Makes 6 to 8 servings.

Your Time: 2 minutes

Cooking and Standing Time: 10 minutes


## QUICK RICE PILAF

1 *package mushroom gravy*
  *mix (makes 1 cup)*
2 *cups water*
2 *tablespoons butter or*
  *margarine*
1 *tablespoon instant minced*
  *onion*

½ *teaspoon salt*
2 *cups packaged precooked*
  *rice*
2 *tablespoons diced toasted*
  *almonds*

Combine gravy mix, water, butter, onion, and salt in a medium-sized saucepan and blend well. Cook over moderate heat (about 250° F.), stirring constantly, until mixture comes to a boil and thickens slightly. Add rice and stir to blend; cover and remove from heat. Let stand 5 minutes. Stir with a fork to fluff rice. Sprinkle with almonds. Makes 6 servings.

Your Time: 4 minutes

Cooking and Standing Time: 8 minutes


## PARSLEY RICE

1⅓ *cups water*
1 *chicken bouillon cube*
¼ *teaspoon salt*
1⅓ *cups packaged precooked*
  *rice*
¼ *cup slivered blanched*
  *almonds*

1 *tablespoon dried parsley*
  *flakes*
2 *teaspoons butter or*
  *margarine*

Place water, bouillon cube, and salt in saucepan; bring to a boil over high heat (about 300° F.). Remove from heat and stir in rice,

almonds, parsley, and butter; cover tightly. Let stand 5 minutes. Stir lightly with a fork before serving. Makes 4 servings.
Your Time: 2 minutes
Cooking and Standing Time: 9 minutes


## SWEET SAUERKRAUT

2 tablespoons butter or margarine
½ cup packaged frozen chopped onion
2 16-ounce cans whole tomatoes, undrained
¼ cup firmly packed dark-brown sugar

1 27-ounce can sauerkraut, drained
1 tablespoon imitation bacon pieces
⅛ teaspoon pepper

Melt butter in a large skillet over moderately low heat (about 225° F.). Add onion and cook until fork-tender. Add tomatoes and crush with the back of a spoon. Add brown sugar, sauerkraut, bacon pieces, and pepper. Bring mixture to a boil and simmer, covered, 20 minutes, stirring occasionally. Makes 6 to 8 servings.
Your Time: 5 minutes
Cooking Time: 30 minutes


## CREAMY ONION SPINACH

1 10-ounce package frozen chopped spinach
1 teaspoon instant minced onion

2 teaspoons water
1 3-ounce package cream cheese, at room temperature

Prepare spinach according to package directions. While spinach is cooking, soak onion in water 5 minutes. Drain any excess water from cooked spinach. Add rehydrated onion and cream cheese; stir constantly until cream cheese is entirely melted. Reheat if necessary. Makes 4 servings.
Your Time: 1 minute
Cooking Time: 10 minutes

## SPINACH WITH MUSHROOM SAUCE

2  *10-ounce packages frozen*     1  *10½-ounce can condensed*
    *chopped spinach*                 *cream of mushroom soup,*
                                      *undiluted*

Cook spinach according to package directions and drain. Stir in soup and heat over moderately low heat (about 225° F.). Makes 6 servings.
Your Time: 1 minute
Cooking Time: 8 minutes

## SAVORY SPINACH

½  *cup commercial sour cream*   1  *10-ounce package frozen*
1  *package dry onion salad*         *chopped spinach,*
    *dressing mix*                    *defrosted*

Heat oven to 375° F. Combine sour cream and salad dressing mix in a bowl; fold into spinach. Pour mixture into an ungreased deep 3-cup casserole. Bake, uncovered, 15 minutes, or until bubbling hot. Makes 4 servings.
Your Time: 2 minutes
Baking Time: 15 minutes

## BARBECUED SUCCOTASH

2  *10-ounce packages frozen*     ⅓ *soup can water*
    *succotash*                   1  *to 2 teaspoons chili*
1  *tablespoon vegetable oil*         *powder*
½  *cup frozen chopped onion*     1½ *teaspoons prepared*
½  *cup frozen chopped green*         *mustard*
    *peppers*                     1  *tablespoon Worcestershire*
1  *10¾-ounce can condensed*          *sauce*
    *tomato soup, undiluted*      1½ *teaspoons salt*

Cook succotash according to package directions; drain. Heat oil in a large skillet over moderately low heat (about 225° F.). Add onion and peppers and cook until tender. Add tomato soup, water, succotash, chili powder, mustard, Worcestershire, and salt. Bring mixture to a boil. Cover and simmer 20 minutes, stirring occasionally. Makes 6 to 8 servings.
Your Time: 6 minutes
Cooking Time: 35 minutes

## BAKED SESAME TOMATOES

4  medium-sized tomatoes
Seasoned salt
Garlic powder
1/3 cup fine dry seasoned bread
   crumbs

2  tablespoons melted butter
   or margarine
Dried parsley flakes
1  tablespoon sesame seeds

Heat oven to 400° F. Cut out stem ends of tomatoes and then cut tomatoes in half horizontally. Arrange tomatoes in a 9-inch-square cake pan. Sprinkle tops of tomatoes generously with seasoned salt and garlic powder. In a small bowl combine bread crumbs and melted butter and blend well. Spread crumb mixture over tops of tomatoes with a spatula. Sprinkle parsley lightly over crumb mixture. Sprinkle sesame seeds over top of each tomato. Bake, uncovered, 20 to 25 minutes, or until tomatoes are fork-tender but still hold their shape. Makes 8 servings.
Your Time: 5 minutes
Baking Time: 20 to 25 minutes

## FRIED TOMATOES

3  medium-sized firm
   tomatoes

1/4 cup fine dry bread crumbs
1/4 cup butter or margarine

Remove stem end of tomatoes and cut into slices about ½ inch thick. Coat slices with bread crumbs. Melt butter in a large skillet over moderate heat (about 250° F.) and lightly brown tomatoes on both sides. Serve immediately. Makes 4 servings.
Your Time: 6½ minutes
Cooking Time: 5 minutes

## TOMATOES AND OKRA

1  10-ounce package frozen
   whole okra
1  8-ounce can stewed
   tomatoes

1/4 teaspoon salt

Cook okra according to package directions; drain. Add stewed tomatoes and salt to okra; cook over low heat (about 200° F.) 5 minutes. Makes 4 servings.
Your Time: 2 minutes
Cooking Time: 15 minutes

## TOMATO PUDDING

1  *cup tomato juice*
1  *8-ounce can tomato sauce*
2  *tablespoons dark corn syrup*
2  *tablespoons instant minced onion*
¼  *teaspoon dried basil leaves*

6  *slices white bread*
¼  *cup melted butter or margarine*
2  *tablespoons grated Parmesan cheese*

Heat oven to 350° F. Mix tomato juice, tomato sauce, corn syrup, onion, and basil in a saucepan; heat over moderately low heat (about 225° F.) until well blended. Cut bread slices into quarters. Arrange half the bread in bottom of an ungreased shallow 1¼-quart baking dish. Brush bread with butter. Cover with half the tomato sauce mixture. Repeat layers once again. Sprinkle with Parmesan cheese. Bake, uncovered, 25 minutes. Makes 6 servings.
Your Time: 6 minutes
Baking Time: 25 minutes

## TOMATO-BEAN RELISH

1  *14½-ounce can sliced tomatoes, undrained*
1  *15-ounce can garbanzo beans, drained*
1  *medium-sized cucumber, peeled and thinly sliced*

1  *package dry French salad dressing mix*
2  *tablespoons wine vinegar*
2  *tablespoons vegetable oil*

Place undrained tomatoes, drained garbanzo beans, and cucumber slices in a bowl. Sprinkle with the dry salad dressing mix; add vinegar and oil and toss to mix. Cover and chill 1 to 2 hours. Drain before serving. Serve with cold sliced meat. Makes 6 servings.
Your Time: 3 minutes
Chilling Time: 1 to 2 hours

## SEASONED TOMATO SCALLOP

2  *16-ounce cans whole tomatoes, undrained*
2  *tablespoons vegetable oil*
½  *teaspoon salt*
*Few grains pepper*

1½ *cups seasoned stuffing croutons*
1  *tablespoon grated Parmesan cheese*

Heat oven to 375° F. Grease a deep 1½-quart casserole with unsalted shortening. Combine tomatoes, vegetable oil, salt, and pepper in a medium-sized bowl. Pour half of tomato mixture into prepared casserole. Top with ¾ cup of the croutons. Add remaining tomato mixture and top with remaining croutons. Sprinkle cheese over croutons. Bake, uncovered, 15 minutes, until thoroughly heated. Makes 4 to 6 servings.

Your Time: 2 minutes
Baking Time: 15 minutes

## VEGETABLE TIMBALES

2 7½-ounce jars junior carrots and peas (baby food)
1 egg, slightly beaten
¼ cup mayonnaise
¼ cup undiluted evaporated milk
1 slice white bread, cubed
⅛ teaspoon salt
Few grains pepper

Heat oven to 350° F. Grease 4 6-ounce custard cups with unsalted shortening. Combine carrots and peas, egg, mayonnaise, evaporated milk, bread cubes, salt, and pepper in a medium-sized bowl. Spoon mixture into prepared custard cups. Place cups in a pan of hot water. Bake, uncovered, 40 minutes, or until mixture is firm. Serve immediately. Makes 4 servings.

Your Time: 6 minutes
Baking Time: 40 minutes

## ROSY VEGETABLE STIR

1 9-ounce package frozen cut green beans
1 12-ounce can whole kernel corn, undrained
1 10¾-ounce can condensed tomato soup, undiluted
2 tablespoons butter or margarine
1 tablespoon instant minced onion
½ teaspoon lemon juice

Cook beans according to package directions over moderately low heat (about 225° F.). Drain well. Add corn, tomato soup, butter, onion, and lemon juice. Heat, stirring occasionally, until mixture bubbles at edges. Makes 6 servings.

Your Time: 7 minutes
Cooking Time: 15 minutes

# CHAPTER

# VI

# *Salads*

Salads can help you beat the clock every time. Particularly green salads. There's nothing easier than assembling a big bowl of assorted crisp greens, perhaps punctuating them with bright touches of tomatoes, pepper rings, radishes, and olives. Or add hard-cooked eggs and cheese to mixed vegetables and toss everything in a dressing you blend yourself, using equal parts of mayonnaise and French dressing and some instant minced onion (we call this recipe Vegetable Macedoine Salad, on page 176).

Quick-to-make salads need not have a hurried look. A vegetable cut just a little differently, a cluster of carrot curls, a sprinkling of ripe-olive circles (you can buy them canned in slices), a handful of croutons (they come by the box, flavored or not) can add character to a salad. Try celery or carrot slices cut on the bias. They look—and some people will even tell you they taste—different. It takes only a minute to run the tines of a fork down the exterior of an unpeeled cucumber. As a result, you get decorative slices with a tiny scalloped edge. Use an egg slicer to make perfect slices of hard-cooked egg to arrange like flower petals atop a salad. Serve with crusty French bread, followed by coffee and your pet dessert, and presto! you've turned out a splendid meal.

When the occasion calls for a somewhat heartier lunch or supper, team up a green salad with a meat or pasta dish. Ravioli Casserole on page 115 and Quick Chili on page 97 are two likely companions for green salads.

Not that you'll want to stop with leafy greens, of course, in your quest for timesaving salads. There are many other easy-to-do salads using meat, fish, vegetables, or fruits. And innumerable combinations of salads and main dishes. Try, for example, the Apple-Raisin Salad on page 164 served with the Baked Ham Steak on page 110. Or the sophisticated Belgian Endive Salad on page 167 with the Cheddar Cheese Fondue on page 61.

Yet another blessing for the cook in a hurry is a molded salad. You can make these salads on the night before you intend to serve them, or even on the morning of your party day. Assembling them is ABC simple: just make sure you allow enough time for them to chill properly.

Molded salads, as you'll discover when you try out the recipes included here, have more than their share of charm. Not only are they incredibly easy to prepare, they're economical, and it's practically impossible to spoil them. Somehow they manage to pop out of their molds and look glamorous on the table with hardly any help at all. One of our very special favorites is the recipe for Quick Lemon-Cheese Molds on page 170. The touch of flaked coconut provides an unexpected flavor.

# *Luncheon or Dinner Accompaniment Salads (Unmolded)*

### The Tossed Green Salad

To make a perfect tossed green salad, start with two "do's." Do chill the serving plates and do tear (not cut) the greens. But don't add moisture-producing foods, such as tomatoes, before you coat the greens with dressing. Chopped chives, radish slices, well-drained artichoke hearts, slices of avocado, and the like may be tossed with the greens. This is our version of the classic green salad with two ways to achieve it. The first is simpler; the second will give a more vivid garlic tinge to the dressing. The ingredients are the same.

## CLASSIC GREEN SALAD

2 *quarts torn salad greens*
1 *clove garlic, peeled and cut*
  *in half*
6 *tablespoons vegetable oil or*
  *olive oil*
2 *tablespoons tarragon, wine,*
  *or other vinegar, or lemon*
  *juice*

½ *teaspoon salt*
¼ *teaspoon freshly ground*
  *pepper*
Pinch *of dry mustard*

For either version, dry washed greens thoroughly, wrap in a towel, and chill well. Put required number of salad plates and a wooden bowl large enough to hold the salad for tossing in the refrigerator to chill.

*Version 1:* Just before serving, rub the wooden salad bowl with the cut surface of the garlic. Discard the garlic. Combine the oil, vinegar or lemon juice, salt, pepper, and mustard in the bowl and stir with a fork to blend. Add the crisp, dry greens. Take the untossed salad to the table along with the chilled serving plates. At the table, toss the greens lightly just to coat each leaf with dressing. Serve at once. Makes 4 large salads or 6 small ones.

*Version 2:* Put the salt, pepper, and mustard, and several pieces of finely minced garlic (half a clove suits most tastes) into the salad bowl. Mash the garlic and seasonings with the back of a spoon until the garlic disappears. Stir the vinegar or lemon juice into the seasonings; then stir in the oil. Add the crisp dry greens. Refrigerate until serving time, up to 1 hour. Do *not* toss until you are ready to serve the salad on chilled plates. Serves 4 to 6.

Your Time: 12 minutes
Chilling Time: 1 hour

## APPLE-RAISIN SALAD

2 *red-skinned apples, halved,*
  *cored, and cut into cubes*
½ *cup dark seedless raisins*
½ *cup coarsely chopped*
  *celery*
¾ *cup mayonnaise or salad*
  *dressing*

2 *tablespoons catsup*
*Lettuce leaves*
2 *tablespoons chopped*
  *walnuts*

In a large bowl combine apples, raisins, celery, mayonnaise, and catsup. Arrange on a bed of lettuce leaves and sprinkle chopped nuts over top. Makes 4 servings.
Your Time: 8 minutes

## ASPARAGUS SALAD

4 large crisp lettuce leaves
1 15-ounce can asparagus
　　spears, drained
1 canned pimiento pod, cut
　　into 4 strips

¼ cup mayonnaise
1 teaspoon lemon juice
2 teaspoons drained capers

Place a lettuce leaf on each of 4 salad plates. Top each with equal amounts of asparagus spears and 1 pimiento strip. Blend together mayonnaise and lemon juice. Top each salad with equal amounts of the dressing. Garnish each with ½ teaspoon capers. Chill about 30 minutes. Makes 4 servings.
Your Time: 7 minutes
Chilling Time: 30 minutes

## MARINATED BEAN SALAD

1 20-ounce can red kidney
　　beans, well drained
1 20-ounce can white kidney
　　beans (cannellini), well
　　drained
1 cup thinly sliced celery
1 cup thinly sliced green
　　peppers

¼ cup thinly sliced peeled
　　onion rings
2 tablespoons chopped
　　canned pimiento
1 tablespoon drained capers
¾ cup bottled Italian salad
　　dressing
Pinch of dried dillweed

Combine all ingredients in a large bowl; cover and refrigerate about 1 hour, or until ready to serve. Makes 6 servings.
Your Time: 12 minutes
Chilling Time: 1 hour

## GREEN BEAN SALAD

1  16-ounce can cut green
   beans, drained
1  small sweet onion, peeled
   and finely diced (about ½
   cup)
¼  cup bottled Italian salad
   dressing

½  teaspoon dried oregano
   leaves
Lettuce leaves
½  teaspoon imitation bacon
   pieces

In a large bowl combine beans, onion, dressing, and oregano and toss
gently. Serve mixture on a bed of lettuce leaves. Sprinkle with bacon
pieces. Makes 4 servings.
Your Time: 5 minutes

## SPICY GREEN BEAN SALAD

1  cup vegetable oil
½  cup vinegar
1  package spaghetti-sauce mix
2  16-ounce cans cut green
   beans, drained

3  cups shredded lettuce
6  slices crisp-cooked bacon,
   crumbled

Combine oil, vinegar and spaghetti-sauce mix. Pour over drained
beans; cover and chill several hours. Just before serving, toss with
lettuce. Sprinkle with crumbled bacon. Makes 8 servings.
Your Time: 7 minutes
Chilling Time: Approximately 2 hours

## ITALIAN GREEN BEAN SALAD

1  canned whole pimiento,
   diced
1  16-ounce can diagonal-cut
   green beans, drained
1  2-ounce can sliced
   mushrooms, drained

3  tablespoons bottled Italian
   salad dressing
¼  teaspoon dried dillweed
½  teaspoon salt
2  teaspoons bottled lemon
   juice

Combine all ingredients in a medium-sized bowl and blend well.
Chill, covered, in refrigerator 8 hours or overnight. Serve as a salad
with cold meat. Makes 4 servings.
Your Time: 2 minutes
Chilling Time: 8 hours or overnight

## BELGIAN ENDIVE SALAD

¼ cup white vinegar
2 tablespoons dry white
   wine
1 6-ounce package Italian
   salad dressing mix
⅔ cup vegetable oil
⅓ cup sliced pitted ripe
   olives

¼ cup diced canned
   pimiento
1 tablespoon freeze-dried
   chives
1½ pounds Belgian endive

Place vinegar and wine in a jar with a tight-fitting screw top. Add contents of package of salad dressing mix; cover and shake well to blend. Add oil; cover and shake well to blend. Add olives, pimiento, and chives. Chill several hours. Shake before using. Separate and arrange endive leaves on a large serving plate or arrange 4 to 5 leaves on individual plates and pour dressing over leaves. Makes about 1½ cups dressing. Makes 8 servings.
Your Time: 6 minutes
Chilling Time: 3 hours

## CELERY AND OLIVE SALAD

2¼ cups thickly sliced celery
1 3½-ounce can pitted black
   olives, quartered
½ cup sliced stuffed green
   olives

⅓ cup chopped fresh parsley
¼ cup bottled Italian salad
   dressing
Lettuce leaves

In a large bowl combine all ingredients except lettuce and marinate, covered, in the refrigerator for at least ½ hour. Serve mixture on lettuce. Makes 4 servings.
Your Time: 6 minutes
Chilling Time: 30 minutes

## TOMATO-MUSHROOM SALAD

3 medium-sized tomatoes, cut
   into wedges
6 medium-sized fresh
   mushrooms, sliced thin
2 tablespoons chopped fresh
   parsley

2 tablespoons lemon juice
¼ cup vegetable oil
¼ teaspoon salt
⅛ teaspoon pepper
Lettuce leaves

In a large bowl combine tomatoes, mushrooms, and parsley. In a small jar with a tight-fitting lid combine lemon juice, oil, salt, and pepper and shake vigorously. Pour dressing over tomatoes and gently mix together. Chill until serving time, if desired. Serve tomato mixture on lettuce. Makes 4 servings.
Your Time: 6 minutes

### MINTED TOMATO-AND-LETTUCE SALAD

*2 medium-sized tomatoes, each cut into 8 wedges*
*¼ cup coarsely chopped fresh mint leaves or 1 tablespoon dried mint leaves*

*¼ cup thin peeled onion rings*
*¼ cup bottled Italian salad dressing*
*4 crisp lettuce leaves*

In a bowl mix together tomatoes, mint leaves, onion, and dressing. Cover and chill 30 minutes, or until ready to serve; stir occasionally. When serving, line each of 4 salad plates with a lettuce leaf and top each with equal portions of the tomato mixture. Makes 4 servings.
Your Time: 11 minutes
Chilling Time: 30 minutes

### WATERCRESS SALAD

*1 bunch watercress, trimmed, rinsed well, and drained*
*¼ cup sliced pimiento-stuffed olives*

*¼ cup bottled clear French salad dressing*

In a large bowl combine watercress, olives, and dressing. Mix gently with a tossing motion. Chill about 20 to 30 minutes before serving. Makes 4 servings.
Your Time: 7 minutes
Chilling Time: 20 to 30 minutes

# Luncheon or Dinner Accompaniment Salads (Molded)

## CRUNCHY BEAN SALAD

1 16-ounce can French-style green beans
1 3-ounce package lemon-flavored gelatin
3 tablespoons dried mixed vegetable flakes

1 tablespoon lemon juice
Ice cubes
¼ cup chopped walnuts
Salad greens
Salad dressing

Drain beans and reserve liquid. Measure liquid and add water, if necessary, to make 1 cup liquid. In a saucepan, heat liquid to boiling over moderate heat (250° F.). Remove from heat and add gelatin; stir until dissolved. Stir in vegetable flakes and lemon juice and let stand 10 minutes. Pour gelatin mixture into a 2-cup measure and add enough ice cubes to make 2 cups liquid. Stir until ice melts and mixture thickens slightly. Combine gelatin mixture, beans, and walnuts; spoon into individual molds. Chill until set, or about 3 hours, and unmold on salad greens. Serve with salad dressing. Makes 6 servings.
Your Time: 9 minutes
Chilling Time: 3 hours

## PICKLED-BEET SALAD

1 16-ounce can pickled sliced beets
1 3-ounce package lemon-flavored gelatin

7 to 10 ice cubes
¾ cup finely chopped celery
Mayonnaise or salad dressing

Drain beets, reserving juice. Chop beets coarsely. Add enough water to juice to make 1 cup. Place liquid in a saucepan over moderately high heat (about 350° F.) and bring to a boil; pour hot liquid over gelatin in a bowl and stir until gelatin is dissolved. Add ice cubes and stir until ice is melted. Stir in chopped beets and celery. Pour mixture into a 1½-quart shallow pan. Chill 3 hours, or until firm. Cut into squares to serve. Serve with a spoonful of mayonnaise. Makes 6 to 8 servings.
Your Time: 8 minutes
Chilling Time: 3 hours

## QUICK LEMON-CHEESE MOLDS

1  3-ounce package
     lemon-flavored gelatin
¾  cup milk, scalded
1  8-ounce package cream
     cheese, cut into chunks

2  egg yolks
½  cup heavy cream
½  cup crushed ice
Salad greens
Flaked coconut

Put gelatin and milk into the container of an electric blender. Cover and blend for 20 seconds. Add cream cheese and egg yolks; blend 15 seconds. Add cream and ice and blend for a few seconds. Pour into 6 individual gelatine molds. Chill until firm, about 1½ hours. Unmold on salad greens and garnish with coconut. Makes 6 servings.
Your Time: 7½ minutes
Chilling Time: 1½ hours

## QUICK CRANBERRY-APPLE SALAD

1¾  cups cranberry-apple juice
1  3-ounce package
     lemon-flavored gelatin
1  large unpeeled red apple,
     cored and cubed

⅓ cup coarsely chopped
     celery
⅓ cup coarsely chopped
     walnuts
Mayonnaise or salad dressing

Heat ¾ cup of the cranberry–apple juice in a saucepan over moderate heat (about 250° F.) until boiling. Remove from heat. Add gelatin and stir until dissolved. Stir in remaining 1 cup cranberry–apple juice. Chill mixture to the consistency of unbeaten egg white. Fold in apple, celery, and nuts. Pour mixture into 6 to 8 individual salad molds. Chill until firm, about 1 hour. Serve on a bed of lettuce. Top with small spoonfuls of mayonnaise. Makes 6 to 8 servings.
Your Time: 7 minutes
Chilling Time: 1 hour

## CRANBERRY-LEMONADE SALAD

2  cups cranberry juice
     cocktail, chilled
2  envelopes unflavored
     gelatine
1  cup canned pineapple juice,
     well chilled
1  6-ounce can frozen pink
     lemonade concentrate

½  cup chopped celery
¼  cup pecans or walnuts
1  11-ounce can mandarin
     oranges, drained
Chicory (optional)

Place 1 cup of the cranberry juice cocktail in a small saucepan. Sprinkle gelatine over juice. Let stand 5 minutes to soften. Place over low heat (about 200° F.) and stir constantly until gelatine is dissolved. Combine gelatine mixture, the remaining 1 cup cranberry juice, pineapple juice, and frozen lemonade in a metal bowl. Stir until lemonade is melted. Chill mixture in a bowl of ice water until the consistency of unbeaten egg white, stirring occasionally. Gently fold in celery, nuts, and oranges. Pour into a 5-cup mold. Chill until firm, about 3 hours. Unmold on a serving platter. Garnish with chicory, if desired. Makes 8 servings.
Your Time: 8 minutes
Chilling Time: 3½ hours

## TWENTY-FOUR-HOUR MIXED-FRUIT SALAD

| | |
|---|---|
| 1 16-ounce can pitted Bing cherries, drained | 1 cup commercial sour cream |
| 1 16-ounce can sliced peaches, drained | Salad greens |
| 1½ cups miniature marshmallows | ½ cup chopped walnuts |

Mix cherries, peaches, marshmallows, and sour cream in a large bowl. Cover and chill in the refrigerator for about 24 hours. Serve on salad greens with a sprinkling of walnuts. Makes 6 servings.
Your Time: 3 minutes
Chilling Time: 24 hours

## MOLDED CHEESE PEARS

| | |
|---|---|
| 1 17-ounce can Bartlett pear halves | 1 cup boiling water |
| Jarred pasteurized Neufchâtel pimiento cheese spread | Lettuce leaves |
| 1 3-ounce package lime-flavored gelatin | Mayonnaise (optional) |

Drain pears, reserving syrup. Measure ¾ cup of the syrup, or add water, if necessary, to make the ¾ cup liquid; set aside. Place a heaping teaspoonful of the cheese spread in the center of each pear. Arrange pear halves, cut side up, in the prepared pie plate. In a medium-sized bowl combine gelatin and boiling water and stir well to

dissolve gelatin. Stir in the reserved ¾ cup pear syrup. Pour gelatin carefully over pears in pie plate. Chill until set, about 3 hours. Cut into wedges and serve on lettuce leaves, with mayonnaise, if desired. Makes 6 servings.
Your Time: 4 minutes
Chilling Time: 3 hours

### RASPBERRY-RHUBARB RING

1  *16-ounce package frozen rhubarb, thawed*
½  *cup water*
1  *10-ounce package frozen raspberries in quick-thaw pouch*

1  *6-ounce package raspberry-flavored gelatin*
2  *cups boiling water*
1  *16-ounce container cream-style cottage cheese*

Cook rhubarb according to the package directions for stewed rhubarb, using the ½ cup water called for on package. Pour rhubarb into a small bowl, cover and place in refrigerator until cool. Thaw raspberries according to package directions; drain, reserving syrup. When rhubarb is cool, drain and reserve the juice. Place gelatin in a large metal bowl. Add the 2 cups boiling water and stir until gelatin is dissolved. Add the reserved raspberry juice and the rhubarb juice and blend well. Place bowl, covered, in the refrigerator until cool. Set bowl with gelatin mixture in a large bowl of ice water and stir occasionally until mixture is the consistency of unbeaten egg white. Fold in rhubarb and raspberries. Pour mixture into a 6½-cup ring mold. Chill until firm, about 3 hours. Unmold on a serving plate. Fill center of ring with cottage cheese. Makes 6 to 8 servings.
Your Time: 15 minutes
Cooling and Chilling Time: about 4½ hours

### BLENDER SUNSHINE SALAD

2  *envelopes unflavored gelatine*
1  *cup chilled orange juice*
½  *lemon, peeled and seeded*
¼  *cup sugar*

¼  *teaspoon salt*
1½ *cups sliced peeled carrots*
1½ *cups undrained crushed pineapple*
*Salad greens*

Sprinkle gelatine over ½ cup of the orange juice in the container of an electric blender; allow to stand for a few minutes. Place the remaining ½ cup orange juice in a small saucepan and bring to a boil over moderate heat (about 250° F.). Add boiling orange juice to gelatine; cover and blend at low speed until gelatine is dissolved. Use a rubber spatula to push gelatine granules from sides of container into mixture. Turn blender to high; add lemon, sugar, and salt. Blend until mixture is smooth. Stop blender. Add carrots and chop by turning to high speed for only a few seconds. Stop and add pineapple; blend a few seconds longer. Turn mixture into a 4-cup mold. Chill until firm, about 2 to 3 hours. Unmold on salad greens. Makes 8 servings.

Your Time: 19 minutes

Chilling Time: 2 to 3 hours

## TOMATO-CHEESE SALAD

2  tablespoons lemon juice
½  cup crushed ice
1  8-ounce can mixed
    vegetables, drained
¼  cup sliced stuffed green
    olives
Salad greens

1  3-ounce package
    lemon-flavored gelatin
¾  cup milk, scalded
1  8-ounce package cream
    cheese, cut into chunks
1  10¾-ounce can condensed
    tomato soup, undiluted

Place gelatin and scalded milk in the container of an electric blender; cover and blend at high speed for 20 seconds. Add cream cheese; cover and blend at high speed for 15 seconds. Add tomato soup, lemon juice, and crushed ice; blend 15 seconds. Stir in vegetables and olives; pour into an 8-inch-square pan. Chill 3 hours, or until set. Cut into squares and serve on salad greens. Makes 9 servings.

Your Time: 7 minutes

Chilling Time: 3 hours

# *Main Dish Salads*

### MOLDED CHICKEN SALAD

1  envelope unflavored
    gelatine
1  cup cold water
1  10½-ounce can condensed
    cream of chicken soup
Few drops Tabasco
2  tablespoons lemon juice
¼  cup mayonnaise or salad
    dressing

1  5-ounce can boned chicken,
    diced
1  5-ounce can water
    chestnuts, drained and
    chopped
⅓ cup toasted salted almonds,
    chopped
1  16-ounce can jellied
    cranberry sauce, sliced

In a small saucepan sprinkle gelatine over ½ cup of the cold water to
soften. Place over low heat (about 200° F.) and stir until gelatine is
dissolved. In a large bowl blend together the remaining ½ cup water
and the soup; stir in the dissolved gelatine. Tabasco, lemon juice, and
mayonnaise. Chill mixture until it is the consistency of unbeaten egg
white. Fold in the remaining ingredients. Turn into a 3-cup mold.
Chill until firm. Unmold and garnish with cranberry sauce slices.
Makes 4 servings.
Your Time: 14 minutes
Chilling Time: 1½ hours

### CUCUMBER AND SHRIMP SALAD

1  4½-ounce can medium-sized
    shrimp, drained
½  cup ice water
2  tablespoons lemon juice
2  medium-sized cucumbers,
    peeled

⅔ cup bottled Italian salad
    dressing
⅛ teaspoon salt
Lettuce leaves

In a small bowl combine shrimp, water, and lemon juice and soak for
at least ½ hour. Cut cucumbers in half lengthwise and slice thin.
Combine cucumber slices, drained shrimp, dressing, and salt in a
bowl and chill 1 hour. Serve on a bed of lettuce leaves. Makes 4
servings.
Your Time: 6 minutes
Chilling Time: 90 minutes

## HAM AND CHEESE SALAD

2 cups cream-style cottage
   cheese
1 cup diced cooked ham or
   canned luncheon meat
¼ cup chopped celery
¼ cup drained pickle relish

2 teaspoons dry Italian salad
   dressing mix
Crisp lettuce cups
Tomato wedges
Parsley sprigs

In a medium-sized bowl combine cottage cheese, diced ham, chopped celery, pickle relish, and salad dressing mix. Chill. Serve salad in lettuce cups with tomato wedges. Garnish with parsley sprigs. Makes about 3½ cups, or 4 to 5 servings.
Your Time: 8 minutes
Chilling Time: 1 hour

## SKILLET POTATO SALAD

6 tablespoons bottled
   French salad dressing
1 16-ounce package frozen
   French fried potatoes
1 12-ounce can luncheon
   meat, cut into
   2-x-½-x-½-inch strips

¼ cup chopped green onions
¼ cup chopped green pepper
1½ cups diced American
   cheese

Heat 2 tablespoons of the dressing in a large skillet over moderately high heat (about 275° F.); add potatoes and cook, stirring occasionally, until potatoes are thoroughly heated. Push potatoes to one side of skillet. Add luncheon meat, onions, and green pepper to empty side of skillet. Cook and stir until onion and green pepper are tender. Reduce heat to very low (about 175° F.). Add cheese and the remaining French dressing; stir gently to combine all ingredients. Heat until cheese melts slightly. Makes 4 servings.
Your Time and Cooking Time: 10 minutes

## SUPER SUPPER SALAD BOWL

1 6-ounce jar marinated
   artichoke hearts, drained
   and liquid reserved
1 3-ounce jar marinated
   mushroom buttons,
   drained and liquid reserved
Bottled clear French salad
   dressing
1 quart torn crisp lettuce,
   loosely packed
1 quart torn crisp chicory,
   loosely packed

1 quart torn crisp romaine
   lettuce, loosely packed
1 pint basket cherry tomatoes
1 medium-sized unpeeled
   cucumber, sliced
¼ cup peeled onion rings
1 avocado, peeled and sliced
   lengthwise
2 tablespoons lemon juice

In a 1-cup measuring cup combine reserved liquid from artichokes and mushrooms with enough French dressing to measure ¾ cup. Cover and chill until ready to use. In a large salad bowl toss together greens, tomatoes, cucumber slices, onion rings, artichoke hearts, mushrooms, and the avocado slices, which have been dipped in the lemon juice. Chill 1 hour. Pour dressing over salad when ready to serve. If desired, line salad bowl with additional romaine leaves and arrange avocado slices with some of the tomatoes on top in a decorative design. Additional French dressing may be served. Makes 8 to 10 servings.
Your Time: 18 minutes
Chilling Time: 1 hour

## VEGETABLE MACEDOINE SALAD

2 tablespoons mayonnaise
2 tablespoons French salad
   dressing
1 teaspoon instant minced
   onion
1 16-ounce can mixed
   vegetables, drained

¼ cup chopped green pepper
¼ cup thinly sliced celery
¼ cup cubed Cheddar cheese
1 hard-cooked egg, shelled
   and chopped

In a small bowl blend together mayonnaise and French dressing; stir in onion and let stand 5 minutes. In a medium-sized bowl combine mixed vegetables, green pepper, celery, cheese, and egg; fold in dressing mixture. Cover and chill 1 hour. Makes 4 to 6 servings.
Your Time: 10 minutes
Chilling Time: 1 hour

# CHAPTER
# VII
# *Breads and Sandwiches*

Sesame Butter Sticks, Coconut-Ball Loaf, Peach Coffee Ring—very different hot breads used for very different purposes, yet in the area of timesaver breads they have a common beginning: refrigerated buttermilk biscuits. Those little compressed biscuits that come sealed in an airtight container can be twisted, rolled, or spread or folded with seasoning or flavored sugars or fruits to produce a variety of breads for coffee time or for dessert. Brown-and-serve rolls can be topped with butter and a sprinkling of sesame seeds for dinner or baked in a sweet-nut syrup to produce Walnut Honey Rolls (page 190), which would make an ideal after-school snack with a glass of milk.

Or you can take a loaf of brown-and-serve French bread. Cut it part way through into slices. Spread each slice with garlic butter for bread to go with a spaghetti meal. Slide chunks of cheese between each slice, bake, and serve as a quick fondue. Spread each slice with butter and sprinkle with cinnamon and sugar to make a quick cinnamon loaf. These are just a few examples of the ways you can produce extraordinarily good breads from the variety of timesaving brown-and-serve, refrigerated, and frozen bread products you will find in your grocery store.

In this chapter you'll find two bread categories and a bonus section on sandwiches that make a meal. One section is devoted to breads that may be served with lunch or dinner. A delightful example is the Lemon French Bread on page 180, which would go beautifully with a

Chicken Salad for lunch or a Lobster Tetrazzini (page 81) for dinner. The second section offers an array of sweet breads guaranteed to make any coffee klatch a memorable one. Would you believe that you can spend eight minutes making beautiful pastries that you can serve—with pride and coffee—twelve minutes later? You will be able to accomplish this bit of magic when you follow the recipe for Almond-Frosted Danish on page 184.

The sandwiches—really super supper dishes—are especially useful for working husbands and wives who have had a hearty business lunch and want a light and easy evening meal. Or they can be the mainstay of a luncheon at home when the bridge club or a committee meeting is scheduled at midday. Sandwiches are a nourishing meal of carbohydrate plus protein provided by meat, fish, poultry, or cheese. Add a bowl of raw vegetables, for nibbling, to give color and texture contrast. Or choose a vegetable-juice cocktail to precede a sandwich meal and follow with a fresh fruit for dessert.

Sandwiches can be plain, but they will look and taste much, much better if they are made to look pretty. You might assemble a sandwich platter with crisp coleslaw in a lettuce cup, some olives, wedges of tomato, and scallions surrounding the sandwiches. Or, if you turn to sandwiches often, keep likely garnishes in tightly covered jars in the refrigerator—crisp dill pickle strips, slices of sweet pickle, tiny gherkins; olives, both stuffed green and ripe; tiny pickled onions; slices of pimiento or little bunches of watercress and parsley, washed and ready to use. Happily, all of these taste as good with hot sandwiches as with cold ones.

# Dinner or Luncheon Breads

## QUICK CHEESE CRESCENTS

*1 container refrigerated crescent dinner rolls (8 rolls)*          *½ cup packaged shredded Cheddar cheese*

Heat oven to 375° F. Grease a cookie sheet with unsalted shortening. Open roll container according to label directions and separate into 8 triangles. Before shaping rolls, sprinkle each triangle with cheese and roll up as directed. Place on prepared cookie sheet. Bake 10 to 12 minutes, or until browned. Serve warm. Makes 8 rolls.
Your Time: 4 minutes
Baking Time: 10 to 12 minutes

## CHEESE-BACON CRESCENT ROLLS

⅓ *cup packaged shredded*     1  *container refrigerated*
   *Cheddar cheese*          *crescent dinner rolls (8*
3  *slices bacon, cooked,*      *rolls)*
   *drained, and crumbled*  1  *tablespoon milk*
1  *tablespoon bacon drippings*  *Caraway seeds*

Heat oven to 375° F. Mix cheese, bacon, and bacon drippings together in a small bowl. Grease a cookie sheet with unsalted shortening. Open roll container according to label directions. Unroll dough and separate into 8 triangles. Spread a thin layer of cheese filling over each triangle of dough. Roll up as directed on package. Place on prepared cookie sheet. Brush with milk and sprinkle lightly with caraway seeds. Bake 10 to 12 minutes, or until golden brown. Serve warm. Makes 8 rolls.
Your Time: 9 minutes
Cooking Time: 15 to 17 minutes

## HOT CHIVE-AND-CHEESE BISCUITS

2  *tablespoons melted butter*    1  *8-ounce container*
   *or margarine*             *refrigerated tender flaky*
1  *tablespoon freeze-dried*     *biscuits (12 biscuits)*
   *chives*
1  *tablespoon grated Parmesan*
   *cheese*

Heat oven to 400° F. Grease a cookie sheet with unsalted shortening. Blend butter, chives, and cheese together. Open biscuit container according to label directions. Split biscuits in half. Place on prepared cookie sheet. Spread filling on bottom halves of biscuits; replace tops and spread with additional filling. Bake 9 to 11 minutes, or until lightly browned. Serve warm. Makes 12 biscuits.
Your Time: 4 minutes
Baking Time: 9 to 11 minutes

## DILLY BISCUIT RING

2  *9½-ounce containers*           1  *teaspoon instant minced*
   *refrigerated tender flaky*         *onion*
   *buttermilk biscuits (10 big*    1  *teaspoon dillseed*
   *biscuits)*                     ½  *teaspoon celery seed*
2  *tablespoons melted butter*    ¼  *teaspoon seasoned salt*
   *or margarine*

Heat oven to 375° F. Open biscuit container according to label
directions. Remove biscuits and separate them. Stand biscuits on
edge around side of 9-inch round pan. Combine butter, onion,
dillseed, celery seed, and seasoned salt. Brush mixture over tops of
biscuits. Bake 25 to 30 minutes, or until golden brown. Serve warm.
Makes 1 ring.
Your Time: 4½ minutes
Baking Time: 25 to 30 minutes

## DILL BREAD STICKS

1  *cup bite-size shredded rice*   1  *8-ounce container*
   *biscuits*                         *refrigerated tender flaky*
2  *tablespoons dillseed*             *biscuits (12 biscuits)*
2  *teaspoons seasoned salt*       2  *tablespoons milk*

Heat oven to 450° F. Lightly grease a cookie sheet with unsalted
shortening. Spread cereal on a cookie sheet and heat in oven 5
minutes, until lightly toasted. In a small bowl crush cereal lightly and
mix with dillseed and salt. Open biscuit container according to label
directions. Separate biscuits and cut each one in half; with the hands
roll each biscuit half on a lightly floured board into a pencil-thin
stick about 4 inches long. Place sticks on waxed paper. Brush each
with milk; roll sticks in crushed cereal mixture. Place sticks on
prepared cookie sheet and bake in a 450° F. oven 10 minutes, or
until lightly browned. Serve warm with soup. Makes 2 dozen sticks.
Your Time: 13 minutes
Baking Time: 15 minutes

## LEMON FRENCH BREAD

¼  *cup butter or margarine*       2  *teaspoons lemon juice*
½  *teaspoon grated lemon peel*    1  *loaf French bread*

Melt butter; add lemon peel and juice. Cool until slightly thickened. Cut bread crosswise into 1-inch slices almost through to bottom crust. Brush butter mixture between slices. Wrap bread in aluminum foil and store in refrigerator until serving time. Place in a preheated 350° F. oven and bake 15 minutes. Serve warm. Makes 4 to 6 servings.
Your Time: 3 minutes
Baking Time: 15 minutes

## SEASONED ITALIAN BREAD

1  *loaf Italian bread (about 12 inches long)*
¼  *cup melted butter or margarine*
2  *teaspoons seasoned dry bread crumbs*

¼  *teaspoon garlic salt*
½  *teaspoon freeze-dried chives*
1  *teaspoon grated Parmesan cheese*

Heat broiler. Split bread in half lengthwise. Brush cut surfaces generously with butter. Sprinkle with bread crumbs, garlic salt, chives, and cheese. Place bread halves on a broiler rack and broil 4 inches from source of heat about 5 minutes, or until golden brown. Serve warm. Makes 4 servings.
Your Time: 5 minutes
Cooking Time: 5 minutes

## LIVER AND CHEESE CRESCENTS

1  *4¾-ounce can liverwurst spread*
⅓  *cup packaged shredded Cheddar cheese*
3  *tablespoons imitation bacon pieces*

1  *container refrigerated crescent dinner rolls (8 rolls)*
*Milk*
*Sesame seeds*

Heat oven to 375° F. In a small bowl combine liverwurst spread, cheese, and bacon pieces and blend well. Open roll container according to label directions. Unroll dough and separate into 8 triangles. Spread some of the liverwurst mixture on each triangle to within ¼ inch of the edges. Starting at the shortest edge of the triangle, roll up tightly as directed on package. Tuck tip of triangle underneath crescent. Brush the top of each crescent with milk and

sprinkle with sesame seeds. Place on an ungreased cookie sheet and bake 15 minutes, or until golden brown. Serve warm as a salad accompaniment. Makes 8 crescents.
Your Time: 6 minutes
Baking Time: 15 minutes

## ONION BREAD STICKS

1   10-to-12-inch loaf Italian          2½ tablespoons dry onion
    bread                                                    soup mix
½ cup softened butter or
    margarine

Heat oven to 375° F. Cut bread in half lengthwise; cut each half crosswise into 12 narrow strips. Blend butter and onion soup mix together in a small bowl. Spread one side of bread sticks with onion butter. Wrap sticks in aluminum foil and heat in oven for 15 minutes. Open foil and heat until bread sticks are crisp, about 5 minutes. Serve warm. Makes 24 bread sticks.
Your Time: 6½ minutes
Baking Time: 20 minutes

## PARMESAN BISCUITS

1   8-ounce container                  ¼ cup grated Parmesan
    refrigerated buttermilk                    cheese
    biscuits (10 biscuits)                 ¼ teaspoon garlic salt
1½ tablespoons melted butter      1   teaspoon dried parsley
    or margarine                                   flakes

Heat oven to 375° F. Open biscuit container according to label directions. Remove biscuits and separate them. Brush tops and sides of each biscuit with melted butter. Combine Parmesan cheese, garlic salt, and parsley in a bowl; dip top and sides of each biscuit into the cheese mixture. Place biscuits on an ungreased cookie sheet and bake 10 to 12 minutes. Serve hot. Makes 10 biscuits.
Your Time: 5 minutes
Baking Time: 10 to 12 minutes

## SESAME CHEESE LOAF

*¼ cup softened butter or*
*margarine*
*1 package cheese sauce mix*
*(makes 1 cup)*

*1 loaf French bread, about 18*
*inches long*
*1 tablespoon sesame seeds*

Heat oven to 400° F. In a small bowl combine butter and cheese sauce mix and stir to blend well. Slice loaf of French bread in half horizontally. Spread cheese mixture on cut surface of bottom half; sprinkle sesame seeds on cheese mixture. Replace top half. Cut loaf diagonally into 1½-inch slices almost through to bottom. Wrap loaf in a large piece of aluminum foil. Bake 15 minutes, or until heated through. Serve immediately. Makes 6 to 8 servings.
Your Time: 5 minutes
Baking Time: 15 minutes

## SESAME BUTTER STICKS

*¼ cup melted butter or*
*margarine*
*1 tablespoon lemon juice*
*1 8-ounce container*
*refrigerated buttermilk*
*biscuits (10 biscuits)*

*2 tablespoons sesame seeds*

Heat oven to 450° F. Combine melted butter and lemon juice. Pour half of butter mixture into an 8-inch-square baking pan. Open biscuit container according to label directions. Remove biscuits and separate them. Roll and twist each biscuit into an 8-inch strip. Place strips in pan. Brush with remaining butter and sprinkle with sesame seeds. Bake 8 to 10 minutes. Serve warm. Makes 10 sticks.
Your Time: 6 minutes
Baking Time: 8 to 10 minutes

## OPEN SESAME BREAD

*2 hard rolls*
*¼ cup melted butter or*
*margarine*

*3 tablespoons sesame seeds*

Heat oven to 350° F. Cut rolls horizontally into ½-inch slices. Brush slices with butter and sprinkle with sesame seeds. Bake on ungreased cookie sheet 8 to 10 minutes. Serve warm. Makes 4 servings.
Your Time: 7 minutes
Baking Time: 8 to 10 minutes

# *Sweet Breads and Coffeecakes*

## ALMOND-FROSTED DANISH

| | |
|---|---|
| 1  8-ounce container refrigerated crescent dinner rolls (8 rolls) | 1  tablespoon softened butter or margarine |
| 1  egg, beaten | 4  teaspoons milk |
| 1  tablespoon granulated sugar | ¼ teaspoon almond extract |
| 1  cup confectioners' sugar | Slices blanched almonds |

Heat oven to 375° F. Lightly grease a cookie sheet with unsalted shortening. Open roll container according to label directions. Unroll crescent dinner rolls into the 2 large rectangular pieces on a lightly floured board. With the fingers press perforations in dough together to seal. Cut each rectangle lengthwise into 6 strips. Twist 2 strips together in the shape of a rope, pinching the ends, and arrange the rope strip on the prepared cookie sheet in the shape of an S. Bring ends to the center to form a figure 8. Repeat with remaining strips. Brush each with the beaten egg and sprinkle with granulated sugar. Bake 10 to 12 minutes, or until golden brown. While pastries are baking, in a small bowl combine confectioners' sugar, butter, milk, and almond extract; blend well. When pastries are done, remove from cookie sheet. Immediately drizzle icing over each and sprinkle with almonds. Serve warm. Makes 6 pastries.
Your Time: 8 minutes
Baking Time: 10 to 12 minutes

## APPLE DANISH SWIRLS

| | |
|---|---|
| 1  14-ounce package refrigerated apple turnovers | 2  teaspoons ground cinnamon |
| 1½ tablespoons dark-brown sugar | |

Place 8 paper liners in a 2½-inch-cup muffin pan. Heat oven to 400° F. Open turnover package according to label directions. Reserve filling and icing. Unroll dough on a wooden board; arrange the 8 rectangles to form a large rectangle about 13 by 7 inches, overlapping the middle edges slightly. Press together seams and perforations firmly to seal well. Spread apple filling from turnover package evenly over the dough. Sprinkle brown sugar and cinnamon over the apple mixture. Starting with a short side, roll up dough in jelly-roll fashion, pressing edges to seal well. Cut roll into 8 slices. Place slices, cut side down, in the paper-lined muffin cups. Bake 18 to 20 minutes, or until golden brown. Let cool in pan 5 minutes. Remove swirls to a wire rack. Drizzle icing from the turnover package over tops. Serve warm. Makes 8 swirls.

Your Time: 9 minutes
Baking and Cooling Time: 23 to 25 minutes

## DUTCH APPLE COFFEECAKE

1  7¾-ounce jar junior Dutch
   apple dessert (baby food)
½ cup sugar
½ cup dark seedless raisins
¼ cup packaged corn flake
   crumbs

¼ cup dark corn syrup
½ teaspoon ground cinnamon
1  8-ounce container
   refrigerated tender flaky
   biscuits (12 biscuits)

Heat oven to 375° F. Grease a 9-inch round cake pan with unsalted shortening. Combine Dutch apple dessert, sugar, raisins, corn flake crumbs, corn syrup, and cinnamon. Pour mixture into the prepared pan. Open biscuit container according to label directions. Arrange biscuits on top of mixture. Bake 25 minutes, or until biscuits are browned on top. Remove from oven and let stand a few minutes; invert onto serving plate. Remove pan. Serve immediately. Makes 4 to 6 servings.

Your Time: 7 minutes
Baking Time: 25 minutes

## APRICOT-NUT ROLLS

1  tablespoon melted butter
   or margarine
⅓ cup apricot jam
¼ cup butterscotch sundae
   sauce

3  tablespoons chopped
   pecans
12  brown-and-serve dinner
   rolls

Heat oven to 400° F. In a small bowl combine butter, apricot jam, and butterscotch sauce; spread over bottom of an ungreased pan just large enough to hold rolls. Sprinkle with nuts. Place rolls in mixture with tops down. Bake 15 minutes. Let stand 1 or 2 minutes before inverting onto a plate. Remove pan and serve immediately. Makes 12 rolls.
Your Time: 4 minutes
Baking Time: 15 minutes

## BLUEBERRY COFFEECAKE

2  cups bite-size shredded rice biscuits, crumbled
¼  cup firmly packed dark-brown sugar
¼  teaspoon ground cinnamon
⅛  teaspoon ground nutmeg
2  tablespoons melted butter or margarine
1  8-ounce container refrigerated buttermilk biscuits (10 biscuits)

1  tablespoon granulated sugar
*1  10-ounce package frozen blueberries in quick-thaw pouch, thawed according to package directions and drained
¼  cup chopped walnuts

Heat oven to 375° F. Grease an 8-inch round cake pan with unsalted shortening. Combine cereal crumbs, brown sugar, cinnamon, and nutmeg in a bowl. Add butter; mix well. Sprinkle half the crumb mixture in bottom of prepared pan. Open biscuit container according to label directions. Place biscuits over crumbs. Mix granulated sugar, blueberries, and walnuts in a bowl; sprinkle over biscuits. Sprinkle with remaining crumb mixture. Bake 25 to 30 minutes. Serve warm. Makes 6 servings.
Your Time: 6 minutes
Baking Time: 25 to 30 minutes

*1¼ cups fresh or canned drained blueberries may be substituted.

## BUTTERSCOTCH CRESCENTS

⅓ cup firmly packed brown sugar
3  tablespoons finely chopped walnuts
2  tablespoons melted butter or margarine

1  container refrigerated crescent dinner rolls (8 rolls)
1  tablespoon dark corn syrup

Heat oven to 375° F. Grease a cookie sheet with unsalted shortening. Mix brown sugar, walnuts, and butter together. Open roll container according to label directions. Unroll dough and separate into triangles. Spread a thin layer of brown sugar filling over each triangle of dough. Roll up as directed on package. Place on greased cookie sheet. Brush with corn syrup. Bake 10 to 12 minutes, or until golden brown. Serve warm. Makes 8 rolls.
Your Time: 7 minutes
Baking Time: 10 to 12 minutes

## UPSIDE-DOWN CARAMEL ROLLS

½ cup vanilla–caramel sundae
   sauce
¼ cup light corn syrup
1 cup finely chopped walnuts

2 containers refrigerated
   butterflake dinner rolls
   (12 small or 6 large rolls
   each)

Heat oven to 375° F. Brush 12 large muffin cups with melted butter. Combine sundae sauce and syrup in a cup; spoon evenly into muffin cups. Sprinkle walnuts over sauce. Open roll containers according to label directions. Remove rolls from package as directed and stand 2 small rolls in each cup. Bake 12 minutes. Let stand 1 or 2 minutes; invert on a rack to remove from pan. Serve warm. Makes 12 rolls.
Your Time: 8 minutes
Baking Time: 12 minutes

## CRESCENT COFFEE ROLLS

½ cup mixed candied fruits
   and peels
2 tablespoons cinnamon sugar
1 tablespoon chopped
   blanched almonds

1 container refrigerated
   crescent dinner rolls (8
   rolls)

Heat oven to 375° F. Chop fruits finely; place in a small bowl and stir in half the cinnamon sugar and all the almonds. Open roll container according to label directions and separate dough into 8 triangles; sprinkle fruit mixture over dough before rolling in crescent shapes. Place on ungreased cookie sheet and sprinkle with the remaining 1 tablespoon cinnamon sugar. Bake 10 to 13 minutes, or until golden brown. Serve hot. Makes 8 rolls.
Your Time: 9 minutes
Baking Time: 10 to 13 minutes

## ORANGE COFFEE RING

¾ cup granulated sugar
1 tablespoon grated orange
   peel
2 8-ounce containers
   refrigerated buttermilk
   biscuits (10 biscuits each)
¼ cup melted butter or
   margarine

1 ounce (⅓ of 3-ounce
   package) cream cheese
¾ cup sifted confectioners'
   sugar
1 tablespoon orange juice
¼ teaspoon vanilla extract
¼ cup flaked coconut

Heat oven to 425° F. Lightly grease a 9-inch round cake pan with unsalted shortening. Combine granulated sugar and grated orange peel in a small bowl. Open biscuit container according to label directions. Remove biscuits from containers and dip each biscuit in melted butter and then in sugar mixture. Arrange in an overlapping circle in prepared pan. Bake 15 to 20 minutes, or until golden brown. In a small bowl cream together cheese, confectioners' sugar, orange juice, and vanilla. While coffee ring is still warm, spread frosting over top and sprinkle with coconut. Serve warm. Makes 8 servings.
Your Time: 12 minutes
Baking Time: 15 to 20 minutes

## CINNAMON COFFEE TWIST

2 containers refrigerated
   crescent dinner rolls (8
   rolls each)
2 tablespoons softened butter
   or margarine

½ cup dark seedless raisins
⅓ cup toasted diced almonds
1 tablespoon cinnamon sugar
¼ cup honey
¼ cup toasted diced almonds

Heat oven to 375° F. Lightly grease a 9-inch round cake pan with unsalted shortening. Open roll container according to label directions. Unroll the dough from both containers and separate into 8 rectangles. Place the 8 rectangles of dough lengthwise on a flat surface and press the seams together to seal them well. Spread butter over dough. Combine raisins, the ⅓ cup almonds, and the cinnamon sugar in a small bowl. Sprinkle mixture evenly over dough. Starting with a long side, roll up dough in jelly-roll fashion to make a long rope. Starting at the center, coil the roll around in prepared cake pan to form a pinwheel. Spread the honey over top of dough. Sprinkle top with remaining ¼ cup almonds. Bake 25 minutes, or until golden brown. Serve warm. Makes 6 servings.
Your Time: 9 minutes
Baking Time: 25 minutes

## COCONUT-BALL LOAF

1  8-ounce container                ⅓ cup honey
   refrigerated buttermilk   1¼ cups shredded coconut
   biscuits (10 biscuits)

Heat oven to 400° F. Open biscuit container according to label directions. Remove biscuits and separate them. Cut each biscuit in half. Place honey in one small bowl and coconut in another. Shape each biscuit half into a ball and dip quickly in honey, then roll in coconut. Arrange balls in 2 layers in an ungreased 8½-x-4½-x-2½-inch loaf pan. Bake 20 to 25 minutes, or until golden brown. Cool 5 minutes. Carefully turn out loaf onto a serving plate. Serve warm. Makes 4 servings.
Your Time: 9 minutes
Baking and Cooling Time: 25 to 30 minutes

## PEACH COFFEE RING

2  8-ounce containers           2  tablespoons melted butter
   refrigerated buttermilk          or margarine
   biscuits (10 biscuits each)  2  tablespoons sugar
1  20-ounce can sliced          ½  teaspoon ground cinnamon
   peaches, well drained        Chopped nuts (optional)

Heat oven to 450° F. Open biscuit containers according to label directions. Remove biscuits and separate them. Place biscuits around the edge of an ungreased 9-inch round cake pan, arranging them on edge with flat sides touching. Insert a peach slice between each biscuit. Brush top with butter. Combine sugar and cinnamon and sprinkle over biscuits. Bake 25 minutes, or until biscuits are golden brown. Garnish with chopped nuts if desired. Serve warm. Makes 8 servings.
Your Time: 8 minutes
Baking Time: 25 minutes

## QUICK PEANUT-BUTTER COFFEECAKE

1  9.5-ounce container          2  tablespoons peanut butter
   refrigerated cinnamon rolls  2  tablespoons jelly or jam
   (8 rolls)                    1  tablespoon milk

Heat oven to 375° F. Lightly grease a cookie sheet with unsalted shortening. Open roll container according to label directions. Remove dough from container and separate into rolls. Arrange

cinnamon rolls overlapping slightly in a circle on the prepared cookie sheet. Reserve frosting. In a small bowl combine peanut butter, jelly, and milk and spread mixture over the tops of rolls. Bake 20 minutes, or until lightly browned. Spread reserved frosting over rolls while still warm. Serve warm. Makes 6 to 8 servings.
Your Time: 7 minutes
Baking Time: 20 minutes

## SURPRISE MUFFINS

1  12-ounce package corn muffin mix
⅓ cup canned whole cranberry sauce

¼ teaspoon grated orange peel

Heat oven to 400° F. Lightly grease 12 2½-inch-cup muffin pans with unsalted shortening. Prepare muffins according to package directions. Fill muffin pans about halfway. In a small bowl combine cranberry sauce and orange peel and drop a teaspoonsful in center of each muffin. Top with rest of batter. Bake 15 minutes or until muffins are brown. Serve warm. Makes 12 muffins.
Your Time: 8 minutes
Baking Time: 15 minutes

## WALNUT HONEY ROLLS

¼ cup honey
2  tablespoons melted butter or margarine
¼ teaspoon ground nutmeg

¼ cup chopped walnuts
12  brown-and-serve cloverleaf rolls

Preheat oven to 400° F. Grease 12 2½-inch-cup muffin pans with unsalted shortening. Combine honey, butter, nutmeg, and chopped nuts. Divide nut mixture evenly into each cup. Place rolls upside down in cups. Bake 15 minutes. Let stand in pans 1 minute after removing from oven. Invert pans on serving plate to remove rolls. Spread with any mixture left in cups. Serve warm. Makes 12 rolls.
Your Time: 4 minutes
Baking Time: 15 minutes

# Supper Sandwiches

## OPEN-FACED CHILI SANDWICHES

1 15½-ounce can chili con    6 slices process American
  carne with beans            cheese
6 slices white bread
¾ cup cream-style cottage
  cheese

In a medium-sized saucepan cook chili over moderate heat (about 250° F.), stirring occasionally, until heated thoroughly. Spread chili evenly over the 6 slices bread. Spread 2 tablespoonfuls of the cottage cheese over the top of each slice; top with a slice of American cheese. Place sandwiches on broiler rack. Broil in preheated broiler 4 inches from heat about 3 minutes, or until cheese is bubbly and lightly browned. Makes 3 servings.
Your Time: 5 minutes
Cooking Time: 8 minutes

## CONTINENTAL CHICKEN SANDWICHES

2 medium-sized tomatoes,    1 2-ounce package blue
  thinly sliced              cheese, crumbled
4 slices white bread, toasted   4 slices bacon, partially
Salt                      cooked
1 4¾-ounce can chicken
  spread

Heat oven to 375° F. Place about 3 tomato slices on each piece of toast. Sprinkle lightly with salt. Spread a fourth of the chicken spread over tomatoes on each sandwich. Sprinkle crumbled blue cheese over chicken layer. Lay a strip of bacon on each sandwich. Place sandwiches on an ungreased cookie sheet. Bake for 10 minutes, or until bacon is crisp. Makes 4 sandwiches.
Your Time: 10 minutes
Baking Time: 10 minutes

## CRUNCHY CHICKEN SANDWICH

1  4¾-ounce can chicken          ⅓ cup chopped walnuts
 spread                          8  slices white bread
1  tablespoon mayonnaise         Pimiento-stuffed olives
½ cup finely chopped peeled
 cucumber

In a small bowl mix together chicken spread, mayonnaise, cucumber, and walnuts; chill for 30 minutes. Cut off crust from bread; mound about 2 tablespoons of filling diagonally across each slice. Bring together 2 remaining corners and secure with a toothpick. Garnish with an olive. Makes 8 sandwiches, or 4 servings.
Your Time: 8 minutes
Chilling Time: 30 minutes

## CORNED-BEEF HERO

1  loaf French bread, about 18    1  3-ounce package pressed
 inches long                       corned beef
⅓ cup commercial sour cream      ½ cup packaged shredded
2  teaspoons frozen chopped           Cheddar cheese
 chives
1  medium-sized tomato, cut
 into ¼-inch slices

Preheat broiler. Slice loaf of French bread in half horizontally. Place halves, cut side up, on a cookie sheet and broil 6 inches from heat about 1 minute, or until lightly toasted. In a small bowl combine sour cream and chives and blend well. Spread sour cream mixture on the bottom half of toasted French bread. Arrange slices of tomato on top of sour cream mixture. Arrange corned beef on top of tomato slices. Sprinkle cheese on top. Place bread on cookie sheet and broil 6 inches from heat 2 to 3 minutes, or until cheese is melted and lightly browned. Top sandwich with the top half of loaf and cut into serving pieces. Makes 3 or 4 servings.
Your Time: 7 minutes
Broiling Time: 3 to 4 minutes

## BAKED FRANKFURTER BOATS

8 *frankfurter buns, split*
¼ *cup melted butter or*
  *margarine*
2 *teaspoons prepared mustard*
2 *teaspoons prepared*
  *horseradish*

¾ *cup packaged shredded*
  *Cheddar cheese*
½ *cup bottled India relish*
8 *frankfurters*

Heat oven to 400° F. Brush the insides of the buns with the melted butter. In a small bowl combine mustard and horseradish; spread over butter. In another small bowl combine cheese and relish. Split frankfurters almost through lengthwise; spoon cheese-relish mixture into the center of each frankfurter. Place a frankfurter, cut side up, on each bun. Arrange on an ungreased cookie sheet and bake 10 minutes, or until buns are lightly browned and cheese is melted. Makes 8 sandwiches.
Your Time: 7 minutes
Baking Time: 10 minutes

## SUPPER GRILLWICHES

8 *slices white bread*
½ *cup peanut butter*
8 *thin slices canned luncheon*
  *meat*

¼ *cup softened butter or*
  *margarine*

Spread 4 slices of the bread thinly with some of the peanut butter; top each slice with 2 pieces of the luncheon meat. Spread the remaining slices of bread with the remaining peanut butter; place, peanut butter side down, on top of meat. Spread the outsides of sandwiches generously with the softened butter. Arrange sandwiches in a large skillet, place over moderately high heat (about 275° F.) and brown about 5 minutes on each side. Serve immediately. Makes 4 sandwiches.
Your Time: 10 minutes
Cooking Time: About 10 minutes

## SPICY LUNCHEON-MEAT SANDWICHES

1 *tablespoon cider vinegar*
2 *tablespoons dark corn syrup*
1 *small clove garlic, peeled and finely chopped*
1 *small bay leaf*
½ *cup water*
1 *12-ounce can luncheon meat*

1 *tablespoon mixed pickling spices, coarsely crushed*
8 *slices rye or pumpernickel bread, buttered*
*Coleslaw (optional)*

In a large saucepan combine vinegar, 1 tablespoon of the corn syrup, garlic, bay leaf, and water. Add the luncheon meat all in one piece. Simmer, covered, over moderate heat (about 250° F.) 10 minutes. Turn loaf over with a spatula. Pour remaining tablespoon corn syrup over loaf. Sprinkle with pickling spices. Simmer, covered, another 10 minutes. Remove meat and cut into ¼-inch slices. Arrange slices on half the buttered bread slices. Top with remaining bread slices. Serve with coleslaw, if desired. Makes 4 servings.
Your Time: 14 minutes
Cooking Time: 20 minutes

## INSIDE-OUT PIZZA

1 *4½-ounce can deviled ham*
½ *cup canned tomato sauce*
½ *teaspoon dried oregano leaves*

8 *slices white bread*
*Melted butter or margarine*
2 *tablespoons grated Parmesan cheese*

In a bowl combine deviled ham, tomato sauce, and oregano. Brush one side of each slice of bread with butter. Spread deviled ham mixture on unbuttered side of 4 of the slices. Sprinkle each with cheese. Top each with a slice of bread, buttered side up. Place sandwiches in preheated waffle iron and bake 10 to 12 minutes. Makes 4 servings.
Your Time: 6 minutes
Cooking Time: 10 to 12 minutes

## QUICKIE BROILED SANDWICHES

1 *2-ounce jar dried beef, shredded*
1 *5-ounce jar cream cheese with chives*

⅓ *cup commercial sour cream*
1 *9-ounce package frozen waffles*
*Paprika (optional)*

Pour boiling water over dried beef and let stand a few minutes; drain well. In a medium-sized bowl combine dried beef, cheese spread, and sour cream. Arrange waffles on an ungreased cookie sheet; spread dried beef mixture over waffles. Place about 5 inches from heat in a preheated broiler and broil about 5 minutes, or until topping is puffy. Sprinkle with paprika, if desired. Makes 6 servings.
Your Time: 8 minutes
Broiling Time: 5 minutes

## TAMALE HERO SANDWICH

| | |
|---|---|
| 1 tablespoon instant minced onion | ½ cup chopped green pepper |
| 2 tablespoons water | 1 15-ounce can tamales |
| 1 12-inch loaf Italian bread | 1 4-ounce package shredded Cheddar cheese |
| 1 15½-ounce can chili con carne | |

Heat oven to 350° F. Mix onion and water together in a small bowl and let stand 5 minutes. Slice bread in half lengthwise. Place bread halves on an ungreased cookie sheet. Spread each half with chili con carne. Sprinkle with onion and green pepper. Arrange 3 tamales on each slice of bread. Sprinkle with cheese. Bake 15 minutes. Serve as an open-faced sandwich and cut into servings. Makes 4 to 6 servings.
Your Time: 9 minutes
Baking Time: 15 minutes

## TURKEY SANDWICH AU GRATIN

| | |
|---|---|
| 16 slices white bread, lightly toasted | 3 tablespoons water |
| Softened butter or margarine | ¼ cup dry sherry |
| 16 thin slices cooked turkey | 2 10½-ounce cans condensed cream of mushroom soup, undiluted |
| ½ cup butter or margarine | |
| 4 cups thinly sliced mushrooms | ½ 4-ounce package (½ cup) shredded Cheddar cheese |
| 3 tablespoons instant minced onion | |

Spread slices of toast lightly with softened butter. Place turkey on 8 of the slices. Cover each with a second slice of toast. Trim off the crusts. Melt the ½ cup butter in a skillet over moderately low heat

(about 225° F.). Add mushrooms and cook about 10 minutes, or until tender, stirring frequently. While mushrooms are cooking sprinkle onion over water in a small bowl and let stand 5 minutes. Add onion, sherry, and mushroom soup to the mushrooms in the skillet and heat until very hot. Place sandwiches in a shallow baking pan with low sides. Spoon mushroom sauce over sandwiches and sprinkle each with cheese. Place sandwiches in a preheated broiler about 4 to 5 inches from heat and broil 3 to 4 minutes, or until cheese is melted. Makes 8 servings.
Your Time: 22 minutes
Cooking Time: About 18 minutes

### WAFFLED HAM-AND-CHEESE SANDWICHES

| | |
|---|---|
| 1  *4½-ounce can deviled ham* | 1  *egg, slightly beaten* |
| 1  *teaspoon prepared* | *⅓ cup milk* |
| *mustard* | 2  *tablespoons butter or* |
| 1  *5-ounce package frozen* | *margarine* |
| *waffles* | |
| 1½  *slices process American* | |
| *cheese* | |

In a small bowl combine deviled ham and mustard. Spread on each of 3 frozen waffles; top each with ½ slice cheese and another waffle to make a sandwich. In a pie plate combine egg and milk. Melt butter in a skillet over moderately high heat (about 350° F.). Dip waffle sandwiches into egg batter and place in the skillet. Cook until golden brown, turning once. Serve warm. If desired, cut each sandwich diagonally into quarters to serve. Makes 3 servings.
Your Time: 3 minutes
Cooking Time: 6 minutes

# CHAPTER
# VIII
# *Desserts*

In stores today, refrigerator and freezer cases are chock full of ready-to-serve puddings, pies and cakes, fruits, and jellied desserts and, indeed, these are all very good and very useful.

If your family expects a dessert with every lunch and dinner, these ready-mades are a convenient solution.

You may hesitate to reach for them always, however, remembering from childhood days that desserts should be "something special," something, even, of a reward. Even time doesn't dissipate that "eat your spinach or you won't get dessert" feeling for most of us.

Actually, desserts can be as rewarding for the cook as they are for the diner. It's fun to make desserts; in fact, it can be quite thrilling to turn out a masterpiece of a cake or pie.

Believe it or not, you can capture this kind of drama using the same prepared desserts available to everyone. Mostly it takes imagination and a realization that the market is filled with an enormous variety of ingredients that can be used to make delicious, healthful, and impressive desserts.

Fruit desserts can be made from fresh, frozen, canned, and dried fruits or even a mixture of them, which means, literally, that no fruit is every out of season. A cold or a hot fruit compote, made with a mixture of fresh, canned, frozen, and dried fruits spiked with a dollop of liqueur and a gentle seasoning of cinnamon or nutmeg will complement most meat- or cheese-based meals.

The parfait, classically a multilayered concoction of ice cream and flavored syrup, can appear in as many guises as your imagination permits. A parfait glass traditionally has a tall bowl and a foot, but you can use any small glass to build a mixture of sweets. Layers of canned chocolate pudding with spoonfuls of marshmallow cream between; mounting layers of various flavors of ice cream; layers of lemon sherbet separated by green crème de menthe; layers of ready-to-serve pudding with fruit relish interspersed, or layers of two flavors of gelatin all make timesaving desserts that look intricate.

Ice creams, from the richest to the most diet-conscious ice milks, are the ever-reliable timesaving dessert. But they lend themselves to great variety of presentation. It takes little time to pack two layers of ice cream of sherbet into a melon-shaped mold and less time to dip the mold into hot water, turn it out onto a leaf-lined platter, and present a majestic-looking bombe. Serve it with a side dish of sundae sauce, and you've achieved a dessert worthy of the most elegant restaurant.

Pies and cakes—those favorite desserts—come in any degree of doneness you prefer. Ready-to-serve pies and cakes come in a variety of flavors on the bakery shelves of supermarkets. Or you can select a fresh-frozen pie or cake to keep in your own freezer until you need to serve it. Canned pie fillings, frozen preformed pie crusts, and refrigerated toppings give you an opportunity to make a pie of your choice that won't take more than five minutes of your time in the kitchen. Cake mixes in "infinite" flavors take the guesswork out of home baking. These are just a few of the ways by which you can *create* a dessert rather than just serving one.

Except perhaps for holidays, when we all loosen our belts a little, desserts should balance a meal. For instance, a hearty stew with bread and salad would best be followed by the light, fresh-tasting Layered Burgundy-Cherry Mold on page 226, whereas a light soup and salad luncheon could be topped by the rich Chocolate Candy Pie on page 230.

We think you'll like the short-cut dessert recipes in this chapter. With them you're not apt to run out of dessert ideas in a hurry, for they cover everything from very special fruit desserts, ice cream desserts, puddings and parfaits, and molded gelatine desserts to easy-to-make pies and tarts, as well as cakes and cookies.

# Fruit Desserts

## APPLE CRISP

½ cup packaged graham
  cracker crumbs
1½ tablespoons melted butter
  or margarine
1 22-ounce can apple pie
  filling

½ teaspoon ground
  cinnamon
1 teaspoon sugar

Heat oven to 375° F. In a small bowl moisten crumbs with the melted butter. Place apple pie filling in the bottom of an ungreased shallow 1-quart casserole. Sprinkle apples with crumbs. Combine cinnamon and sugar in a small bowl and sprinkle over crumbs. Bake, uncovered, 30 minutes. Serve warm. Makes 4 servings.
Your Time: 5 minutes
Baking Time: 30 minutes

## BAKED APPLES À LA MODE

2 15-ounce cans baked apples
  (or 4 baked apples),
  undrained
½ cup dark seedless raisins

2 tablespoons light-brown
  sugar
¼ teaspoon ground cinnamon
Vanilla ice cream

Heat oven to 400° F. Stuff center of each apple with raisins. Place apples in a shallow baking dish. Sprinkle tops with brown sugar and cinnamon. Bake, uncovered, 10 to 15 minutes, or until thoroughly heated. Serve apples hot with a scoop of vanilla ice cream. Makes 4 servings.
Your Time: 4 minutes
Baking Time: 10 to 15 minutes

## ROSY BAKED APPLE SLICES

½ cup granulated sugar
¼ cup firmly packed
   light-brown sugar
½ teaspoon ground
   cinnamon
¼ teaspoon ground nutmeg
1 8-ounce can jellied
   cranberry sauce

1 20-ounce can apple slices,
   undrained
⅓ cup sliced blanched
   almonds
1½ cups miniature
   marshmallows

Heat oven to 350° F. Combine sugar, brown sugar, cinnamon, and nutmeg in a mixing bowl. Stir cranberry sauce with a spoon until thoroughly broken up. Add cranberry sauce, apple slices, and almonds to sugar mixture and stir to combine thoroughly. Spoon apple mixture into an ungreased shallow 1½-quart baking dish. Sprinkle marshmallows over the top. Bake, uncovered, 25 to 30 minutes, or until apples are heated and marshmallows are melted and brown. Serve warm. Makes 6 servings.
Your Time: 6 minutes
Baking Time: 25 to 30 minutes

## BLUEBERRY HALO

1 4-serving package instant
   vanilla pudding
Milk
½ cup graham cracker
   crumbs

½ teaspoon ground
   cinnamon
1½ cups blueberries, washed
   and drained

Prepare pudding according to package directions, using amount of milk called for on package. Chill 5 minutes. Stir graham cracker crumbs and cinnamon together in a medium-sized bowl. Fold in 1 cup of the berries. Spoon blueberry-crumb mixture and vanilla pudding in alternate layers into sherbet glasses, ending with a pudding layer. Arrange remaining blueberries in circle around edge of pudding. Makes 4 to 6 servings.
Your Time: 9 minutes
Chilling Time: 5 minutes

## CHERRY AMBROSIA

1 30-ounce can pitted dark
  sweet cherries
1 cup commercial sour cream
2 tablespoons apricot jam

2 tablespoons chopped
  toasted almonds
¼ cup toasted flaked coconut

Drain cherries and place them on absorbent paper to dry thoroughly. In a bowl thoroughly combine sour cream, jam, and almonds. Carefully fold in cherries. Sprinkle coconut over top. Chill 30 minutes. Makes 4 to 6 servings.
Your Time: 6 minutes
Chilling Time: 30 minutes

## RUSSIAN CHERRIES

1 8-ounce jar red currant jelly
3 tablespoons light rum
1 17-ounce can pitted dark
  sweet cherries, chilled and
  drained

½ cup commercial sour cream

Blend red currant jelly and rum together in a serving bowl. Stir in chilled cherries. Refrigerate until serving time, or at least 30 minutes. Serve topped with sour cream. Makes 4 servings.
Your Time: 3 minutes
Chilling Time: 30 minutes

## CRANBERRY DELIGHT

1 cup sifted all-purpose flour
2¼ teaspoons baking powder
¾ teaspoon salt
¼ teaspoon ground
  cinnamon
¾ cup instant granular whole
  wheat cereal

⅓ cup sugar
1 egg, well beaten
⅓ cup vegetable oil
1 16-ounce can whole-berry
  cranberry sauce
Sweetened whipped cream
  (optional)

Heat oven to 400° F. Grease an 8-inch-square cake pan with unsalted shortening. Sift together flour, baking powder, salt, and cinnamon into a medium-sized bowl. Blend in cereal and sugar. Combine egg, oil, and cranberry sauce in a small bowl. Add to dry ingredients all at once. Stir only until flour is moistened. Pour batter into prepared pan; bake, uncovered, 40 minutes, or until golden brown. Serve warm with sweetened whipped cream, if desired. Makes 6 servings.
Your Time: 8 minutes
Baking Time: 40 minutes

## MIXED FRUIT AMBROSIA

2  10-ounce packages frozen
    mixed fruit in quick-thaw
    pouches, thawed according
    to package directions

3  tablespoons crème de cacao
    liqueur
Flaked coconut

In a medium-sized bowl mix together fruit and liqueur. Spoon into 4 sherbet glasses. Top each with coconut. Chill 1 hour. Makes 4 servings.
Your Time: 5 minutes
Chilling Time: 1 hour

## POUND CAKE WITH FRUIT À LA MODE

4  ½-inch-thick slices pound
    cake, toasted
1  10-ounce package frozen
    mixed fruits in quick-thaw
    pouch, thawed according
    to package directions and
    drained

2  tablespoons light rum
Vanilla ice cream

Place a slice of toasted pound cake on each of 4 individual plates. In a small bowl combine fruit and rum. Spoon fruit mixture evenly over cake. Top each with a small scoop of ice cream. Makes 4 servings.
Your Time: 4 minutes

## FESTIVE FRUIT BOWL

1 10-ounce package frozen
  mixed fruits in quick-thaw
  pouch, thawed according
  to package directions
1 16-ounce can orange and
  grapefruit sections,
  undrained

1 large banana, peeled and
  sliced
2 tablespoons dry white wine

Combine all ingredients in a bowl. Chill 30 minutes. Makes 4 servings.
Your Time: 3 minutes
Chilling Time: 30 minutes

## BUTTERSCOTCH PEACH TRIFLE

1 17-ounce can peach slices
1 4-serving-size package
  instant butterscotch
  pudding

1½ cups light cream
6 ladyfingers, split
¼ cup toasted slivered
  almonds

Drain canned peach slices, reserving ¼ cup juice. Prepare instant butterscotch pudding as package directs, using the 1½ cups light cream and the ¼ cup peach juice in place of the milk called for on the package. In each of 6 serving dishes arrange 2 ladyfinger halves and about 3 peach slices. Spoon pudding over the peaches. Sprinkle each serving with almonds. Chill 1 hour. Makes 6 servings.
Your Time: 6½ minutes
Chilling Time: 1 hour

## PEACH MELBA WITH COCONUT CREAM

⅔ cup sweetened condensed
  milk, undiluted
½ cup water
¼ teaspoon salt
1½ teaspoons vanilla extract
¼ teaspoon almond extract

1 cup chilled heavy cream
1 3½-ounce can flaked
  coconut
1 16-ounce can cling peach
  halves, drained
4 tablespoons raspberry jam

In a medium-sized bowl combine condensed milk, water, salt, and vanilla and almond extracts. In a small bowl whip cream until it forms soft peaks; fold in coconut. Fold whipped cream mixture into condensed milk mixture. Pour into an 8½-x-4½-x-2½-inch loaf pan. Cover and place pan in freezer for 4 hours, or until firm. At serving time, place a peach half in each dessert dish with a scoop of the frozen coconut cream topped with a spoonful of raspberry jam. Makes 4 servings.

Your Time: 9 minutes

Chilling Time: 4 hours

## MELBA PEACHES FLAMBÉ

| | |
|---|---|
| 1 10-ounce package frozen raspberries in quick-thaw pouch, thawed according to package directions | ¼ cup cold water |
| | 1½ tablespoons cornstarch |
| | 1 29-ounce can cling peach halves, drained |
| ½ cup currant jelly | ¼ cup brandy |

Place thawed raspberries in a saucepan. Mash berries with a spoon or masher. Add jelly and bring to a boil over moderately low heat (about 225° F.). Add water slowly to cornstarch in a small bowl and blend thoroughly. Stir cornstarch mixture into raspberries and cook over moderate heat (about 250° F.), stirring constantly, until thickened and clear. Remove from heat and strain mixture into a chafing dish or electric skillet. Discard pulp and seeds. Add drained peach halves. Just before serving, heat peaches until sauce bubbles, basting frequently with the sauce. Warm brandy in a small saucepan over low heat (about 200° F.). Remove brandy from heat and ignite. Pour over peaches. Immediately spoon peaches into serving dishes and top with some of the raspberry sauce. Makes 6 servings.

Your Time and Cooking Time: 15 minutes

## MINCEMEAT-STUFFED PEACHES

| | |
|---|---|
| 1 16-ounce can cling peach halves, drained | Vanilla ice cream |
| ½ cup jarred mincemeat with brandy and rum | |

Heat oven to 325° F. Place peach halves cut side up in a shallow baking dish. Fill centers of peaches with mincemeat. Bake, uncovered, 5 to 7 minutes. Serve warm with ice cream. Makes 4 servings.
Your Time: 3 minutes
Baking Time: 5 to 7 minutes

## RUM TAFFY PEACHES

1  *29-ounce can peach halves*  
½  *cup dark molasses*  
3  *tablespoons sugar*  
3  *tablespoons lemon juice*  

2  *tablespoons light rum or 1 teaspoon rum flavoring*  
*Vanilla ice cream*

Drain peach halves and reserve ½ cup of the peach syrup. Combine peach syrup with molasses, sugar, lemon juice, and rum in a large skillet. Simmer over moderately low heat (about 225° F.) about 5 minutes. Add peach halves; cover and cook 5 minutes longer. Serve warm or chilled with ice cream. Makes 6 servings.
Your Time: 4 minutes
Cooking Time: 10 minutes

## PEARS À LA CRÈME

1  *29-ounce can pear halves, chilled*  
1½  *tablespoons cornstarch*  
3  *tablespoons light-brown sugar*  

1½  *teaspoons lemon juice*  
2  *tablespoons light rum or rum flavoring*  
*Pressurized ready-whipped cream*

Drain pears, reserving syrup. Chill pears. In a saucepan mix cornstarch and sugar together. Gradually add pear syrup and lemon juice, stirring until smooth. Cook over moderate heat (about 250° F.), stirring constantly, until mixture comes to a boil. Cool and stir in rum. Chill 1 hour. Place a pear half in center of each dessert plate. About 1 inch around pear make a ring of whipped cream. Spoon sauce over pear. Makes 6 to 8 servings.
Your Time: 7 minutes
Chilling Time: 1 hour

## PEARS FLAMBÉ

| | |
|---|---|
| 1  29-ounce can pear halves | 1  cup orange marmalade |
| 2  tablespoons butter or | ¼  cup brandy |
|    margarine | Commercial sour cream |

Drain pear halves. Heat butter and marmalade in a skillet over moderately low heat (about 225° F.) until melted. Add pears and heat thoroughly, basting frequently with the marmalade mixture. Just before serving, warm brandy slightly in a small saucepan over low heat (about 200° F.). Pour warmed brandy over pears and set aflame. Serve pear halves with marmalade sauce and a spoonful of sour cream. Makes 6 to 8 servings.
Your Time: 6 minutes
Cooking Time: 5 minutes

## PEARS WITH GOLDEN SAUCE

| | |
|---|---|
| 1  29-ounce can pear halves | Few grains salt |
| 1  egg | 1  3-ounce package cream |
| 2  tablespoons undiluted |    cheese, at room |
|    frozen orange juice |    temperature |
|    concentrate | |

Drain pears and reserve ½ cup of the syrup. With rotary beater beat egg well in top of a double boiler. Add orange juice, reserved pear syrup, and salt; beat until blended. Place over simmering water and cook 6 to 8 minutes, stirring occasionally, until thickened. Add cream cheese and beat until smooth. Serve sauce warm or cold over pear halves. Makes 6 to 8 servings.
Your Time: 6 minutes
Cooking Time: 6 to 8 minutes

## WAFFLED PEAR DESSERT

| | |
|---|---|
| ½ cup thawed frozen orange | 1  cup frozen whipped |
|    juice concentrate, |    topping, thawed |
|    undiluted | 1  5-ounce package frozen |
| ⅓ cup bottled maple-blended |    waffles, thawed |
|    syrup | 1  17-ounce can pear halves, |
| ⅛ teaspoon salt |    drained |
| 1  egg yolk | Maraschino cherries |

Combine orange juice concentrate, maple syrup, salt, and egg yolk in a saucepan. Place over low heat (about 200° F.) and cook, stirring constantly, until mixture is slightly thickened. Chill for 20 minutes. Fold in whipped topping. Toast waffles and place one on each of 6 serving plates. Top each with a scant ¼ cup of the orange mixture. Place a pear half, cut side up, on top of mixture. Spoon equal amounts of orange mixture into each pear half. Garnish with maraschino cherries. Makes 6 servings.
Your Time: 10 minutes
Cooking Time: 10 minutes
Chilling Time: 20 minutes

## RASPBERRIES IN PORT WINE

*3 10-ounce packages frozen
    red raspberries in
    quick-thaw pouch, thawed
    according to package
    directions*

*½ cup port wine
½ teaspoon grated lime peel
1 tablespoon lime juice
Sweetened whipped cream
    (optional)*

Put thawed raspberries in a serving bowl; stir in remaining ingredients, except whipped cream. Chill 1 hour, or until ready to serve. Serve with sweetened whipped cream, if desired. Makes 6 to 8 servings.
Your Time: 5 minutes
Chilling Time: 1 hour

## STRAWBERRY-APPLE WHIP

*1 3½-ounce package
    strawberry-flavored
    whipped dessert mix
½ cup chilled evaporated
    milk, undiluted
1 15-ounce jar sweetened
    applesauce*

*¼ teaspoon ground nutmeg
1 10-ounce package frozen
    sliced strawberries,
    undrained*

Place dessert mix and evaporated milk in a small, deep, narrow bowl. Beat at high speed on electric mixer for 1 minute, or with rotary beater until thickened. Fold in applesauce and nutmeg. Beat for 2 minutes. Turn into individual serving dishes or a 3-cup mold. Cover and chill 2 to 3 hours, or until firm. About 20 minutes before serving

time, place package of strawberries in warm water to thaw. Serve strawberries over whip. Makes 4 to 6 servings.
Your Time: 6 minutes
Chilling Time: 2 to 3 hours

## STRAWBERRY WHIP

1  *pint fresh strawberries,*
   *rinsed and hulled*
2  *tablespoons sugar*
1  *teaspoon grated orange peel*
2  *tablespoons orange liqueur*
   *or orange juice*

1  *cup thawed frozen whipped*
   *topping*
*Fresh mint sprigs (optional)*

In a bowl combine strawberries, sugar, peel, and liqueur. Mix to blend. Cover and chill 2 hours. Just before serving, fold in whipped topping. Serve in individual dessert dishes. Garnish each serving with a small sprig of mint if desired. Makes 4 servings.
Your Time: 7 minutes
Chilling Time: 2 hours

## STRAWBERRY TRIFLE

1  *11-ounce package jelly roll*
⅓ *cup light rum*
1  *4-serving package vanilla*
   *instant pudding*
½ *cup heavy cream*
*Milk*

1  *pint strawberries, washed,*
   *hulled, and sliced*
1  *cup chilled heavy cream*
1  *tablespoon confectioners'*
   *sugar*

Slice jelly roll into 8 slices and sprinkle with 3 tablespoons of the rum. Prepare pudding according to package directions, substituting the ½ cup heavy cream for ½ cup of the milk called for on the package. Stir in the remaining rum. Let stand 5 minutes. Arrange slices of cake upright in an overlapping row around sides of a deep 1½-quart casserole. Place a slice of cake on the bottom. Pour in vanilla pudding. Arrange strawberries over top. Whip the 1 cup cream and the sugar until mixture holds its shape; spoon over strawberries. Chill at least 2 hours. Makes 6 servings.
Your Time: 5 minutes
Standing Time: 5 minutes
Chilling Time: 2 hours

# Ice-Cream Desserts

### HOT APRICOT SUNDAE

2  tablespoons cornstarch
⅛ teaspoon ground allspice
Few grains salt
1  12-ounce can apricot nectar

½ cup light corn syrup
1  tablespoon bottled lemon
   juice
Vanilla ice cream

In a saucepan mix together cornstarch, allspice, and salt. Gradually stir in apricot nectar and corn syrup. Place over moderate heat (about 250° F.) and bring mixture to a boil; boil 1 minute, stirring constantly. Remove saucepan from heat and stir in lemon juice. Serve sauce warm over ice cream. (Unused sauce may be covered and stored in the refrigerator and reheated.) Makes about 2 cups sauce.
Your Time and Cooking Time: 14 minutes

### CHERRY SUNDAE

1  21-ounce can cherry pie
   filling
1  tablespoon grated orange
   peel

¼ teaspoon ground cinnamon
2  tablespoons cherry liqueur
   (optional)
Vanilla ice cream

In a bowl mix together cherry pie filling, grated peel, cinnamon, and liqueur. Cover and chill 2 hours. Serve sauce over ice cream. Sauce may be stored tightly covered in the refrigerator for a week or more. Makes 2 cups sauce.
Your Time: 5 minutes
Chilling Time: 2 hours

### SHERRIED FRUIT SUNDAE

1  17-ounce can fruit cocktail,
   drained

2  tablespoons sweet sherry
Vanilla ice cream

In a bowl mix together drained fruit and sherry. Cover and chill 2 hours. Serve sauce over scoops of ice cream. Makes 1½ cups sauce.
Your Time: 1½ minutes
Chilling Time: 2 hours

## BAKED ALASKA WAFFLES

1  *5-ounce package frozen*
   *waffles (6 waffles)*
¼ *cup creamy peanut butter*
3  *large egg whites, at room*
   *temperature*
¼ *teaspoon cream of tartar*

*Few grains salt*
6  *tablespoons sugar*
½  *teaspoon almond extract*
1  *pint brick ice cream (flavor*
   *of your choice)*

Arrange waffles on a cookie sheet. Spread some of the peanut butter on each. In the small bowl of an electric mixer combine egg whites, cream of tartar, and salt. Beat until soft peaks form. Gradually add sugar 1 tablespoon at a time, beating well after each addition, until glossy and stiff peaks form. Stir in almond extract. Cut ice cream into 6 slices. Place 1 slice on each waffle. Spread with meringue, completely covering ice cream and sides of waffles. If desired, freeze until ready to use. Heat oven to 500° F. Bake 3 to 4 minutes, or until meringue is lightly browned. Serve immediately. Makes 6 servings.
Your Time: 15 minutes
Baking Time: 3 to 4 minutes

## BANANA-SPLIT CUPS

1  *cup quick*
   *chocolate-flavored mix*
½  *cup heavy cream*
6  *packaged individual dessert*
   *sponge cups*

1  *8¼-ounce can crushed*
   *pineapple, undrained*
3  *small bananas, peeled and*
   *cut into halves, crosswise*
1  *pint vanilla ice cream*

Combine chocolate-flavored mix and cream in a saucepan over moderately low heat (about 225° F.). Bring to a boil, stirring occasionally. Remove from heat. Place a dessert sponge cup on each of 6 dessert plates; spoon crushed pineapple into each one. Split banana pieces almost through and place on pineapple. Top with a small scoop of ice cream. Spoon warm chocolate syrup over each serving. Makes 6 servings.
Your Time: 4 minutes
Cooking Time: 10 minutes

## QUICK BISCUIT TORTONI

1   *4½-ounce container (2 cups) frozen whipped topping, thawed*
2   *tablespoons cognac*
¼   *cup canned diced roasted almonds*

¼   *cup flaked coconut*
1   *egg white, at room temperature*
*Canned diced roasted almonds (optional)*

In a mixing bowl gently mix together whipped topping, cognac, almonds, and coconuts. Beat egg white until stiff but not dry. Fold beaten egg white into topping mixture. Spoon into 6 muffin-sized foil baking cups. Sprinkle with additional nuts, if desired. Freeze several hours, or overnight. Makes 6 servings.
Your Time: 12 minutes
Freezing Time: Several hours

## CRÈME DE MENTHE ICE CREAM

1   *quart vanilla ice cream*      ½   *cup crème de menthe*

Soften ice cream only slightly. Scoop or spoon the ice cream into 2 freezer trays. Do not smooth down. Spoon ¼ cup crème de menthe per freezer tray between the scoops of ice cream. Freeze until firm, or at least 1 hour. Makes 6 to 8 servings.
Your Time: 5 minutes
Freezing Time: 1 hour

## ICE-CREAM SQUARES

1¼   *cups finely crushed vanilla wafer crumbs (about 34 cookies)*
¾   *cup sugar-and-honey wheat germ*
½   *cup firmly packed light-brown sugar*

¾   *teaspoon ground cinnamon*
½   *cup melted butter or margarine*
1   *quart vanilla ice cream, softened*

Grease a shallow 2-quart baking dish with unsalted shortening. Combine vanilla wafer crumbs, wheat germ, brown sugar, cinnamon, and melted butter in a medium-sized bowl and blend well. Reserve ⅓ cup of mixture for topping. Press remaining crumb mixture over bottom and sides of prepared baking dish. Spoon the softened ice cream over crumbs; spread top of ice cream smooth with a spatula. Sprinkle with reserved crumb mixture. Cover and freeze 3 to 4 hours, or until firm for easy cutting. Makes 8 servings.
Your Time: 8 minutes
Chilling Time: 3 to 4 hours

## LEMONADE SHERBET

1  13-fluid-ounce can        1  6-ounce can frozen
     evaporated milk, undiluted        lemonade concentrate,
                                                thawed

Pour evaporated milk into a loaf pan and freeze until ice crystals form around edges. Chill mixing bowl and rotary beater while milk is in freezer. Turn milk into bowl and whip with rotary beater until stiff. Add lemonade and beat until blended. Pour into loaf pan, cover, and place in freezer for 1½ hours, or until firm. Makes 6 servings.
Your Time: 10 minutes
Freezing Time: 1½ hours

## PEANUT-BUTTER–ICE-CREAM RINGS

2  tablespoons light corn syrup      ¼ teaspoon vanilla extract
2  tablespoons butter or              2  cups ready-to-eat
     margarine                              high-protein cereal
¼  pound marshmallows             ¼  cup shredded coconut
¼  cup chunk-style peanut         Vanilla ice cream
     butter                                  Chocolate syrup (optional)

Combine corn syrup, butter, marshmallows, and peanut butter in a medium-sized saucepan. Cook over very low heat (about 175° F.), stirring constantly, until marshmallows are melted and mixture is smooth. Remove from heat; stir in vanilla. Combine cereal and coconut in a large mixing bowl. Pour marshmallow mixture over cereal; toss to combine thoroughly. Cool slightly. Shape with the hands into thin rings about 3 inches in diameter. Let stand until cool, or about 30 minutes. Just before serving, fill with ice cream and serve with chocolate sauce, if desired. Makes about 10 rings.

Your Time: 13 minutes
Cooking Time: 5 minutes
Cooling Time: 30 minutes

## PEACH MELBA PARFAIT

1½ cups coarsely chopped peeled fresh peaches
1½ tablespoons sugar
1½ teaspoons lemon juice
2 cups fresh raspberries

2 tablespoons sugar
1½ pints vanilla ice cream
6 peach slices
6 raspberries

In a bowl sprinkle chopped peaches with the 1½ tablespoons sugar and the lemon juice; chill at least ½ hour. Put raspberries through fine sieve or food mill to remove seeds. Sprinkle the purée with the 2 tablespoons sugar and chill at least ½ hour. Prepare parfaits by spooning ¼ cup peaches into each glass. Top with following layers in each: ¼ cup ice cream, ¼ cup raspberries, and ¼ cup ice cream. Garnish with peach slice and raspberry. Serve immediately. Makes 6 servings.

Your Time: 19 minutes
Chilling Time: 30 minutes

## PEACHES À L'ORANGE

1  29-ounce can cling peach halves, chilled and drained
1  pint orange sherbet

Orange liqueur
Mint sprigs (optional)

Place a peach half cut side up in each of 5 or 6 stemmed sherbet glasses. (Number of peach halves in the can will vary according to their size.) Place a scoop of sherbet in the center of each peach half. Pour 1 tablespoon orange liqueur over each. Serve immediately. Each serving may be garnished with a sprig of fresh mint, if desired. Makes 5 to 6 servings.

Your Time: 5 minutes

## PINEAPPLE-MINT PARFAIT

1  20-ounce can crushed
    pineapple
½ teaspoon peppermint
    extract

3  drops green food coloring
1½ pints vanilla ice cream

Drain pineapple. Mix drained pineapple, mint extract, and food coloring in a bowl. Chill for 1 hour. (Drained juice may be used as beverage.) Spoon alternate layers of pineapple and ice cream into parfait glasses. Makes 6 servings.
Your Time: 7 minutes
Chilling Time: 1 hour

# Puddings and Parfaits

### APPLE CRUMBLE

3  tablespoons butter or
    margarine
8  cake-type doughnuts,
    crumbled
2  16-ounce jars sweetened
    applesauce

½ cup dark seedless raisins
2  tablespoons sugar
½ teaspoon ground cinnamon
Sweetened whipped cream
    (optional)

Melt butter in a skillet over low heat (about 200° F.). Add doughnut crumbs and cook over moderately high heat (about 300° F.) until crumbs are slightly browned. Combine applesauce, raisins, sugar, and cinnamon in a bowl. Alternate layers of browned crumbs and applesauce mixture in 8 individual dessert dishes. Top with whipped cream, if desired. Makes 8 servings.
Your Time: 8 minutes
Cooking Time: 5 minutes

### EASY APRICOT WHIP

1  package fluffy white
    frosting mix
⅔ cup boiling water
1  30-ounce can apricot halves,
    drained and finely
    chopped

3  tablespoons lemon juice
¼ cup chopped toasted
    almonds

Place frosting mix in large bowl of electric mixer. Add boiling water and beat at low speed 1 minute until blended. Beat at high speed until frosting thickens. Gradually add apricots, beating constantly until soft peaks form. Fold in lemon juice and nuts. Spoon into sherbet glasses; chill 2 hours. Makes 8 to 10 servings.
Your Time: 11 minutes
Chilling Time: 2 hours

## CREAMY BANANA PUDDING

1 *18-ounce can ready-to-serve vanilla pudding*
1 *4½-ounce container (2 cups) frozen whipped topping, thawed*

2 *small bananas, peeled and thinly sliced*
2 *tablespoons chocolate sprinkles*

Turn the pudding into a mixing bowl. Fold in whipped topping. Gently stir in bananas and the chocolate sprinkles. Spoon into sherbet glasses. Top with additional chocolate sprinkles, if desired. Chill about 2 hours. Makes 6 to 8 servings.
Your Time: 10 minutes
Chilling Time: 2 hours

## BROWN-BREAD PUDDING

2½ *cups milk*
1 *16-ounce can brown bread with raisins*
2 *tablespoons butter or margarine*

½ *cup jarred cranberry-orange relish*
¾ *teaspoon salt*
*Whipped cream or ice cream (optional)*

Pour milk into a medium-sized saucepan. Place over moderately low heat (about 225° F.) until milk bubbles at edges. Crumble brown bread into hot milk. Add butter, cranberry-orange relish, and salt. Cook 4 to 5 minutes longer, or until most of the milk is absorbed. Break up lumps of brown bread with a fork so that pudding is fairly smooth. Serve warm with whipped cream or ice cream, if desired. Makes 6 to 8 servings.
Your Time: 9 minutes
Cooking Time: 9 to 10 minutes

## CRACKER PUDDING

1  4-serving package instant          1  cup packaged graham
    *toasted coconut pudding*             *cracker crumbs*
2  *cups milk*

In a medium-sized bowl prepare the instant coconut pudding according to package directions, using the 2 cups milk. Stir in the graham cracker crumbs and blend well. Spoon into serving dishes and refrigerate until set, or at least 30 minutes. Makes 4 servings.
Your Time: 4 minutes
Chilling Time: 30 minutes

## CRANBERRY-BREAD PUFF PUDDING

¼  *cup butter or margarine*            6  *tablespoons granulated*
4  *slices white bread, cut into*            *sugar*
   *½-inch cubes*                         ¼  *teaspoon vanilla extract*
1  *16-ounce can jellied*                 ¼  *teaspoon almond extract*
   *cranberry sauce, cut into*        ⅓  *cup all-purpose flour*
   *½-inch cubes*                         ⅛  *teaspoon baking powder*
2  *eggs, separated, at room*            ¼  *teaspoon salt*
   *temperature*                          *Confectioners' sugar*

Heat oven to 375° F. Grease an 8-inch round cake pan with unsalted shortening. Heat butter in skillet over moderate heat (about 250° F.); add bread cubes and cook and stir until lightly browned. Pour into the bottom of the prepared pan. Cover with cranberry sauce cubes. In a bowl beat egg whites with rotary beater until stiff peaks form. Beat egg yolks well in bowl; gradually add sugar and vanilla and almond extracts, beating until thick and lemon-colored. Fold in flour, baking powder, and salt. Gently fold in beaten egg whites. Pour batter over cranberry sauce, covering it completely. Bake, uncovered, 20 to 25 minutes, or until golden brown. Cool about 5 minutes and sprinkle with confectioners' sugar; serve warm. Makes 6 to 8 servings.
Your Time: 15 minutes
Baking Time: 20 to 25 minutes

## HEAVENLY CHOCOLATE CRÈME

1 4-ounce package sweet
  cooking chocolate
4 egg yolks
¼ cup slivered toasted
  almonds
2 tablespoons coffee liqueur
4 egg whites, at room
  temperature

⅛ teaspoon salt
½ cup chilled heavy cream
⅛ teaspoon almond extract
1 1-ounce square
  unsweetened chocolate,
  grated

Melt sweet chocolate in top of a double boiler over hot water. In a bowl beat egg yolks with rotary beater until thick and lemon-colored. Gradually add chocolate, beating until blended. Stir in almonds and coffee liqueur. In a large bowl beat egg whites and salt until stiff peaks form; fold in chocolate mixture. Spoon into serving dishes. Chill at least 2 hours. Whip cream and almond extract together in a bowl until mixture holds its shape. Spoon over crème before serving. Garnish with grated chocolate. Makes 8 servings.
Your Time: 14 minutes
Chilling Time: 2 hours

## CHOCOLATE CREAM

2 envelopes unflavored
  gelatine
½ cup cold milk
¾ cup milk, heated to
  boiling
1 egg
¼ cup sugar
⅛ teaspoon salt
1 6-ounce package
  semisweet chocolate
  pieces

1 teaspoon vanilla extract
1 cup heavy cream
1½ cups ice cubes or crushed
  ice (10 to 12 cubes)
½ cup walnuts
Whipped cream (optional)

Sprinkle gelatine over cold milk in container of electric blender. Allow to stand a few minutes to soften gelatine. Add hot milk; cover

and turn blender on low speed until gelatine is dissolved. Scrape sides of container with rubber spatula. Add egg, sugar, salt, and chocolate pieces. Turn blender on high and blend until mixture is smooth and chocolate is melted. Add vanilla and cream. Turn blender on low speed and add ice, a little at a time, until all has been added and ice is melted. Add walnuts and blend just until walnuts are chopped. Pour at once into 8 individual serving dishes. Chill about 10 minutes. Garnish with whipped cream, if desired. Makes 8 servings.
Your Time: 10 minutes
Chilling Time: 10 minutes


## MOCK CRÈME BRÛLÉE

2 4-serving-size packages
   vanilla pudding and pie
   filling
1 quart dairy half-and-half
1 cup packaged graham
   cracker crumbs

⅓ cup finely chopped walnuts
¼ cup firmly packed
   dark-brown sugar

Prepare pudding according to package directions, substituting half-and-half for milk called for on package. Cool slightly. Combine crumbs and chopped walnuts; spread evenly over bottom of an ungreased shallow 1½-quart baking dish. Carefully pour in pudding. Sprinkle top with brown sugar. Broil in preheated broiler 3 to 4 inches from heat until sugar melts and forms a crust, or about 3 to 5 minutes. Watch carefully so that sugar does not burn. Chill, uncovered, for 1 hour. Makes 8 servings.
Your Time: 13 minutes
Cooking Time: 8 to 10 minutes
Chilling Time: 1 hour


## COFFEE-MACAROON PUDDING

2 cups milk
¼ cup heavy cream
2 tablespoons sugar
2½ teaspoons instant coffee
   powder or granules

⅛ teaspoon almond extract
1 4-serving-size package
   coconut cream instant
   pudding

In a medium-sized bowl, combine milk, cream, sugar, instant coffee powder, and almond extract. Stir to blend well. Add pudding mix

and beat slowly with a rotary beater just until well blended, about 1 minute. Pour at once into individual serving dishes. Chill until set, or about 5 minutes. Makes 4 or 5 servings.
Your Time: 4 minutes
Chilling Time: 5 minutes

## CINNAMON TWIST–PINEAPPLE COBBLER

1 21-ounce can pineapple pie
   filling

1 container refrigerated
   cinnamon rolls with icing
   (8 rolls)

Heat oven to 375° F. Turn pineapple pie filling into a 9-inch metal pie pan. Open roll container according to label directions. Place the rolls around the edge. Reserve the can of icing. Bake, uncovered, 25 minutes. Remove from oven and spread rolls with the icing. Serve warm. Makes 8 servings.
Your Time: 4 minutes
Baking Time: 25 minutes

## PEACH AND WALNUT COBBLER

1 21-ounce can peach pie
   filling
1 cup packaged pancake mix
¼ cup sugar
¾ cup coarsely chopped
   walnuts
1 teaspoon ground nutmeg

1 egg, slightly beaten
⅓ cup milk
3 tablespoons melted butter
   or margarine
Sweetened whipped cream
   (optional)
Vanilla ice cream (optional)

Heat oven to 425° F. Grease a deep 1½-quart casserole with unsalted shortening. Pour peach pie filling into prepared casserole. Combine pancake mix, sugar, walnuts, and nutmeg in a mixing bowl. Combine beaten egg, milk, and melted butter in another bowl. Add egg mixture to dry ingredients and stir until batter is smooth. Pour batter over pie filling. Bake, uncovered, 25 minutes. Top of cobbler may be covered with foil during the last 5 minutes to prevent excessive browning. Serve warm with cream or vanilla ice cream, if desired. Makes 6 servings.
Your Time: 7 minutes
Baking Time: 25 minutes

## PEPPERMINT CRUNCH

1¼ cups crushed peppermint       Chocolate sauce (optional)
   candy
2 cups chilled heavy cream,
   whipped

Place some of the candy in the container of an electric blender and blend at high speed until crushed. Repeat with rest of candy. Fold crushed candy into the whipped cream. Pour mixture into an ungreased 8-inch-square cake pan. Wrap tightly with aluminum foil and freeze until firm, or about 2 to 3 hours. Do not stir. At serving time, spoon into dessert dishes. Top with chocolate sauce, if desired. Makes 6 servings.
Your Time: 7 minutes
Freezing Time: 2 to 3 hours

## HIGHLAND MIST

1 4½-ounce container (2          ⅓ cup chopped candied
   cups) frozen whipped               cherries
   topping, thawed              Slivered toasted almonds
½ teaspoon almond extract
1 cup crumbled soft coconut
   macaroons (about 6
   1¾-inch cookies)

In a medium-sized bowl blend together whipped topping and almond extract. Fold in crumbled macaroons and chopped cherries. Chill about 30 minutes. Serve sprinkled with toasted almonds. Makes 6 servings.
Your Time: 4 minutes
Chilling Time: 30 minutes

## QUICK RICE PUDDING

2 cups milk, heated              ½ teaspoon vanilla extract
⅔ cup packaged precooked         1 tablespoon butter or
   rice                               margarine
3 tablespoons sugar              ½ teaspoon ground cinnamon
½ teaspoon salt

Heat oven to 350° F. Grease a deep 1-quart casserole with unsalted shortening. Combine all ingredients in the prepared casserole. Bake, uncovered, 45 minutes. Stir every 15 minutes during baking and once more after removing pudding from oven. If a brown top is desired, place baked pudding under preheated broiler for a few minutes. Serve warm or chilled. Makes 6 servings.
Your Time: 4 minutes
Baking Time: 45 minutes

## ORANGE-BANANA RICE PUDDING

1⅔ *cups orange juice*
1⅓ *cups packaged precooked*
   *rice*
 ¼ *teaspoon salt*
 ⅓ *cup honey*
 1 *medium-sized banana,*
    *peeled and thinly sliced*

 ¾ *cup chilled heavy cream*
 1 *tablespoon confectioners'*
    *sugar*
 ¼ *cup flaked coconut*

Heat orange juice in a small saucepan just to a boil. Mix rice, salt, and honey in a bowl. Add orange juice. Chill in refrigerator 2 hours, or until rice is softened and most of the orange juice is absorbed. Fold in bananas just before serving. Whip cream and confectioners' sugar until mixture holds its shape. Garnish each serving with a puff of cream and sprinkling of coconut. Makes 6 servings.
Your Time: 6 minutes
Chilling Time: 2 hours

## PINEAPPLE RICE PUDDING

 1 *17-ounce can ready-to-serve*
    *rice pudding*
 1 *8¼-ounce can crushed*
    *pineapple, drained*
 ½ *cup frozen whipped*
    *topping, thawed, plus*
    *topping for garnish*

 4 *stemmed red maraschino*
    *cherries*

In a bowl mix together rice pudding and pineapple. Fold in the ½ cup whipped topping. Spoon into 4 serving glasses. Top each with an additional dollop of whipped topping. Garnish each serving with a

cherry. Chill about 1 hour, or until ready to serve. Makes 4 servings.
Your Time: 8 minutes
Chilling Time: 1 hour


## SOUTHERN SQUASH PUDDING

2  *10-ounce packages frozen*
   *mashed squash, thawed*
½ *cup dark corn syrup*
⅓ *cup melted butter or*
   *margarine*
½ *teaspoon ground cinnamon*
½ *teaspoon ground nutmeg*
1 *teaspoon salt*

1 *egg*
½ *cup light cream*
⅓ *cup honey*
¼ *cup finely chopped pecans*
   *or walnuts*
*Sweetened whipped cream*
   *(optional)*

Heat oven to 375° F. In a bowl mix squash, corn syrup, butter, cinnamon, nutmeg, and salt. In another bowl beat together egg and light cream. Stir egg mixture into squash mixture. Pour into an ungreased deep 1½-quart casserole. Pour honey over top of pudding. Sprinkle with nuts. Bake, uncovered, 1 hour, or until pudding starts to thicken. Serve warm. If desired, top with sweetened whipped cream. Makes 6 to 8 servings.
Your Time: 6 minutes
Baking Time: 1 hour


## CHERRY-CHOCOLATE SOUFFLÉ

1  *22-ounce can cherry pie*
   *filling*
4  *eggs, separated, at room*
   *temperature*

¼ *cup confectioners' sugar*
3 *tablespoons unsweetened*
   *cocoa*

Heat oven to 425° F. Grease eight 6-ounce baking cups with unsalted shortening. Divide cherry pie filling among the prepared cups. Place in oven on a tray for 5 minutes. In a medium-sized bowl beat egg whites until stiff but not dry. In a large bowl beat egg yolks; add sugar and cocoa and beat until thick and fluffy. Fold beaten whites into egg yolk mixture. Spoon over hot cherry pie filling. Bake, uncovered, near the top of the oven for 8 to 10 minutes. Cool a few minutes before serving. Makes 8 servings.
Your Time: 10 minutes
Baking Time: 13 to 15 minutes

## TUTTI-FRUTTI DESSERT

1 11-ounce can mandarin
   orange segments
Fruit juice (apricot nectar,
   orange, or pineapple)
2 tablespoons sugar
½ teaspoon salt

⅔ cup packaged precooked
   rice
6 maraschino cherries, diced
½ cup chilled heavy cream,
   whipped

Drain mandarin oranges; reserve syrup. Add enough fruit juice to mandarin orange syrup to make 1 cup liquid. Put fruit juice, sugar, salt, and rice in saucepan. Bring to boil over moderately low heat (about 225° F.), then simmer 3 minutes. Remove from heat. Cover and let stand 10 minutes. Fluff rice with a fork; cover and chill well for at least 2 hours. Reserve 4 mandarin orange sections for garnish and fold remaining sections, cherries, and cream into rice. Serve in sherbet glasses, each topped with an orange section. Makes 4 servings.
Your Time: 6 minutes
Cooking Time: 6 minutes
Chilling Time: 2 hours

## FRUIT MÉLANGE PARFAIT

1 3½-ounce package
   strawberry-flavored
   whipped dessert mix
2 tablespoons sugar
½ cup milk
½ cup water
1 14-ounce jar
   cranberry-orange relish

1 cup diced peeled banana
¼ cup chopped pecans or
   walnuts
Whipped cream (optional)
Whole pecans or walnuts
   (optional)

Combine dessert mix and sugar in a bowl. Add milk and beat with an electric mixer at high speed for 1 minute, or until thick. Gradually add water at low speed; then beat at high speed for 2 minutes. Chill mixture, uncovered, in refrigerator for 10 minutes. Fold in ½ cup of the cranberry-orange relish, the banana, and the chopped nuts. Cover and chill in refrigerator for 1 hour, or until set. Serve in parfait glasses, spooning whipped mixture and remaining cranberry-orange relish alternately into glasses. If desired, garnish with whipped cream and whole pecans or walnuts. Makes 8 servings.
Your Time: 12 minutes
Chilling Time: 1 hour 10 minutes

## CRUNCHY CHEESE PARFAIT

½ cup malted cereal granules   2 cups milk
2 tablespoons dark-brown       1 cup cream-style cottage
   sugar                          cheese
2 tablespoons melted butter    1 4-serving package banana
   or margarine                   cream instant pudding

Place cereal, brown sugar, and butter in a small bowl; blend well. In a medium-sized bowl beat milk and cottage cheese with a rotary beater until smooth. Add pudding mix and beat as package directs. Alternate layers of pudding and cereal mixture in parfait glasses. Chill until set, or about 30 minutes. Makes 4 servings.
Your Time: 9 minutes
Chilling Time: 30 minutes

## ORANGE PARFAIT

1 11-ounce can mandarin    1½ cups crushed ice
   orange segments          Whipped cream (optional)
1 3-ounce package
   orange-flavored gelatin

Drain mandarin oranges, reserving the syrup. Add enough water to syrup to make ¾ cup. Place liquid in a saucepan over moderate heat (about 250° F.) until boiling. Place boiling liquid and gelatin in the container of an electric blender. Cover and blend on low speed about 30 seconds, or until gelatin is dissolved. Add crushed ice and blend 30 seconds longer, or until ice is melted. Pour gelatin into 6 parfait glasses, dividing evenly among the glasses. Drop mandarin oranges into the glasses, also dividing them evenly among the glasses. Do not stir. Chill about 30 minutes, or until set. Serve with whipped cream, if desired. Makes 6 servings.
Your Time: 4 minutes
Chilling Time: 30 minutes

## STRAWBERRY PARFAITS

½ cup boiling water            ¼ cup rosé wine
1 3-ounce package             1 2-ounce package dessert
   strawberry-flavored gelatin    topping mix
1 10-ounce package frozen     Mint sprigs (optional)
   halved strawberries,
   undrained

In a bowl add the boiling water to strawberry gelatin and stir until dissolved. Add frozen strawberries and stir until strawberries are separated. Add rosé wine. Chill about 1 hour, or until thickened. Prepare topping mix according to package directions. Alternate layers of the strawberry mixture and whipped topping in 4 parfait glasses. Garnish each with a sprig of mint, if desired. Makes 4 servings.
Your Time: 17 minutes
Chilling Time: 1 hour

## TAPIOCA PARFAIT

1 17-ounce can ready-to-serve tapioca pudding
¼ teaspoon ground cinnamon

1 cup jarred cranberry-orange relish
Whipped topping

In a bowl combine tapioca and cinnamon and mix well. Spoon about 1 tablespoon relish into each of 4 parfait glasses. Spoon half of the tapioca mixture into the glasses. Repeat again with relish and tapioca. Top with whipped topping. Chill in the refrigerator for about 1 hour, or until serving time. Makes 4 servings.
Your Time: 6 minutes
Chilling Time: 1 hour

## COCONUT ENGLISH TRIFLE

1 3-ounce package egg custard mix
2 cups milk
1 packaged 8-inch sponge cake layer

⅓ cup sweet sherry
½ cup raspberry preserves
¼ cup shredded coconut

Prepare egg custard mix according to package directions, using the 2 cups milk. Remove from heat. Place the sponge cake layer in an ungreased deep 9-inch pie pan. Pour the sherry evenly over the top of the cake. Spread the surface of the cake evenly with the raspberry preserves. Slowly pour the slightly cooled custard over the sponge layer, allowing the custard to soak into and around the cake. Chill 1 hour. Before serving, sprinkle the shredded coconut over the top to within 1 inch from edge of cake. Makes 4 to 6 servings.
Your Time: 10 minutes
Chilling Time: 1 hour

## MOCK ZABAGLIONE

*1 quart strawberries, washed      2 tablespoons confectioners'
   and hulled                          sugar
3 tablespoons granulated          ½ teaspoon vanilla extract
   sugar                           1 tablespoon sweet sherry
1 cup heavy cream*

Slice strawberries into a medium-sized bowl; sprinkle with granulated sugar. Chill ½ hour. In a small bowl whip cream, confectioners' sugar, and vanilla until soft peaks form. Stir in sherry. Fold into strawberries. Pour into a 9-x-5-x-2¾-inch loaf pan; cover and place in freezer for about 45 minutes, until thoroughly chilled but not frozen. Makes 6 to 8 servings.
Your Time: 12 minutes
Chilling and Freezing Time: 1¼ hours

*Note: 3½ cups of either raspberries, blueberries, or sliced peaches may be substituted for strawberries.

# Molded Gelatine Desserts

## LAYERED BURGUNDY-CHERRY MOLD

1 3-ounce package               2 tablespoons red Burgundy
   cherry-flavored gelatin          wine
¾ cup boiling water             Pressurized ready-whipped
1½ cups crushed ice                cream

In the container of an electric blender combine gelatin and boiling water. Cover and blend on low speed 30 seconds, or until gelatin is dissolved. Add the crushed ice and the wine. Cover and blend on high speed until ice is melted, about 30 seconds. Pour into a 4-cup ring mold. (Gelatin also may be poured into individual serving dishes, if desired.) Chill at least 30 minutes, or until set. Gelatin will separate into two layers on chilling. Loosen sides of mold with a spatula and unmold onto a serving plate. Decorate edge of mold with rosettes of cream. Makes 6 servings.
Your Time: 3 minutes
Chilling Time: 30 minutes

## MOLDED CRANBERRY CAKE

1  12-ounce package frozen
    pound cake, thawed
3  cups orange juice
1  6-ounce package
    strawberry-flavored gelatin

1  16-ounce can whole-berry
    cranberry sauce
2  cups commercial sour cream
¼  cup orange marmalade
½  teaspoon ground nutmeg

Cut pound cake into ½-inch cubes. In a saucepan heat 1 cup of the orange juice over moderate heat (about 250° F.) until boiling. Remove from heat. Add gelatin; stir until dissolved. Stir in remaining orange juice. Chill until mixture is the consistency of unbeaten egg white. Fold in cranberry sauce. Spoon part of gelatin into a 1½-quart mold. Add a layer of cake cubes. Continue layering, ending with gelatin. Chill until firm, or about 2 hours. Combine sour cream, orange marmalade, and nutmeg in a serving bowl; cover and chill at least 15 minutes. Unmold cranberry cake and serve with sour cream mixture. Makes 10 to 12 servings.
Your Time: 15 minutes
Chilling Time: 2 to 2½ hours

## MOUSSE AU CHOCOLAT

1  envelope unflavored
    gelatine
½  cup cold water
2  18-ounce cans
    ready-to-serve chocolate
    pudding
1  4½-ounce container (2
    cups) frozen whipped
    topping, thawed

Chopped pistachio nuts
    (optional)
Frozen whipped topping,
    thawed (optional)

Sprinkle gelatine over cold water in a small saucepan. Place over low heat (about 200° F.), stirring occasionally, until gelatine is melted. Cool slightly. Put chocolate pudding into a medium-sized bowl. Stir gelatine mixture into pudding. Fold in whipped topping. Fasten a foil collar around the top of a 3- or 4-cup soufflé dish. Pour chocolate mixture into dish; chill until firm, or about 2 to 3 hours. Remove collar before serving. If desired, garnish with chopped pistachio nuts and additional whipped topping. Makes 6 servings.
Your Time: 5 minutes
Cooking Time: 5 minutes
Chilling Time: 2 to 3 hours

## MAPLE VELVET

1 envelope unflavored
   gelatine
¼ cup cold water
1 cup sugar
2 cups light cream
¾ cup bottled maple-blended
   syrup

2 cups commercial sour cream
1 10-ounce package frozen
   strawberries in quick-thaw
   pouch, thawed according
   to package directions
   (optional)

In a small bowl sprinkle gelatine over cold water to soften. Combine sugar, cream, and maple syrup in the top of a double boiler. Place over hot, not boiling, water and heat until lukewarm. Stir occasionally. Add softened gelatine and heat until sugar and gelatine are dissolved, stirring frequently. Remove from heat. Chill until mixture is the consistency of unbeaten egg whites. Fold in sour cream; blend thoroughly. Pour into sherbet glasses or dessert dishes; chill until set, or about 2 to 3 hours. Garnish with thawed frozen strawberries, if desired. Makes 8 to 10 servings.
Your Time: 12 minutes
Chilling Time: 2 to 3 hours

## LUSCIOUS RASPBERRY DESSERT

1 3-ounce package
   raspberry-flavored gelatin
1¼ cups boiling water
1 10-ounce package frozen
   red raspberries in
   quick-thaw pouch
1 3-ounce package cream
   cheese, at room
   temperature

1 tablespoon milk
½ cup marshmallow whip
¼ cup flaked coconut
¼ teaspoon almond extract

In a bowl dissolve gelatin in boiling water. Remove raspberries from pouch; add to gelatin and stir until thawed. Spoon into sherbet glasses. Chill several hours, or until set. In a bowl beat cheese and milk until fluffy. Gradually add marshmallow whip, beating until blended. Fold in coconut and almond extract. Spoon over gelatin just before serving. Makes 5 to 6 servings.
Your Time: 9 minutes
Chilling Time: 2 to 3 hours

## STRAWBERRY-WINE GELATIN

1   10-ounce package frozen
        strawberries in
        quick-thaw pouch,
        thawed according to
        package directions
Water
2   envelopes unflavored
        gelatine

1   cup sugar
1 ⅓ cups rosé wine
    ⅓ cup lemon juice
Pressurized ready-whipped
        cream
Ground mace

Drain strawberries and reserve juice. Measure juice and add enough water to make 1⅔ cups liquid. Sprinkle gelatine on 1 cup of the juice mixture in saucepan to soften. Place over low heat (about 200° F.), stirring constantly, until gelatine is dissolved, about 3 minutes. Add sugar and stir until dissolved. Remove from heat. Stir in the remaining ⅔ cup juice mixture, the wine, and lemon juice. Chill until the consistency of unbeaten egg white. Fold in strawberries. Pour into a 5-cup mold and chill about 2 to 3 hours, or until set. Unmold and serve with whipped cream and a sprinkling of mace. Makes 6 servings.
Your Time: 6 minutes
Chilling Time: 2½ to 3½ hours

## WHIPPED CHEESE MOLD

1   3-ounce package
        lemon-flavored gelatin
½ cup boiling water
1   8-ounce package cream
        cheese, softened
1   16-ounce container
        cream-style cottage cheese

1   cup frozen whipped
        topping, thawed
2   10-ounce packages frozen
        halved strawberries in
        quick-thaw pouch, thawed
        according to package
        directions

In a small bowl dissolve lemon gelatin in the boiling water. Cool slightly. In a bowl beat cream cheese and cottage cheese with an electric hand mixer or rotary beater until smooth. Stir in slightly cooled gelatin mixture. Fold in the whipped topping. Pour into a 4-cup mold and chill until firm, or about 2 hours. Unmold and serve with strawberries. Makes 8 servings.
Your Time: 9 minutes
Chilling Time: 2 hours

# *Pies and Pastries*

### APRICOT ISLAND PIE

| | |
|---|---|
| 1 cup packaged corn flake crumbs | 1 22-ounce can apricot pie filling |
| 2 tablespoons sugar | ½ cup commercial sour cream |
| ⅓ cup softened butter or margarine | 1 cup flaked or shredded coconut |

Butter bottom and sides of an 8-inch pie plate. In a bowl mix cereal crumbs and sugar; cut in butter with a pastry blender until all crumbs are coated. With the back of a spoon, firmly press crumbs over bottom and sides of prepared pie plate. Combine pie filling, sour cream, and coconut; mix well. Spoon filling into crust and chill 2 to 3 hours. Makes 6 servings.
Your Time: 8 minutes
Chilling Time: 2 to 3 hours

### CHOCOLATE CANDY PIE

| | |
|---|---|
| 1 package fluffy white frosting mix | ½ cup finely chopped walnuts |
| 2 teaspoons instant coffee granules or powder | 1 teaspoon vanilla extract |
| ½ cup boiling water | 1 6-ounce package semisweet chocolate |
| 20 packaged chocolate chip cookies, finely crushed | pieces |
| | Vanilla ice cream |

Heat oven to 350° F. Butter a 9-inch pie plate. Prepare frosting mix according to package directions and place in a mixing bowl. Dissolve instant coffee in the boiling water. Add coffee mixture, crushed cookies, 6 tablespoons of the chopped walnuts, and vanilla to prepared frosting; blend thoroughly. Pour into prepared pie plate. Bake 35 to 40 minutes, or until a cake tester inserted in the center comes out clean. Cool on a wire cake rack. Place chocolate pieces in a small saucepan over low heat (about 200° F.) and cook, stirring occasionally, until melted. Spread melted chocolate over top of cooled pie and sprinkle with the remaining 2 tablespoons chopped walnuts. Chill until chocolate is firm. Cut into small wedges and serve with a small scoop of ice cream. Makes 10 servings.
Your Time: 8 minutes
Baking Time: 35 to 40 minutes
Chilling Time: 15 minutes

## CREAMY CHOCOLATE PIE

1  *4-ounce package*
   *chocolate-flavored*
   *whipped dessert mix*
2  *tablespoons light rum*
1  *4½-ounce container (2*
   *cups) frozen whipped*
   *topping, thawed*

1  *8-inch ready-to-use*
   *packaged graham cracker*
   *pie crust*
   *Chocolate sprinkles*

In a bowl prepare chocolate dessert mix according to package directions. Stir in rum and chill until mixture mounds slightly when dropped from a spoon, about 10 to 15 minutes. Fold in 1 cup of the topping and turn mixture into the pie crust. Chill about 2½ hours. When ready to serve, decorate pie with the remaining topping and the chocolate sprinkles. Makes 6 to 8 servings.
Your Time: 11 minutes
Chilling Time: 2¾ hours

## CHOCOLATE-MINT CHIFFON PIE

1  *envelope unflavored*
   *gelatine*
½  *cup cold water*
1  *17½-ounce container frozen*
   *dark-chocolate-flavor*
   *pudding, thawed but still*
   *cold*
½  *teaspoon peppermint*
   *extract*

2  *egg whites, at room*
   *temperature*
1  *8-inch ready-to-use*
   *packaged graham cracker*
   *pie crust*
   *Whipped topping*

In a saucepan sprinkle gelatine over the cold water to soften. Place over low heat (about 200° F.) and heat, stirring constantly, until gelatine is dissolved. Put chocolate pudding in a bowl; gradually stir gelatine into pudding and blend until smooth. Stir in peppermint extract. Chill until the mixture mounds slightly when dropped from a spoon, about 3 minutes. Meanwhile beat the egg whites in a bowl until stiff but not dry. Gently fold them into pudding mixture and turn it into pie crust. Chill several hours, or overnight. Cut into wedges and serve with the whipped topping. Makes 6 to 8 servings.
Your Time: 15 minutes
Chilling Time: Several hours

## CRANBERRY-ORANGE PIE

1  9-inch frozen pastry shell
1  16-ounce can whole-berry
    cranberry sauce
½  cup firmly packed
    light-brown sugar
1  3-ounce package
    orange-flavored gelatin

¾  cup chilled heavy cream,
    whipped
½  cup chopped walnuts
¼  cup chilled heavy cream,
    whipped

Bake and cool pastry shell according to package directions. Place cranberry sauce and brown sugar in a saucepan and heat over moderate heat (about 250° F.), stirring frequently, until mixture starts to bubble. Remove from heat. Add gelatin and stir until dissolved. Chill until mixture starts to thicken. Fold in the ¾ cup cream (whipped) and the nuts and spoon mixture into cooled pastry shell. Chill 3 to 4 hours, or until firm. Before serving, garnish top with the remaining ¼ cup cream (whipped). Makes 6 servings.
Your Time: 11 minutes
Baking and Cooking Time: 15 minutes
Chilling Time: 3 to 4 hours

## FRUIT-GLAZED CREAM PIE

1  4-serving-size package
    instant vanilla pudding and
    pie filling
1  cup heavy cream
1  cup milk
1  9-inch frozen pastry shell,
    baked and cooled

1  17-ounce jar fruits for salad
1  tablespoon cold water
1  tablespoon cornstarch
2  tablespoons red cinnamon
    candies

Prepare pudding according to package directions, using the 1 cup cream and the 1 cup milk. Pour into prepared pastry shell. Let stand until set. Drain the fruits well and reserve ⅔ cup of the fruit syrup. Arrange fruits on top of pie filling. Stir the cold water and cornstarch together in a small bowl. Combine cornstarch mixture, the ⅔ cup reserved fruit syrup, and cinnamon candies in a saucepan. Place over moderate heat (about 250° F.) and cook, stirring constantly, until mixture is thickened and clear. Cool slightly. Spoon mixture over fruits on pie. Chill 1 to 2 hours, or until glaze is set. Makes 6 to 8 servings.
Your Time: 13 minutes
Baking Time: 10 minutes
Chilling Time: 1 to 2 hours

## FRUIT SALAD CREAM PIE

1 *6.5-ounce package graham cracker crust mix*
2 *tablespoons melted butter or margarine*
½ *cup chilled heavy cream*
⅓ *cup firmly packed light-brown sugar*
½ *cup commercial sour cream*

1 *11-ounce can mandarin orange segments, drained*
1 *13¼-ounce can pineapple chunks, drained*
1 *16-ounce can pitted dark sweet cherries, drained*
½ *cup flaked coconut*

Prepare crumb crust in a 9-inch pie plate, adding the melted butter as directed on package for a firm, rich crust. Pour cream into a small bowl and whip with a rotary beater until it starts to thicken. Gradually add brown sugar and beat until stiff. Fold in sour cream. Measure 1 cup of the cream mixture into a medium-sized bowl; fold in well-drained fruits and coconut. Pour into prepared crust. Spread remaining cream filling over top of pie. Chill pie at least 3 hours before serving. Makes 8 servings.
Your Time: 11 minutes
Chilling Time: 3 hours

## PLANTATION FRUIT PIE

1 *unbaked frozen apple or peach pie*
¾ *cup commercial sour cream*
1 *egg, slightly beaten*

2 *tablespoons sugar*
⅛ *teaspoon almond extract*
¼ *cup toasted coconut*

Preheat oven and bake pie according to package directions. Remove from oven and cool pie for about 15 minutes. In a bowl combine sour cream, egg, sugar, and almond extract. Spoon mixture over top crust of cooled pie. Bake in a 325° F. oven for 10 to 15 minutes, or until topping is set. Remove pie from oven and sprinkle topping with toasted coconut. Cool pie about 15 minutes before serving. Makes 6 servings.
Your Time: 5 minutes
Cooking Time: 50 to 55 minutes

## PEACHES AND CREAM PIE

1 *9-inch frozen pastry shell,*      1 *cup frozen whipped*
   *baked and cooled*                    *topping, thawed*
1 *4-serving-size package*           1 *8-ounce can sliced peaches,*
   *instant coconut cream*              *well drained*
   *pudding*

Prepare instant pudding as directed on package. Pour pudding into cooled pastry shell. Chill until set, or about 30 minutes. Spread whipped topping over pie. Arrange peach slices on top. Chill. Makes 6 servings.
Your Time: 6 minutes
Baking and Chilling Time: 1 hour

## GRAPE CHIFFON PIE

1 *9-inch frozen pastry shell*       1 *cup unsweetened grape*
1 *3½-ounce package*                    *juice, chilled*
   *vanilla-flavored whipped*      *Pressurized ready-whipped*
   *dessert mix*                          *cream*

Bake pastry shell according to package directions. Cool completely. Prepare whipped dessert mix according to package directions, using the grape juice in place of the milk and water called for on the package. Pour mixture into pastry shell and chill until firm, or about 1 hour. Serve topped with whipped cream. Makes 6 servings.
Your Time: 5 minutes
Baking and Chilling Time: 75 minutes

## RAISIN PIE

1 *egg*                              1 *cup dark seedless raisins*
1 *cup commercial sour cream*        1 *9-inch frozen pastry shell,*
1 *teaspoon vanilla extract*            *thawed, unbaked*
¼ *teaspoon salt*                    *Whipped topping (optional)*
⅛ *teaspoon ground nutmeg*
½ *cup firmly packed*
   *light-brown sugar*

Heat oven to 350° F. In a mixing bowl beat egg slightly. Stir in sour cream, vanilla, salt, and nutmeg. Add brown sugar and blend until smooth; stir in raisins. Turn into pie shell. Bake 30 to 35 minutes, or

until knife inserted in center comes out clean. Serve at room temperature with whipped topping, if desired. Makes 6 servings.
Your Time: 8 minutes
Baking Time: 30 to 35 minutes

## STRAWBERRY CREAM PIE

1 envelope unflavored gelatine
⅔ cup water
1 18-ounce can ready-to-serve vanilla pudding
½ teaspoon vanilla extract

¼ teaspoon almond extract
8 packaged ladyfingers; split
1 10-ounce package frozen sliced strawberries, thawed
1 tablespoon quick-cooking tapioca

Combine gelatine and water in a small saucepan. Place over moderately low heat (about 225° F.) and stir until gelatine is dissolved. Put pudding in a bowl. Add gelatine to pudding and beat with a rotary beater until smooth. Stir in vanilla and almond extracts. Cool slightly. Arrange split ladyfingers on the bottom and end to end around the sides of an ungreased 9-inch pie plate. Pour pudding into ladyfinger shell. Chill until almost set. Drain strawberries, reserving syrup. Combine strawberry syrup and tapioca in a saucepan. Place over moderate heat (about 250° F.) and cook, stirring constantly, until thickened. Stir in strawberries. Spread glaze over pie. Chill until pie is firm, or at least 2 hours. Makes 6 servings.
Your Time: 10 minutes
Chilling Time: 2 hours

## QUICK ORANGE-WALNUT PASTRIES

1 package active dry yeast
¼ cup warm water
1 tablespoon sugar
1 egg yolk
1 package pie-crust mix for a 2-crust 9-inch pie

½ cup finely chopped walnuts
1 cup canned ready-to-spread vanilla frosting
1 tablespoon grated orange peel

In a large bowl dissolve yeast in the warm water. Blend in sugar and egg yolk. Add pie-crust mix and blend well with a fork. Add ¼ cup of the walnuts and mix well. Divide dough into 24 portions. Flatten each portion with fingers to a ¼-inch-thick round. Place on cookie sheets 2 inches apart. Cover and let dough rise in a warm place (about 85° F.) 1 hour. Heat oven to 375° F. Bake pastries 10 to 15 minutes, or until golden brown. Meanwhile, in a small bowl combine the 1 cup vanilla frosting and the orange peel and blend well. Spread frosting over warm pastries. Sprinkle tops with the remaining ¼ cup walnuts. Serve warm. Makes 24 pastries.

Your Time: 8 minutes
Rising Time: 1 hour
Baking Time: 10 to 15 minutes

## PINEAPPLE TARTS

*18 slices white bread*
*½ cup sweetened condensed*
*    milk, undiluted*
*¼ cup finely chopped pecans*
*    or walnuts*

*1 22-ounce can pineapple*
*    pie filling*
*Sweetened whipped cream*

Heat oven to 400° F. Grease a cookie sheet with unsalted shortening. Cut 18 rounds from the bread slices with a 2¾-inch cookie cutter. Place 6 of the rounds on prepared cookie sheet. Brush bread rounds with condensed milk. Cut centers from the remaining 12 rounds with a 2-inch cookie cutter. Use rings of bread for sides of tarts. (Extra bread pieces may be used for bread pudding or bread crumbs.) Place a ring of bread on each round of bread and brush with condensed milk. Then top with a second ring and brush again with condensed milk. Sprinkle with pecans. Bake 10 minutes and cool. At serving time, spoon pineapple filling into tarts and garnish with cream. Makes 6 tarts.

Your Time: 9 minutes
Baking Time: 10 minutes

## SUGAR COOKIE TARTS

*1 roll refrigerated sugar*
*    cookies*

*3 tablespoons strawberry jam*
*Granulated sugar*

Heat oven to 375° F. Cut cookie dough into ¼-inch-thick slices. Flatten slices slightly with the palm of the hand. Place about ½ teaspoon strawberry jam in centers of half the cookie slices. Top each filled cookie with another cookie slice. Using a fork, press outside edges of cookies together. Place tarts 2 inches apart on

ungreased cookie sheets and bake 10 to 15 minutes, or until golden brown. Remove tarts from oven and sprinkle with granulated sugar. Cool on a wire rack. Makes about 1½ dozen large cookie tarts.
Your Time: 15 minutes
Baking Time: 10 to 15 minutes

# *Cakes*

### APPLE-CINNAMON UPSIDE-DOWN CAKE

1 teaspoon butter or
  margarine
½ cup crab apple jelly
¼ cup dark seedless raisins

1 9.5-ounce container
  refrigerated cinnamon rolls
  with icing
½ cup shredded coconut

Heat oven to 375° F. Combine butter, jelly, raisins, and the icing from the package of cinnamon rolls in an ungreased 8-inch round cake pan. Place on surface unit of range and cook over low heat (about 200° F.) until jelly is melted and mixture is bubbly, stirring occasionally. Sprinkle coconut over hot topping in pan. Open roll container according to label directions. Separate dough into the 8 rolls and arrange, cinnamon topping down, over hot mixture. Bake 18 to 22 minutes, or until golden brown. Invert pan on serving plate. Let stand a few seconds and remove pan. Serve warm. Makes 6 to 8 servings.
Your Time: 3 minutes
Baking Time: 18 to 22 minutes

### APRICOT-ANGEL-FOOD TORTE

1 packaged 10-inch angel
  food cake
2 12-ounce jars apricot
  preserves

⅛ teaspoon almond extract
1 2-ounce package
  dessert-topping mix

Cut angel food cake into 3 horizontal layers. In a small bowl combine 1½ cups apricot preserves with almond extract. Spread about ⅓ cup of the apricot mixture between cake layers. Prepare topping mix according to package directions. Fold in remaining

apricot mixture. Chill cake and topping about 1 hour. Serve a spoonful of the topping with slices of the cake. Makes 8 to 10 servings.
Your Time: 9 minutes
Chilling Time: 1 hour

## GLAZED APRICOT TORTE

1  *18-ounce roll refrigerated*          2  *tablespoons lemon juice*
   *sugar cookies*                        1  *8¾-ounce can apricot*
1  *tablespoon grated lemon*                *halves, drained*
   *peel*
1  *12-ounce jar apricot*
   *preserves*

Heat oven to 375° F. Cut 25 ¼-inch-thick slices from the cookie roll; arrange 18 of the slices in the bottom of an ungreased 9-inch springform pan. Sprinkle with the lemon peel. Cut the remaining 7 slices in half crosswise and arrange, cut edge down, around the inside rim of pan. Reserve remaining dough. Place pan in oven about 5 minutes, or long enough for cookie dough to soften; smooth out dough with a spatula to form a solid crust. Return to oven for about 15 to 20 minutes, or until lightly browned. (Crust will puff up slightly.) Cool about 15 minutes. Combine apricot preserves and lemon juice. Reserve about 3 tablespoons of the mixture; spread remainder evenly over cookie crust. Cut the reserved cookie dough into quarters lengthwise. Place a portion at a time on a flat surface and with the hands work each into a strip about 8 inches long. Place 2 of the strips of dough across apricot filling in one direction and press to rim at edge to fasten. Repeat with the remaining 2 strips of dough in the opposite direction. Arrange apricot halves in the outside spaces between strips of dough. Spoon reserved apricot mixture over apricots to glaze. Reduce oven temperature to 350° F. Bake torte, uncovered, about 30 to 35 minutes, or until strips are lightly browned. Cool torte completely on a wire cake rack. Remove outside rim of pan before serving. Makes 8 servings.
Your Time: 12 minutes
Baking Time: 50 to 60 minutes

## EGGNOG ANGEL CAKE

| | |
|---|---|
| 1  packaged 8-inch angel food cake | ¼  teaspoon ground nutmeg |
| 5  tablespoons softened butter or margarine | 2  tablespoons brandy |
| 2  cups confectioners' sugar | 1½  cups heavy cream, chilled |
| 2  egg yolks | 2  tablespoons confectioners' sugar |
| 2  teaspoons vanilla extract | ¼  cup finely crushed peanut brittle |

Cut the cake crosswise into 4 even layers. In a bowl, work together butter and 1½ cups of the confectioners' sugar until creamy. Blend in egg yolks. Add the remaining ½ cup confectioners' sugar, 1 teaspoon of the vanilla, and the ¼ teaspoon nutmeg; blend well. Gradually stir brandy into butter mixture. Spread filling between cake layers, allowing about ½ cup for each layer. In a bowl combine cream, the 2 tablespoons confectioners' sugar, and the remaining 1 teaspoon vanilla. Whip until stiff peaks form. Frost top and sides of cake with mixture. Draw the back of a spoon up the sides of the frosting at intervals to form a design. Chill 1 hour. Before serving, sprinkle crushed peanut brittle around outside edge of top of cake. Makes 12 servings.
Your Time: 18 minutes
Chilling Time: 1 hour

## PEACH BLOSSOM ANGEL FOOD

| | |
|---|---|
| 1  4-serving package vanilla pudding and pie filling | 1  6-inch packaged angel food cake |
| Milk | ½  cup chilled heavy cream |
| ½  teaspoon almond extract | ¼  cup slivered almonds |
| 1  22-ounce can peach pie filling | |

Prepare pudding according to package directions, but using ¼ cup less milk than the amount called for on the package. Cool; then stir in almond extract. Reserve ½ cup of the pudding; fold peach pie filling into the remainder. Cut cake into ½-inch slices and arrange in a

standing row around edge of an ungreased shallow 2-quart rectangular baking dish. Tear any remaining cake slices into small pieces and fold into pudding; pour pudding into cake-lined baking dish. In a small bowl whip cream until it holds its shape and fold in the reserved ½ cup pudding. Spoon cream over top of pudding and garnish with almonds. Chill 2 to 3 hours. Makes 8 servings.
Your Time: 13 minutes
Chilling Time: 2 to 3 hours

## COFFEE FLUFF SURPRISE

1 *6-ounce package semisweet chocolate pieces*
1 *teaspoon shortening*
8 *packaged dessert sponge cups*
1 *egg white, at room temperature*
1 *tablespoon instant coffee powder*

2 *tablespoons granulated sugar*
1 *cup chilled heavy cream*
1 *teaspoon vanilla extract*
2 *tablespoons confectioners' sugar*

Melt chocolate and shortening in the top of a small double boiler over hot, not boiling, water. Spread tops of sponge cups with chocolate mixture; allow a generous tablespoon for each. Chill a few minutes in refrigerator until chocolate just begins to set. In a medium-sized bowl, beat egg white and coffee powder together until soft peaks form. Add granulated sugar and beat until stiff peaks form. In a bowl beat cream, vanilla, and confectioners' sugar together until mixture holds its shape. Fold cream into egg white mixture. Spoon over chocolate in sponge cups. Serve immediately. Makes 8 servings.
Your Time: 12 minutes
Cooking Time: 6½ minutes
Chilling Time: 5 minutes

## EIGHT-MINUTE CHEESECAKE

½ cup packaged corn flake
  crumbs
½ teaspoon ground cinnamon
½ teaspoon ground nutmeg
1 tablespoon melted butter or
  margarine
2 envelopes unflavored
  gelatine
1 teaspoon grated lemon peel

2 tablespoons lemon juice
½ cup hot milk
¼ cup sugar
2 egg yolks
1 8-ounce package cream
  cheese
1 cup finely crushed ice
½ cup heavy cream

In a bowl combine corn flake crumbs, cinnamon, nutmeg, and butter. Sprinkle half of crumb mixture over bottom of 8-inch springform pan. Place gelatine, grated lemon peel, and lemon juice in the container of an electric blender. Add milk and blend at high speed 40 seconds. Add sugar, egg yolks, and cream cheese; blend at high speed 10 seconds. Add crushed ice and cream and blend 15 seconds. Pour mixture immediately into pan. Sprinkle with reserved crumbs. Chill 1½ hours. Makes 8 servings.
Your Time: 8 minutes
Chilling Time: 1½ hours

## CHERRY-GLAZED CHEESECAKE

1½ teaspoons unflavored
  gelatine
3 tablespoons water
½ of a 21-ounce can
  cherry-pie filling
1 teaspoon grated lemon
  peel

Red food coloring (optional)
1 17-ounce frozen
  cheesecake with
  sour-cream topping
2 tablespoons chopped
  pistachio nuts

Sprinkle gelatine over water in top of double boiler; place over boiling water and heat until gelatine is melted. Spoon pie filling into a bowl and stir gelatine into pie filling; add lemon peel and a few drops red food coloring if desired. Chill until slightly thickened. Remove cheesecake from foil pan and place on serving plate. Spoon cherry filling over top of cake. Sprinkle nuts in a border around top of cake. Let stand in refrigerator about 1½ hours, or until cake is thawed, before serving. Makes 6 servings.

Your Time: 3 minutes

Chilling and Standing Time: 1 hour 45 minutes

## QUICK CHOCOLATE TORTE

½ cup semisweet chocolate
    pieces
1 3-ounce package cream
    cheese, at room
    temperature
1½ tablespoons milk
2¼ cups confectioners' sugar
    Few grains salt

½ teaspoon vanilla extract
2 packaged 8-inch sponge
    cake layers
¼ cup raspberry jam
¼ cup apricot jam
¼ cup slivered blanched
    almonds

Place chocolate pieces in top of a double boiler over hot water; stir until melted. In a bowl blend cream cheese and milk together. Gradually add confectioners' sugar, salt, and vanilla, mixing well. Add melted chocolate and mix until smooth. If necessary, add additional milk to give a good consistency for spreading. Cut each cake layer in half horizontally to make 4 layers. Place the bottom half of one layer on a serving plate; spread with raspberry jam. Top with a second layer and spread with half the chocolate frosting. Top with the third layer and spread with apricot jam. Place last layer on top and frost with remaining chocolate frosting. Sprinkle with nuts. Makes 8 servings.

Your Time: 12½ minutes

Cooking Time: 5 to 10 minutes

## CHOCO-NUT CAKE

¾ cup firmly packed
    light-brown sugar
1 cup coarsely chopped
    peanuts
¼ cup creamy peanut butter
¼ cup butter or margarine

¼ cup evaporated milk,
    undiluted
2 packaged 8-inch sponge
    cake layers
1 6-ounce package semisweet
    chocolate pieces

Combine brown sugar, nuts, peanut butter, butter, and evaporated milk in a small bowl. Stir until smooth. Place cake layers on a cookie sheet. Spread one layer with the peanut mixture; top the other with chocolate pieces. Place in preheated broiler about 5 inches from heat and broil until chocolate pieces begin to melt and nut mixture begins to brown, or about 4 minutes. Remove layers from broiler; with a small spatula spread chocolate evenly over cake. Place nut-topped layer over chocolate-topped layer. Makes 8 servings.
Your Time: 10 minutes
Broiling Time: 4 minutes

## ONE-TWO-THREE CHOCOLATE CAKE

*½ cup whole bran cereal*
*1 cup strong cold coffee*
*¼ cup vegetable oil*
*1 tablespoon cider vinegar*
*1 teaspoon vanilla extract*
*1¼ cups sifted all-purpose flour*

*1 cup sugar*
*¼ cup unsweetened cocoa*
*1 teaspoon baking soda*
*1 teaspoon ground cinnamon*
*½ teaspoon salt*
*Ice cream (optional)*

Heat oven to 350° F. Combine cereal and coffee in an ungreased 8-inch square cake pan. Let stand until most of the coffee has been absorbed, 10 to 15 minutes. Add oil, vinegar, and vanilla to cereal in the pan and stir to blend thoroughly. Sift together flour, sugar, cocoa, baking soda, cinnamon, and salt. Add sifted dry ingredients to mixture in pan and stir until smooth. Place pan in oven and bake 35 minutes, or until a cake tester inserted in the center comes out clean. Cool on a wire cake rack. Cut into squares to serve. If desired, serve with ice cream. Makes 6 to 8 servings.
Your Time: 11 minutes
Standing and Baking Time: 40 to 50 minutes

## COCONUT CAKE WITH LEMON SAUCE

*½ cup red currant jelly*
*1 6-or-8-inch ready-to-use packaged angel, sponge or chiffon cake*
*1 3½-ounce can flaked coconut*

*1 18-ounce can ready-to-serve lemon or vanilla pudding*
*¼ cup sweet or cream sherry*

In a saucepan over low heat (about 200° F.) heat jelly, stirring constantly, until it is smooth. Brush jelly over sides and top of cake.

Sprinkle immediately with coconut and chill about 30 minutes. Meanwhile in a bowl blend pudding and sherry together. Cut the cake into slices and serve each with some of the sauce. Makes 8 to 10 servings.
Your Time: 12 minutes
Chilling Time: 30 minutes

## CRANBERRY-FILLED SNOWBALL CAKES

*1 12-ounce package frozen
    pound cake, thawed*
*1 14-ounce jar
    cranberry-orange relish,
    well drained*
*½ cup sweetened condensed
    milk, undiluted*

*1 4-ounce can shredded
    coconut*
*Sweetened whipped cream
    (optional)*

Heat oven to 375° F. Cut pound cake crosswise into 14 slices. Spread half the slices generously with cranberry-orange relish. Top with remaining slices. Brush sides and top of each stack with the condensed milk. Sprinkle with coconut to coat surfaces. Place stacks on ungreased cookie sheets and bake 4 to 5 minutes, or until coconut is lightly browned. Cool. If desired, serve topped with whipped cream. Cakes may be served while still warm, if desired. Makes 7 servings.
Your Time: 8 minutes
Baking Time: 4 to 5 minutes

## CRUMB CAKE

*2½ cups complete pancake
    mix (contains egg, milk,
    and shortening)*
*⅓ cup sugar*
*1 cup water*
*1 teaspoon vanilla extract*
*¼ cup firmly packed
    light-brown sugar*

*½ teaspoon ground
    cinnamon*
*2 tablespoons softened
    butter or margarine*
*Confectioners' sugar*

Heat oven to 375° F. Grease a 9-inch-square baking pan with unsalted shortening and dust with flour. In a mixing bowl mix together 2 cups of the pancake mix and the ⅓ cup sugar. Stir in water and vanilla, stirring just enough to moisten the dry ingredients. Turn batter into prepared pan. In a small bowl mix together the remaining ½ cup pancake mix, brown sugar, and cinnamon. Cut in butter with a pastry blender or 2 knives to form coarse crumbs. Using your fingers, sprinkle the crumb mixture evenly over the batter. Bake 20 to 25 minutes. Cool on a wire cake rack. Sprinkle top with confectioners' sugar. Makes 9 servings.

Your Time: 11 minutes
Baking Time: 20 to 25 minutes

## SICILIAN CHEESE LOAF

*¼ cup light rum*
*¼ cup superfine sugar*
*½ cup mixed candied fruits*
*and peels*
*1 12-ounce package frozen*
*pound cake, thawed*
*1 16-ounce container*
*cream-style cottage cheese*

*⅓ cup superfine sugar*
*½ teaspoon lemon extract*
*1 1-ounce square sweet*
*cooking chocolate,*
*coarsely grated*

In a small bowl, mix rum and the ¼ cup sugar until sugar is dissolved. Stir in candied fruits. Slice cake into 6 horizontal layers about ¼ inch thick. In a medium-sized bowl beat cottage cheese with an electric mixer until almost smooth. Add the ⅓ cup sugar and the lemon extract; mix until blended. Drain fruits, reserving rum. Fold fruit into cheese. Sprinkle rum over cake slices. Spread a thin layer of the cheese filling over bottom slice of cake. Sprinkle with a little of the chocolate. Repeat with remaining slices and stack slices to form a loaf. Spread remaining cheese filling over top and sides of cake. Sprinkle top of cake with chocolate and chill 3 to 4 hours. Makes 8 to 10 servings.

Your Time: 19 minutes
Chilling Time: 3 to 4 hours

## CINNAMON PANCAKES

*12 frozen pancakes*
*Softened butter or margarine*
*1 tablespoon sugar*
*1 tablespoon ground*
*cinnamon*

*2 10-ounce packages frozen*
*sliced strawberries in*
*syrup, thawed, undrained*

Heat oven to 450° F. Remove frozen pancakes from freezer. Cover a large cookie sheet with aluminum foil and place pancakes on sheet. Spread each pancake generously with butter. Combine sugar and cinnamon and sprinkle on pancakes. Heat pancakes in oven about 10 minutes, or until sugar mixture is melted. Heat strawberries in saucepan over moderately low heat (about 225° F.) until the juice just reaches the boiling point. Serve the hot strawberries over pancakes. Makes 6 servings.
Your Time: 7 minutes
Cooking Time: 10 minutes

## FRUIT AND CREAM SHORTCAKE

1 *8½-ounce can pineapple*     1 *11-ounce can mandarin*
   *tidbits*                            *orange segments, drained*
1 *cup commercial sour cream*   ¼ *cup chopped walnuts or*
1 *cup miniature*                        *pecans*
   *marshmallows*                1 *9-ounce package pound*
1 *3½-ounce can flaked*         *cake*
   *coconut*                      *Maraschino cherries*

Drain pineapple tidbits and reserve ¼ cup juice. In a medium-sized bowl fold together pineapple, sour cream, marshmallows, coconut, orange segments, nuts, and the ¼ cup juice. Chill for 1 hour. Cut pound cake into 6 slices. Spoon fruit mixture over cake slices and garnish with cherries. Makes 6 servings.
Your Time: 5 minutes
Chilling Time: 1 hour

## HONEY-NUT CAKE DESSERT

1 *package yellow cake mix (2*    1 *cup honey*
   *layers)*                          ½ *cup water*
1 *cup coarsely chopped*      *Whipped topping (optional)*
   *pecans or walnuts*
1 *6-ounce package*
   *butterscotch-flavored*
   *pieces*

Heat oven to 350° F. Lightly grease a 12¾-x-9-x-2-inch cake pan with unsalted shortening. Prepare cake mix according to package directions and stir in pecans. Turn batter into prepared cake pan.

Sprinkle with the butterscotch pieces. In a saucepan mix together honey and water. Place over moderately low heat (about 225° F.) and heat just to boiling. Pour over batter; do not mix. Bake 35 minutes, or until a cake tester inserted in the center comes out clean. Serve warm with whipped topping, if desired. Makes 8 to 10 servings.
Your Time: 15 minutes
Baking Time: 35 minutes

## LITTLE LEMON CAKES

*1 package lemon pie filling*
   *(enough for an 8-inch pie*
   *shell)*

*8 packaged dessert sponge*
   *cups*
*¼ cup toasted flaked coconut*

Prepare lemon pie filling according to directions on package. Cool slightly; pour into sponge cups. Sprinkle with toasted coconut. Chill for 30 minutes. Makes 8 servings.
Your Time: 6 minutes
Chilling Time: 30 minutes

## LEMON-MARBLED GINGERBREAD

*1 package gingerbread mix*  *1 18-ounce can ready-to-serve*
                                    *lemon pudding*

Heat oven to 350° F. Grease a 9-inch-square cake pan with unsalted shortening and dust with flour. Prepare gingerbread mix according to package directions. Pour batter into prepared pan. Drop pudding by tablespoonfuls on batter and run a knife zigzag through batter to marble it. Bake 30 to 35 minutes. Cool on a wire cake rack. Makes 8 servings.
Your Time: 6 minutes
Baking Time: 30 to 35 minutes

## HONEY-BUTTER FINGERS

*6 tablespoons whipped honey*
   *spread*
*1 9-ounce package frozen*
   *French toast (6 slices)*

*2 tablespoons sesame seeds*

Spread 1 tablespoon honey spread on each slice of French toast. Sprinkle about 1 teaspoon sesame seeds over each slice. Cut each slice in thirds and crosswise in half again. Place pieces on an ungreased cookie sheet and place in preheated broiler 4 inches from heat; broil about 3 minutes, or until golden brown and crisp. Serve hot. Makes 3 dozen fingers.
Your Time: 4 minutes
Broiling Time: 3 minutes

## DOUBLE-DECKER ORANGE CREAM CAKE

*10 ladyfingers*
*1 cup chilled heavy cream*
*1 tablespoon honey*
*3 tablespoons undiluted frozen orange juice concentrate*

*Fresh orange sections (optional)*

Line an 8½-x-4½-x-2½-inch loaf pan with waxed paper. Split ladyfingers and place a layer, crust side down, in the loaf pan. In a bowl whip cream and honey until they hold their shape; stir in orange juice. Spread half of the cream mixture over ladyfingers. Repeat layers again and top with a layer of ladyfingers. Cover and chill 6 to 8 hours or overnight. Invert cake on serving platter. Garnish with fresh orange sections, if desired. Makes 6 to 8 servings.
Your Time: 7 minutes
Chilling Time: 6 to 8 hours

## PEANUT-BUTTER CUPCAKES

*1 package yellow cake mix (2 layers)*
*½ cup chunk-style peanut butter*

*1 16.5-ounce can ready-to-use chocolate frosting*
*⅓ cup chunk-style peanut butter*

Heat oven to 350° F. Line 2½-inch-cup muffin pans with paper baking cups. Prepare cake mix according to package directions, adding the ½ cup peanut butter with the water and eggs. Spoon batter into prepared muffin cups; fill about ⅔ full. Bake 20 to 25 minutes, or until cake tester inserted in center of a cupcake comes out clean. Place cupcakes on wire cake rack to cool. Meanwhile in a bowl blend frosting with the ⅓ cup peanut butter. Frost cupcakes. Makes 30 to 36 cupcakes.
Your Time: about 28 minutes
Baking Time: 20 to 25 minutes

## RAISIN PUDDING CAKE

1  11¾-ounce package
cupcake mix
1  cup dark seedless raisins
1½ cups water
1  cup dark corn syrup

2  tablespoons butter or
margarine
Whipped cream (optional)
Vanilla ice cream (optional)

Heat oven to 350° F. Grease an 8-inch-square cake pan with unsalted shortening. Prepare cupcake batter as directed on package. Stir in raisins. Pour batter into prepared pan. Place water, corn syrup, and butter in a saucepan. Place over moderate heat (about 250° F.), stirring occasionally, until butter melts. Pour syrup mixture slowly over batter in pan. Do not stir. Bake about 45 minutes. Serve warm with whipped cream or vanilla ice cream, if desired. Makes 6 to 8 servings.
Your Time: 9 minutes
Baking Time: 45 minutes

## MOCHA-RASPBERRY TORTE

1  teaspoon instant coffee
powder or granules
3  tablespoons confectioners'
sugar
½ teaspoon vanilla extract
½ cup toasted slivered
almonds

1  12-ounce frozen pound
cake, partially thawed
½ cup raspberry preserves
1  cup chilled heavy cream
1  tablespoon quick
chocolate-flavored mix

While cake is still slightly frozen, slice it horizontally into 5 equal layers. Spread about 2 tablespoons of the raspberry preserves on the bottom layer. Top with another cake layer. Spread about 2 more tablespoons of the preserves over second cake layer. Repeat until all the cake layers are used and cake is reassembled. Place cream in the small bowl of an electric mixer with chocolate mix, coffee powder, sugar, and vanilla. Beat until mixture forms soft peaks. Spread whipped cream over sides and top of cake. Chill until serving time, or about 2 hours. When ready to serve, sprinkle with almonds. Makes 8 servings.
Your Time: 9 minutes
Chilling Time: 2 hours

## QUICKIE SHORTCAKE

*1 cup washed, hulled, and
   sliced fresh strawberries*
*1 cup peeled, sliced fresh
   peaches*
*½ cup orange juice*
*24 shortbread cookies*
*½ cup chilled heavy cream*

*2 tablespoons confectioners'
   sugar*
*½ teaspoon ground
   cinnamon*
*½ teaspoon ground nutmeg*
*4 whole strawberries*

In a bowl combine strawberries, peaches, and orange juice. Arrange 5 cookies in each of four dessert dishes. Spoon in fruit. In a bowl whip cream, sugar, cinnamon, and nutmeg until mixture holds its shape. Spoon over fruit and top each serving with a cookie and a whole strawberry. Makes 4 servings.
Your Time: 9 minutes

*Note:* Any fresh summer fruit may be substituted.

# Cookies

## CHOCOLATE-CHIP BARS

*2 13-ounce packages cookie
   mix with semisweet
   chocolate pieces*
*½ cup butter or margarine*

*1 package fluffy white
   frosting mix*
*1 cup packaged chopped
   pecans or walnuts*

Heat oven to 350° F. Place cookie mixes in a mixing bowl. Reserve chocolate pieces. Using a pastry blender or 2 knives, cut butter into dry mix until mixture resembles coarse corn meal. With the back of a spoon, press mixture onto the bottom and sides of an ungreased 15½-x-10½-x-1-inch jelly-roll pan. Bake 20 minutes, or until crust is just set. Prepare frosting mix according to package directions; fold in reserved chocolate pieces and ½ cup of the chopped nuts. Spread over crust in pan. Sprinkle with the remaining ½ cup chopped nuts. Bake 25 to 30 minutes, or until lightly browned. Cool on a wire rack. Cut into about 1¼-x-2½-inch bars. Makes about 4 dozen bars.
Your Time: 14 minutes
Baking Time: 45 to 50 minutes

## CHOCOLATE QUICKIES

1 cup chunk-style peanut
   butter
⅔ cup sweetened condensed
   milk, undiluted

3 tablespoons unsweetened
   cocoa

Heat oven to 350° F. Grease a large cookie sheet with unsalted shortening. In a bowl combine peanut butter, condensed milk, and cocoa. Drop batter by teaspoonfuls onto prepared cookie sheet. Bake about 10 minutes. Remove from cookie sheet and cool on wire rack. Makes 2½ dozen.
Your Time: 8 minutes
Baking Time: 10 minutes

## COCONUT DROPS

1 4-ounce can shredded or
   flaked coconut
⅓ cup sweetened condensed
   milk, undiluted

⅛ teaspoon salt
¼ teaspoon vanilla extract

Heat oven to 350° F. Combine all ingredients in a medium-sized bowl. Stir until well blended. Cover a cookie sheet with brown paper. Drop coconut mixture by teaspoonfuls onto brown paper. Bake 15 minutes, or until coconut is lightly browned. Remove cookies immediately from the brown paper with a small spatula; cool on wire rack. Makes about 1½ dozen cookies.
Your Time: 5 minutes
Baking Time: 15 minutes

## MINTED MINIATURE ÉCLAIRS

¾ cup chilled heavy cream
2 teaspoons confectioners'
   sugar
1 tablespoon crème de
   menthe

12 ladyfingers, split
½ cup canned
   ready-to-spread
   refrigerated fudge
   frosting

In a bowl, whip cream and sugar with rotary beater until soft peaks form. Add crème de menthe and whip until mixture holds its shape. Spread cream filling over 12 of the ladyfinger halves. Spread fudge frosting over the tops of the remaining halves. Place frosted ladyfingers over cream filling. Allow 2 éclairs to a serving. Makes 6 servings.
Your Time: 13 minutes


## FUDGE-NUT COOKIE SQUARES

1  *8-ounce package cream*      1  *egg*
    *cheese, at room*            1  *teaspoon vanilla extract*
    *temperature*                1  *roll refrigerated fudge nut*
¼  *cup sugar*                       *slice-and-bake cookies*

Heat oven to 350° F. In the small bowl of an electric mixer beat the cream cheese at medium speed until fluffy, gradually adding the sugar. Beat in egg and vanilla; set aside. Cut cookie dough into 48 ⅛-inch-thick slices. Place 24 slices in an ungreased 12¾-x-9-x-2-inch baking pan in even rows. Pour cheese mixture evenly over slices. Top with the remaining 24 slices in the same pattern as the bottom layer. Bake 25 minutes, or until a cake tester inserted in the center of a cookie comes out clean. Cool on a wire cake rack and cut into squares. Makes 24 squares.
Your Time: 15 minutes
Baking Time: 25 minutes


## GRAHAM-PEANUT CHEWS

⅓ *cup butter or margarine*       4  *cups graham-flavored*
32  *marshmallows*                    *cereal*
½  *cup creamy peanut butter*

Butter a 9-inch-square pan lightly. Place the butter and marshmallows in a saucepan over moderately low heat (about 225° F.) and cook, stirring constantly, until melted and smooth. Stir in peanut butter and heat a few minutes. Remove from heat and add cereal, tossing to coat evenly. Turn mixture into prepared pan and press down evenly with the back of a spoon. Cool thoroughly in refrigerator, about 45 minutes. Cut into about 1½-x-2-inch rectangles. Makes about 2 dozen bars.
Your Time: 7 minutes
Cooling Time: 45 minutes

## EASY LEMON COOKIES

1  4-serving-size package
    lemon instant pudding
¾ cup prepared buttermilk
    biscuit mix

3  eggs
¼ cup vegetable oil

Heat oven to 400° F. Grease a cookie sheet with unsalted shortening. Combine pudding mix, biscuit mix, eggs, and vegetable oil in a bowl. Drop by rounded teaspoonfuls onto prepared cookie sheet. Bake 8 to 10 minutes or until edges start to brown. Remove cookies to wire cake rack to cool. Makes about 2 dozen.
Your Time: 6 minutes
Baking Time: 8 to 10 minutes

## NO-BAKE PEANUT BUTTER SQUARES

1¼ cups packaged graham
    cracker crumbs
¼ cup sugar
½ teaspoon ground
    cinnamon
½ teaspoon ground nutmeg

⅓ cup light corn syrup
½ cup chunk-style peanut
    butter
1  6-ounce package
    semisweet chocolate
    pieces

Combine cracker crumbs, sugar, cinnamon, and nutmeg in a mixing bowl. Add corn syrup and peanut butter and work together until thoroughly combined. Press into an 8-inch-square cake pan. Place chocolate pieces in a saucepan over low heat (about 200° F.) and heat, stirring occasionally, until melted. Spread over mixture in pan. Chill about 1 hour. Cut into 2-inch squares. Makes 16.
Your Time: 9 minutes
Chilling Time: 1 hour

## REFRIGERATOR BROWNIES

3  cups finely crushed vanilla
    wafers
2  cups miniature
    marshmallows
1  cup chopped salted peanuts
1  cup sifted confectioners'
    sugar

1  12-ounce package
    semisweet chocolate pieces
1  cup evaporated milk,
    undiluted
2  teaspoons evaporated milk,
    undiluted

Generously grease a 9-inch-square cake pan with unsalted shortening. Mix vanilla wafers, marshmallows, nuts, and confectioners' sugar in large mixing bowl. Combine chocolate pieces and the 1 cup evaporated milk in a small saucepan. Cook and stir over low heat (about 200° F.) until chocolate is melted and mixture is smooth. Reserve ½ cup of chocolate mixture for glaze. Using a fork, stir remainder of chocolate mixture into the crumb mixture until well blended. Press mixture evenly into prepared pan. Stir the 2 teaspoons evaporated milk into the remaining ½ cup chocolate mixture. Spread glaze evenly over brownies. Chill until glaze is set, or about 1 hour. May be stored, well wrapped, in refrigerator for several days. Cut into about 36 squares.
Your Time: 15 minutes
Chilling Time: 1 hour


## POLKA-DOT BARS

*1½ cups quick-cooking rolled oats*
*1 14-ounce can sweetened condensed milk, undiluted*
*½ teaspoon salt*
*1 teaspoon vanilla extract*
*½ cup chunk-style peanut butter*
*1 6-ounce package semisweet chocolate pieces*

Heat oven to 350° F. Grease an 8-inch-square cake pan with unsalted shortening. In a bowl mix together oats, milk, salt, and vanilla. Stir in peanut butter and chocolate pieces. Pour batter into prepared pan. Bake 30 minutes, or until lightly browned. Cool about 10 minutes before removing from pan. Cool on a wire rack and cut into bars. Makes 32 1-x-2-inch bars.
Your Time: 6 minutes
Baking Time: 30 minutes


## SCOTCH LACE WAFERS

*1 4-serving-size package butterscotch pudding and pie filling*
*2 cups quick-cooking rolled oats*
*½ cup chopped pecans or walnuts*
*¾ cup softened butter or margarine*
*½ cup sugar*
*1 teaspoon vanilla extract*
*Ice cream or fruit (optional)*

Heat oven to 350° F. In a bowl, thoroughly blend together all the ingredients with the fingers. Shape into balls the size of small walnuts; place 3 inches apart on ungreased cookie sheets. Flatten balls slightly with a fork. Bake 12 to 15 minutes. Cool on cookie sheet before removing. Makes 3 dozen. Serve with ice cream or fruit, as desired.

Your Time: 14 minutes

Baking Time: 12 to 15 minutes

## SIX-LAYER COOKIES

*¼ pound butter or margarine*
*1 cup packaged graham*
*cracker crumbs*
*1 cup shredded coconut*
*1 12-ounce package*
*semisweet chocolate pieces*

*1 14-ounce can sweetened*
*condensed milk, undiluted*
*1 cup chopped walnuts*

Heat oven to 350° F. Place butter in a 12¾-x-9-x-2-inch pan and melt over moderately low heat (about 225° F.). Remove from heat. Sprinkle graham cracker crumbs in an even layer over the melted butter. Sprinkle coconut over crumbs, then sprinkle chocolate pieces in an even layer over the coconut. Pour condensed milk evenly over chocolate and top with the chopped walnuts. (Do not stir.) Bake 30 to 35 minutes. Let cool completely in pan before cutting into bars. Makes 30 1½-x-2½-inch bars.

Your Time: 11 minutes

Baking Time: 30 to 35 minutes

## WALNUT CANDY BARS

*1 13-ounce package cookie*
*mix with semisweet*
*chocolate pieces*
*½ cup miniature spiced*
*gumdrops*

*½ cup miniature*
*marshmallows*
*1½ cups chopped walnuts*

Heat oven to 375° F. Grease a 9-inch-square cake pan with unsalted shortening and line the greased pan with waxed paper. Prepare cookie mix according to package directions. Stir in gumdrops, marshmallows, and 1 cup of the walnuts. Spread evenly in paper-lined pan. Sprinkle top with remaining walnuts. Bake 25 to 30

minutes, or until a cake tester inserted in the center comes out clean. Cool in pan about ½ hour. Loosen sides and turn out onto a cutting board. Remove waxed paper; turn the cake right side up. Using a sharp thin knife, cut cake lengthwise into 3 strips; cut each strip into 6 bars. Makes 18 bars.
Your Time: 15 minutes
Baking Time: 25 to 30 minutes
Cooking Time: 25 to 30 minutes

## NO-BAKE WINE-NUT BALLS

1  *12-ounce package vanilla
   wafers (about 3 cups
   finely crushed)*
1  *cup semisweet chocolate
   pieces*
3  *tablespoons light corn syrup*

½  *cup dry white wine*
¾  *cup confectioners' sugar*
1  *cup chopped pecans or
   walnuts*
   *Confectioners' sugar*

Crush vanilla wafers in the container of an electric blender on high speed, a few at a time. Pour into a large bowl. Place chocolate pieces in the top of a double boiler. Cook over simmering water, stirring occasionally, until melted. Combine melted chocolate, corn syrup, wine, the ¾ cup confectioners' sugar, and the pecans with vanilla wafers in bowl; blend well. Chill 30 minutes. With the hands, shape mixture into 1-inch balls. Balls may be served immediately, but flavor improves on standing 2 to 3 days in a tightly covered container. Before serving, roll each ball in confectioners' sugar to coat well. Makes about 40 balls.
Your Time: 13 minutes
Chilling Time: 30 minutes

# CHAPTER

# IX

# *Other Ways to Save Meal Preparation Time*

Other than the use of ready-to-serve foods, there are three major techniques for time-saving meal preparation.

## *Main Dishes to Make Ahead*

There are, first, make-ahead meals planned on the assumption that you can spend time the night before or earlier in the day in pre-preparation of a main dish that can be refrigerated, ready to heat and serve. This is a form of making your own convenience food, which, of course, allows a greater touch of individuality and also allows you to prepare more accurately the amount you expect to use at a given meal, because you're not limited by commercial portions. Make-ahead meals are particularly useful when you'll be home late. Perhaps you're going to a cocktail party and want to ask some friends to come home and share supper with you. Maybe it's an afternoon meeting that may run late. Or, of course, make-aheads are the perfect solution for informal dinner entertaining when you want to stay with guests—and not in the kitchen.

## PARTY BEEF STROGANOFF

1½ pounds ½-inch slices beef
   tenderloin, cut into thin
   strips
2 tablespoons all-purpose
   flour
¼ cup butter or margarine
½ pound mushrooms, sliced
½ cup thinly sliced peeled
   onion
1 clove garlic, peeled and
   pressed
¾ cup water
1 package instant beef broth
   mix

½ teaspoon salt
⅛ teaspoon pepper
½ teaspoon Worcestershire
   sauce
1 tablespoon chopped fresh
   dillweed or ½ teaspoon
   dried dillweed
½ cup dry white wine
½ cup commercial sour
   cream (added when ready
   to serve)
2 cups cooked rice
   (optional)

Place beef strips in a paper bag with the flour and shake to coat pieces evenly. Melt butter in a large skillet over moderately low heat (about 225° F.). Add mushrooms, onion, and garlic and cook until onion is lightly browned; remove vegetables with a slotted spoon and reserve. Increase heat to moderately high (about 300° F.). Add beef strips; cook and stir until beef is browned, adding a little more butter if necessary. Add water and stir to loosen browned bits in bottom of skillet. Add the mushroom-onion mixture to skillet and stir in instant broth mix, salt, pepper, Worcestershire, and dill. Simmer, uncovered, over moderately low heat (about 225° F.) 5 minutes. Stir in wine and cook 3 minutes longer. Cool. Spoon mixture into a refrigerator container; cover and refrigerate. To serve, heat about 15 minutes in the top of a double boiler over boiling water, stirring occasionally. Stir in sour cream. Serve with cooked rice, if desired. Makes 4 servings.

*Party Beef Stroganoff may be prepared ahead and stored in the refrigerator for 2 days.*

## OLD-FASHIONED BEEF STEW

*1½ pounds boneless beef
    chuck, cut into 1½-inch
    cubes*
*1½ tablespoons flour*
*2 tablespoons vegetable oil*
*1 cup water*
*1 16-ounce can tomatoes,
    undrained*
*4 whole cloves*
*1 bay leaf*
*1½ teaspoons salt*
*⅛ teaspoon pepper*

*½ cup diced celery*
*2 small onions, peeled and
    quartered*
*2 medium-sized carrots,
    peeled and quartered*
*2 medium-sized potatoes,
    peeled and cut into
    eighths*
*1 medium-sized green
    pepper, seeded and cut
    into 8 squares*

Roll beef cubes in flour to coat them thoroughly. Heat oil in a Dutch oven over moderately high heat (about 300° F.); add beef; cook until browned on all sides. Add water and tomatoes; stir in cloves, bay leaf, salt, and pepper. Simmer, covered, over low heat (about 200° F.) 1½ hours. Add celery, onions, carrots, and potatoes. Continue to simmer, covered, ½ hour longer, or until meat and vegetables are almost tender. Add green pepper during last 10 minutes of cooking. Remove stew from heat and cool. Cover Dutch oven and refrigerate. To serve, place over low heat (about 200° F.) and heat, stirring occasionally, until bubbling. Makes 4 to 6 servings. *This beef stew may be prepared ahead and stored in the refrigerator 2 to 3 days.*

## SOUTHWEST CHILI

*1 tablespoon vegetable oil*
*1 pound ground beef round*
*¼ cup sliced peeled onion*
*1 clove garlic, peeled and
    pressed*
*2 teaspoons chili powder or ¼
    teaspoon chili powder and
    1 canned green chili
    pepper pod, seeded and
    sliced*

*½ teaspoon salt*
*Pinch of ground cumin*
*1 16-ounce can tomatoes,
    undrained*
*1 16-ounce can pinto or red
    kidney beans, well drained*

Heat oil in a large saucepan over moderate heat (about 250° F.). Cook beef, onion, and garlic until onion is soft and beef is browned, stirring frequently. Stir in chili powder, salt, cumin, and tomatoes. Break up any large tomato pieces with a wooden spoon. Stir in beans. Bring chili to a boil; reduce heat to moderately low (about 225° F.) and simmer, uncovered, for 10 minutes. Cool. Spoon mixture into a refrigerator container; cover and refrigerate. To serve, heat about 15 minutes in the top of a double boiler over boiling water, stirring occasionally. Makes 1 quart, or 4 servings.

*This chili may be made ahead and refrigerated for 1 or 2 days.*

## CHAFING-DISH MEATBALLS WITH SOUR CREAM

1 *pound ground beef sirloin*
2 *tablespoons chili sauce*
1 *tablespoon finely chopped pimiento-stuffed olives*
1 *tablespoon chopped fresh parsley*
1 *teaspoon instant minced onion*
½ *teaspoon Worcestershire sauce*
1 *teaspoon salt*
¾ *teaspoon monosodium glutamate*

⅛ *teaspoon pepper*
2 *tablespoons flour*
2 *tablespoons butter or margarine*
¾ *cup canned beef broth, undiluted*
1 *cup commercial sour cream*
¼ *teaspoon onion salt*
*Chopped fresh parsley (optional)*

In a large bowl mix together beef, chili sauce, olives, parsley, onion, Worcestershire, salt, monosodium glutamate, and pepper. Shape mixture into 1-inch balls; roll each in flour. Cover and refrigerate 12 to 24 hours. When ready to serve, melt the butter in a large skillet over moderately low heat (about 225° F.). Add meatballs and brown on all sides, shaking skillet to keep the round shape. Add the broth and simmer, uncovered, over moderate heat (about 250° F.) 10 to 15 minutes, or until liquid cooks down and balls are glazed. Turn meatballs into a chafing dish, leaving a space in the center. Place chafing dish over warm water. Combine sour cream and onion salt; pour into center of chafing dish to serve as a dip for meatballs. Garnish with chopped parsley, if desired. Makes 4 servings.

*Prepared meatballs may be stored in the refrigerator for 24 hours.*

## MEAT LOAF RING

1  pound ground beef round
1  egg, slightly beaten
½ cup seasoned fine dry bread
  crumbs
½ cup milk
½ teaspoon salt
⅛ teaspoon pepper
½ cup (2 ounces) shredded
  Cheddar cheese

2  hard-cooked eggs, shelled
  and each cut into 8 wedges
2  cups hot mashed potatoes
  or hot cooked instant
  mashed potatoes
Paprika
Fresh parsley sprigs

Heat oven to 375° F. Lightly oil a 1-quart ring mold. Place beef in a large mixing bowl; combine egg, bread crumbs, milk, salt, and pepper; add mixture to beef and combine thoroughly. Divide the meat mixture in half. Press one half of the mixture into the bottom of the prepared ring mold, leaving a ½-inch-deep center depression all the way around. Sprinkle Cheddar cheese in the depression. Arrange the egg wedges evenly around the ring mold on top of the cheese. Press the other half of the meat mixture into the ring mold, making sure to seal all edges.* Bake, uncovered, 30 minutes. Remove meat loaf to serving dish and fill center with potatoes. Sprinkle potatoes with paprika. Garnish with parsley. Makes 4 servings.

*Meat loaf ring may be prepared up to this point the night before and refrigerated, ready for baking.

## MOCK WELLINGTON

1  pound ground beef chuck
⅓ cup finely chopped celery
⅓ cup finely chopped peeled
  onion
1  cup fine dry bread crumbs
1  egg, well beaten
½ cup (2 ounces) shredded
  Cheddar cheese
1  teaspoon garlic salt

1  teaspoon salt
⅛ teaspoon pepper
⅔ cup tomato sauce
½ package pie crust mix or 1
  stick pie crust mix
1  3-ounce can broiled sliced
  mushrooms, drained
1  egg, slightly beaten

Heat oven to 375° F. Place beef in a large mixing bowl; mix together in another bowl celery, onion, bread crumbs, the well-beaten egg, the

Cheddar cheese, garlic salt, salt, pepper, and tomato sauce; add to beef and combine thoroughly. Shape meat mixture into a 4-x-7-inch loaf.* Bake loaf in an ungreased shallow 1½-quart baking dish for 30 minutes. Remove meat loaf from the oven and allow it to cool in the baking dish 10 minutes on a wire rack. Heat oven to 425° F. While the meat loaf is cooling, prepare pie crust mix according to package directions. Roll out the dough into a rectangle large enough to cover the meat loaf completely. Arrange the mushroom slices in the center of the pie crust, forming a rectangle about the size of the meat loaf. Place the meat loaf upside down on the mushrooms. Bring the pastry up around the sides of the meat loaf to enclose it completely; seal the edges well. Place meat loaf on an ungreased cookie sheet, sealed side down. Make several diagonal slits along the top edge of the pastry to allow steam to escape. Brush pastry well with the slightly beaten egg. Bake, uncovered, 15 to 20 minutes, or until the pastry is browned. Makes 4 servings.

*Meat loaf may be made up to this point the night before and refrigerated, ready for baking.

## SPICY SHORT RIBS

| | |
|---|---|
| 3½ pounds beef short ribs, cut into 2½-inch serving pieces | 1 bay leaf |
| 2 tablespoons flour | ½ teaspoon Worcestershire sauce |
| 1 tablespoon vegetable oil | ½ teaspoon prepared horseradish |
| 1 medium-sized onion, peeled and sliced | 1½ teaspoons salt |
| ½ cup dry red wine | ⅛ teaspoon pepper |
| 2 tablespoons dark-brown sugar | 1 cup water |

Trim larger fat layers from the ribs and roll the ribs in the flour to coat evenly. Heat oil in a heavy Dutch oven over moderately high heat (about 275° F.). Add ribs and brown well on all sides. Add onion and cook until golden brown. Remove any excess fat drippings. Stir in wine, sugar, bay leaf, Worcestershire, horseradish, salt, and pepper. Add water and stir to mix well. Bring mixture to a boil. Reduce heat to low (about 200° F.); cover tightly and simmer about 2 hours, until meat is fork-tender, stirring occasionally. Remove meat pieces from gravy. Cool meat and gravy quickly. Store meat and gravy separately, tightly covered. When ready to serve, skim off and discard solidified fat from gravy and meat. Combine

meat and gravy in a heavy Dutch oven and heat to serving temperature over moderately low heat (about 225° F.), stirring frequently. Makes 4 servings.
*These short ribs may be stored in the refrigerator 1 or 2 days.*

## CHILI AND FRANKFURTER CASSEROLE

| | |
|---|---|
| 1 tablespoon vegetable oil | 1 8-ounce can tomato sauce |
| 1 pound ground beef round | ½ pound cocktail frankfurters |
| 1 teaspoon salt | 3 cups mashed potatoes |
| ⅛ teaspoon pepper | (leftover or made from |
| 3 to 4 teaspoons chili powder | instant mashed potatoes) |

Heat oven to 350° F. In a large skillet heat oil over moderately high heat (about 275° F.). Add beef and cook, stirring frequently, until browned. Drain off any excess fat. Stir in salt, pepper, chili powder, and tomato sauce. Simmer mixture, uncovered, over moderately low heat (about 225° F.) for 10 minutes. Pour chili into an ungreased shallow 2-quart casserole. Arrange frankfurters on the chili. Spoon a ring of mashed potatoes around edge of casserole.* Bake, uncovered, 45 minutes. If desired, after baking, the casserole may be placed under the broiler (about 3 to 4 inches from heat) for 5 minutes to brown the potatoes. Makes 4 to 6 servings.

*This casserole may be prepared up to this point the night before and refrigerated, ready for baking.

## EASY CHICKEN WITH ONIONS

| | |
|---|---|
| 3 large whole chicken breasts, split | 1 10½-ounce can condensed cream of mushroom soup, undiluted |
| ½ teaspoon salt | |
| ½ teaspoon pepper | 2 tablespoons dry sherry |
| 12 to 16 tiny white peeled onions or 1 8½-ounce can onions, drained | 4 ounces (1 cup) Cheddar cheese, coarsely shredded |

Wash and pat chicken breasts dry and place them in an ungreased shallow 3-quart baking dish; sprinkle lightly with salt and pepper. Add onions. Mix soup and sherry in a small bowl; pour over chicken breasts. Sprinkle with cheese. Cover and refrigerate. About 1¾ hours before serving time, heat oven to 350° F. Bake chicken, covered, for 45 minutes. Uncover and bake 30 to 45 minutes, or until fork-tender. Makes 6 servings.
*Refrigerator Storage Time: 1 day*

## CAMBRIDGE CHICKEN WITH HAM

½ cup all-purpose flour
2 teaspoons salt
⅛ teaspoon pepper
1 3-to-3½-pound broiler-fryer chicken, cut up
½ cup butter or margarine
¼ cup chopped green onions or scallions
1 4-ounce can mushrooms, drained

¾ pound lean cooked ham, diced
1 cup dry red wine
1 clove garlic, peeled and minced
Pinch dried thyme leaves
Salt and pepper to taste

Mix flour, the 2 teaspoons salt, and the ⅛ teaspoon pepper in a paper or plastic bag. Wash and pat chicken pieces dry. Add a few pieces of chicken at a time and shake until chicken is well coated. Heat butter in a large skillet over moderate heat (about 250° F.); add chicken and cook until browned. Arrange chicken in an ungreased shallow 2-quart casserole. Mix together all remaining ingredients in a bowl and pour over chicken. Heat oven to 350° F. Bake chicken, covered, for 1 hour. Remove casserole from oven and cool for a short time before placing in refrigerator overnight. About 1¼ hours before serving time, heat oven to 300° F. Spoon some of the wine mixture from bottom of casserole over chicken. Cover and bake 1 hour. Makes 6 servings.
*Refrigerator Storage Time: 24 hours*

## CHICKEN KIEV

4 whole chicken breasts, split
1 stick (8 tablespoons) chilled butter or margarine
Salt and pepper
3 tablespoons snipped fresh chives

⅓ cup flour
2 eggs, slightly beaten
1⅓ cups fine dry bread crumbs
Vegetable oil

Wash and pat chicken breasts dry. Bone and skin chicken breasts, or ask the butcher to bone them. Pound with a meat mallet to flatten each piece of chicken to a thickness of about ⅛ inch. Divide butter into 8 portions and shape with fingers into cylindrical pieces about 1½ inches long. Place a butter piece toward one end near one edge of each piece of chicken. Sprinkle each piece of chicken lightly with salt, pepper, and a little less than 1 teaspoon of the chives. Roll up breasts, turning in edges to seal while rolling. Roll each piece of chicken in flour to coat; shake off any excess. Dip chicken in beaten egg and then roll in bread crumbs to coat. Place chicken on an ungreased cookie sheet. Cover and refrigerate at least 6 hours. When ready to cook, fill an electric skillet half full with oil; heat to 360° F. (Or use a large skillet over moderately high heat [about 350° F.].) Fry chicken rolls about 7 minutes on each side. Drain on paper towels and serve; or, if desired, Chicken Kiev may be kept warm in a 200° F. oven for about 30 minutes before serving. Makes 4 to 6 servings.

*Prepared Chicken Kiev may be stored in the refrigerator about 1½ days before cooking.*

## PARTY CHICKEN

4 *large whole chicken breasts, split, skinned, and boned*
8 *slices raw bacon*
1 *4-ounce package chipped beef*
1 *10½-ounce can condensed cream of mushroom soup, undiluted*
1 *cup commercial sour cream*

Wash and pat chicken breasts dry. Wrap each split chicken breast with a strip of bacon. Cover the bottom of a greased shallow baking dish (about 8-x-12-x-2 inches) with the chipped beef. Arrange chicken breasts on chipped beef. In a small bowl mix soup and sour cream and pour mixture over chicken. Cover and refrigerate. About 3¼ hours before serving time, heat oven to 275° F. Bake chicken, uncovered, for 3 hours. Makes 8 servings.

*Refrigerator Storage Time: 24 hours*

## CHICKEN POT PIE

*Simmered Chicken and Stock*
   *(recipe below)*
1  *8-ounce can small whole*
   *white onions, well drained*
1  *16-ounce can small whole*
   *white potatoes, drained*
1  *10-ounce package frozen*
   *peas, cooked until almost*
   *tender and drained*
1  *cup peeled and sliced*
   *carrots, cooked until*
   *almost tender and drained*

2  *cups seasoned chicken stock*
2  *cups milk*
⅓ *cup flour*
1  *tablespoon chopped canned*
   *pimiento*
*Salt and pepper*
*Enough pastry for a 2-crust*
   *9-inch pie, made from a*
   *mix or your favorite*
   *pastry recipe*

Combine cooked chicken pieces, onions, potatoes, peas, and carrots in an ungreased deep 2½-quart freezer-to-oven casserole; set aside. In a large saucepan bring to a boil over moderate heat (about 250° F.) the chicken stock and 1½ cups of the milk. Blend together the remaining ½ cup milk and the flour; quickly stir into boiling mixture. Boil 1 minute, stirring constantly. Remove from heat; stir in pimiento and add a little salt and pepper, if necessary. Pour sauce over chicken and vegetables; cool. Roll out pastry to a thickness of ⅛ inch. Cover casserole with pastry and press down pastry over edges of dish. Trim off excess pastry. Make a few slashes in the top to allow steam to escape when baking. If desired, cut a circle from center of pastry and decorate with leaves cut from the pastry trimmings. Cover and refrigerate until ready to bake. Heat oven to 400° F. Bake 30 to 35 minutes, until mixture is thoroughly heated and crust is golden brown. Makes 4 to 6 servings.
*This Chicken Pot Pie may be stored in the refrigerator for 1 day.*


## SIMMERED CHICKEN AND STOCK

1  *large whole broiler-fryer*
   *chicken (3 to 3½ pounds)*
2  *stalks celery with leaves,*
   *halved*
1  *whole medium-sized peeled*
   *onion*

3  *sprigs parsley*
½ *teaspoon dried rosemary*
   *leaves*
1  *bay leaf*
1  *teaspoon salt*
¼ *teaspoon peppercorns*

Wash chicken. In a large saucepan or Dutch oven combine chicken, celery, onion, parsley, rosemary, bay leaf, salt, and peppercorns. Add water to cover chicken halfway, about 1½ quarts. Bring to boil over moderate heat (about 250° F.); then reduce the heat to low (about 200° F.). Cover; simmer 30 to 40 minutes, or until chicken is fork-tender. Remove chicken and strain stock; set aside and cool. Bone chicken into large pieces. Measure and reserve stock for Chicken Pot Pie. Pour any remaining stock into a freezer container, leaving ½ inch head space; seal and freeze for future use as soup or a casserole base.

*Freezer Storage Time for stock: About 2 months*

## LAMB EN BROCHETTE

*1 cup bottled clear French dressing*
*2 tablespoons lemon juice*
*½ teaspoon Worcestershire sauce*
*¼ teaspoon dried marjoram leaves*
*1½ pounds lean boneless lamb, cut into 1½-to-2-inch cubes*

*8 medium-sized mushrooms (about ½ pound)*
*1 medium-sized green pepper, seeded and cut into 8 pieces*
*8 cherry tomatoes*

In a bowl mix together French dressing, lemon juice, Worcestershire, and marjoram. Pour dressing mixture over lamb in a shallow ungreased baking dish; cover and refrigerate 12 to 24 hours. When ready to serve, arrange alternately on 4 long or 8 short skewers. Skewers lamb cubes, mushrooms, green pepper pieces, and tomatoes. Broil or grill 5 to 6 inches from source of heat 10 to 12 minutes on top and the same time on bottom, brushing frequently with some of the marinade. Makes 4 servings.

*Lamb en Brochette may be stored in the refrigerator about 24 hours.*

## LASAGNA

8 ounces of lasagna noodles
    (about 12 noodles)
1 tablespoon olive oil
1 pound ground beef round
½ clove garlic, peeled and
    minced
1 tablespoon dried parsley
    flakes
½ teaspoon salt
½ teaspoon dried oregano
    leaves
½ teaspoon dried sweet basil
    leaves
½ teaspoon sugar

1 6-ounce can tomato paste
1 15-ounce can tomato sauce
¼ cup water
1 16-ounce container ricotta
    or cottage cheese
1 egg, slightly beaten
1 tablespoon dried parsley
    flakes
½ teaspoon salt
⅛ teaspoon pepper
1 pound mozzarella cheese,
    thinly sliced
½ cup grated Parmesan cheese

Cook lasagna noodles according to package directions; rinse with cold water and drain. While the noodles are cooking, heat oil in a large skillet over moderately high heat (about 275° F.); add beef and cook, stirring frequently, until browned. Drain off any excess fat. Stir in garlic, the 1 tablespoon parsley flakes, the ½ teaspoon salt, the oregano, basil, sugar, tomato paste, tomato sauce, and water. Bring mixture to a boil; then reduce heat to moderately low (about 225° F.) and simmer, uncovered, for 15 minutes. Heat oven to 375° F. In a small bowl combine the ricotta cheese, egg, the 1 tablespoon parsley flakes, the ½ teaspoon salt, the pepper, and ¼ of the sliced mozzarella, finely diced. Pour enough of the meat sauce into an ungreased shallow 2-quart baking dish to just cover the bottom. Add layers of ⅓ of the noodles, ⅓ of the ricotta cheese mixture, ⅓ of the Parmesan cheese, ⅓ of the remaining mozzarella cheese slices, and ⅓ of the remaining meat sauce. Repeat layers twice more, ending with the meat sauce.* Bake, covered, 25 minutes, until the sauce is hot and cheeses are melted. Remove cover and bake 5 minutes longer. Allow lasagna to stand 5 minutes before cutting into serving squares. Makes 6 to 8 servings.

*Lasagna may be prepared up to this point the night before and refrigerated, ready for baking.

## BAKED MACARONI AND CHEESE

1  10¾-ounce can condensed
   Cheddar cheese soup,
   undiluted
1  10½-ounce can condensed
   cream of celery soup,
   undiluted

2  cups milk
1  cup (4 ounces) shredded
   Cheddar cheese
2  cups uncooked elbow
   macaroni
Tomato slices

In a large bowl mix together the two soups; gradually stir in milk. Mix in cheese and uncooked macaroni. Turn soup mixture into an ungreased shallow 1½-quart casserole or baking dish. Cover and refrigerate 12 to 24 hours. When ready to serve, heat oven to 350° F. Bake, covered, 15 minutes; stir mixture gently. Bake, uncovered, 45 minutes. Top with tomato slices and bake, uncovered, 15 minutes longer. Makes 4 to 6 servings.

*This macaroni and cheese casserole may be stored overnight in the refrigerator.*


## POLYNESIAN PORK

2  tablespoons vegetable oil
½  cup sliced peeled onion
1½ pounds boneless pork
   shoulder, cut into
   wafer-thin slices
½  cup water
½  cup cider vinegar
½  cup sugar
1  tablespoon soy sauce
½  teaspoon ground ginger
½  teaspoon salt
Few grains pepper
2  tablespoons flour

1  8¾-ounce can pineapple
   tidbits, drained, with the
   syrup reserved
1  cup diagonally sliced
   celery
1  cup slivered seeded green
   pepper (about 1
   medium-sized pepper)
1  5-ounce can bamboo
   shoots, drained and sliced
   (optional)
2  to 3 cups hot cooked rice
   (optional)

Heat oil in a large skillet over moderate heat (about 250° F.). Add onion and cook until golden brown. Remove onion with a slotted spoon and reserve. To the same skillet add pork and brown quickly over moderately high heat (about 300° F.), stirring frequently. Stir in water, vinegar, sugar, soy sauce, ginger, salt, and pepper. Simmer, covered, over low heat (about 200° F.) 20 minutes, or until pork is fork-tender. Remove any excess fat. Blend together flour and reserved pineapple syrup. Bring pork mixture to a boil over moderately high heat (about 350° F.); quickly stir in flour mixture and boil 1 minute, stirring constantly. Add cooked onion, celery, green pepper, and pineapple, and the bamboo shoots, if desired. Over low heat (about 200° F.) simmer, covered, 10 minutes. Remove from heat and cool. Pour mixture into a refrigerator container; cover and refrigerate. To serve, heat mixture in the top of a double boiler over boiling water until thoroughly heated. Serve with cooked rice, if desired. Makes 4 to 6 servings.

*This pork dish may be refrigerated 1 to 2 days before heating to serve.*


## BAKED SEAFOOD SALAD

| | |
|---|---|
| 1  cup coarsely chopped seeded green pepper | 1  5-ounce can lobster meat, drained and flaked |
| ½  cup finely chopped peeled onion | 1  7-ounce can tuna, drained and flaked |
| 2  cups coarsely chopped celery | 1  teaspoon Worcestershire sauce |
| 2  cups mayonnaise | 1  teaspoon salt |
| 2  7½-ounce cans crab meat, drained and flaked | Few grains pepper |
| | Dash Tabasco |
| 2  4½-ounce cans shrimp, drained | 1¼  cups crumbled potato chips |

In a large bowl gently mix together all ingredients except potato chips. Pour mixture into deep 2½-quart casserole. Cover and refrigerate several hours, or overnight. About 1 hour before serving time, heat oven to 350° F. Sprinkle top of casserole with potato chips. Bake, uncovered, 40 to 45 minutes, or until well heated. Do not overbake. Makes 6 to 8 servings.

*Refrigerator Storage Time: 24 hours*

## CURRIED SHRIMP

1 *10½-ounce can condensed cream of mushroom soup, undiluted*
1 *4-ounce can mushrooms, undrained*
½ *teaspoon Worcestershire sauce*
¼ *teaspoon dry mustard*
½ *teaspoon curry powder*
⅛ *teaspoon pepper*
¾ *pound shelled and deveined cooked fresh shrimp or 2 or 3 4½-ounce cans, drained and washed*

1 *tablespoon melted butter or margarine*
½ *cup slivered blanched almonds*
2 *cups hot cooked rice*
*Fruit salad (optional)*
*Chutney*

In a large bowl mix together soup, mushrooms, Worcestershire, mustard, curry powder, pepper, and shrimp. Cover mixture and refrigerate. Heat oven to 350° F. Mix melted butter and almonds on an ungreased cookie sheet and place in oven for about 6 minutes, turning frequently, until almonds are lightly toasted. About 30 minutes before serving time, heat curried shrimp in top of double boiler over boiling water until piping hot. Stir in almonds. Serve over hot fluffy rice, with a fruit salad, if desired. Serve with chutney. Makes 4 servings.
*Refrigerator Storage Time: 24 hours*

## SHRIMP CREOLE

2 *tablespoons olive oil*
1½ *pounds shelled and deveined fresh shrimp*
½ *cup thinly sliced peeled onion*
1 *8-ounce can tomato sauce with tomato bits*
1 *cup slivered seeded green pepper (about 1 medium-sized pepper)*

½ *cup sliced celery*
¾ *teaspoon salt*
⅛ *teaspoon garlic powder*
⅛ *teaspoon chili powder*
1½ *to to 2 cups hot cooked rice or noodles*

Heat the oil in a large skillet over moderate heat (about 250° F.). Add shrimp and cook just until shrimp turns pink, stirring frequently. Remove with a slotted spoon and reserve. To the same skillet add onion and cook until lightly browned. Stir in tomato sauce, green pepper, celery, salt, garlic powder, and chili powder. Simmer gently, uncovered, over moderately low heat (about 225° F.) 10 minutes. Remove mixture from heat; combine with shrimp and cool. (Mixture will appear dry.) Pour mixture into a refrigerator container; cover and refrigerate. To serve, heat creole about 15 minutes in the top of a double boiler over boiling water, stirring occasionally. Serve over cooked rice or noodles. Makes 3 to 4 servings.

*The prepared Shrimp Creole may be stored in the refrigerator 1 or 2 days.*

## CHINESE CASSEROLE

2  *7-ounce cans solid-pack tuna*
1  *10½-ounce can condensed cream of mushroom soup, undiluted*
¼  *cup water*
1  *tablespoon soy sauce*
1  *cup whole unsalted cashew nuts*
1  *4-ounce can button mushrooms, drained*
¼  *cup finely chopped peeled onion or green onion tops*
1  *cup chopped celery*
1  *3-ounce can chow mein noodles*

Drain tuna and break into bite-size pieces. In a large bowl mix mushroom soup, water, and soy sauce; add tuna, cashew nuts, mushrooms, onion, celery, and 1 cup of the noodles. Pour mixture into an ungreased deep 1-quart casserole. Cover and refrigerate. About 55 minutes before serving time, heat oven to 375° F. Sprinkle remaining 1 cup noodles over casserole and bake, uncovered, for 40 minutes. Makes 4 to 6 servings.

*Refrigerator Storage Time: 1 day*

## TUNA À LA KING

*⅓ cup butter or margarine*
*¼ pound mushrooms, sliced*
*½ cup slivered seeded green*
 *pepper*
*1 small onion, peeled and*
 *thinly sliced*
*⅓ cup all-purpose flour*
*2½ cups milk*
*½ cup light cream*
*1 teaspoon Worcestershire*
 *sauce*

*¾ teaspoon salt*
*⅛ teaspoon dry mustard*
*Few grains ground nutmeg*
*Dash of Tabasco*
*2 canned pimientos, cut into*
 *strips*
*3 7-ounce cans tuna, well*
 *drained and broken into*
 *large pieces*
*6 slices toast (optional)*

Melt butter in a saucepan over moderately low heat (about 225° F.). Cook mushrooms, green pepper, and onion until crisp-tender, about 3 minutes. Quickly stir in flour and blend until smooth. Gradually stir in milk, blending well. Stir in cream. Bring mixture to a boil over moderate heat (about 250° F.). Stir in Worcestershire, salt, mustard, nutmeg, and Tabasco; boil 1 minute, stirring constantly. Remove pan from heat and stir in pimiento and tuna. Cool. Pour mixture into a refrigerator container; cover and refrigerate. To serve, heat for about 15 minutes in the top of a double boiler over boiling water, stirring occasionally. Serve on toast if desired. Makes 1½ quarts. Makes 6 servings.
*Tuna à la King may be stored in the refrigerator 1 or 2 days.*

## VEAL CUTLET CASSEROLE

*¼ cup butter or margarine*
*⅓ cup coarsely chopped*
 *peeled onion*
*1½ pounds Italian-style veal*
 *cutlets, cut into 2-inch*
 *strips*
*1 8-ounce package medium*
 *egg noodles, cooked and*
 *drained*
*2 10½-ounce cans condensed*
 *cream of mushroom*
 *soup, undiluted*

*1 cup commercial sour*
 *cream*
*3 tablespoons chopped*
 *canned pimiento*
*¼ teaspoon dried marjoram*
 *leaves*
*Chopped fresh parsley*

Melt butter in a large skillet over moderately low heat (about 225° F.). Add onion and cook until almost tender; remove with a slotted spoon and reserve. To the same skillet add veal; cook over moderately high heat (about 300° F.) until lightly browned and tender, about 5 minutes. To veal in skillet add the onion, noodles, soup, sour cream, pimiento, and marjoram, and mix together. Turn mixture into an ungreased shallow 2-quart casserole or baking dish; cover and refrigerate. When ready to serve, heat oven to 425° F. Bake, covered, 30 minutes, or until mixture is bubbling hot. Garnish with chopped parsley. Makes 6 servings.
*This casserole may be stored in the refrigerator about 2 days.*

## VEAL VERMOUTH

2 *pounds veal cutlets, cut into serving-size pieces or a little smaller*
*Salt and pepper to taste*
*Grated Parmesan cheese*
*Butter or margarine About ½ cup*
2 *large onions, peeled and chopped*
4 *or 5 carrots, peeled and sliced not too thin*

1 *cup sliced mushrooms (about ½ pound)*
3 *chicken bouillon cubes*
1½ *cups boiling water*
½ *cup dry vermouth or any dry white wine*
2½ *cups hot cooked noodles, rice, or mashed potatoes (optional)*

Sprinkle cutlets with salt, pepper, and Parmesan cheese. Heat about half the butter in a large heavy skillet; cook cutlets over moderately high heat (about 300° F.) until lightly browned. Place veal in an ungreased deep 3-quart casserole. Add remaining butter to skillet and heat over moderate heat (about 250° F.); add onions, carrots, and mushrooms and cook until almost tender. Dissolve chicken bouillon cubes in boiling water; stir in wine. Pour wine mixture over vegetables and then pour mixture over veal cutlets. Cover and refrigerate. About 1¼ hours before serving time, heat oven to 325° F. Bake casserole, covered, for 1 hour. If desired, serve juices over noodles, rice, or mashed potatoes. Makes 6 to 8 servings.
*Refrigerator Storage Time: 24 hours*

## *Main Dishes to Make and Freeze:*

The second technique for saving time when you prepare a meal is to make meals ahead to put in the freezer. Depending on your amount of freezer storage space and how often you can set aside a good part of a day or an evening to devote to cooking, you can use this technique extensively or very little.

Many women who claim not to like cooking very much would rather go at it in one intensive session of preparation and feel they have a freezer full of meals they can depend on for several weeks. This technique allows for quantity buying, often when the meat ingredient of the main dish is on sale. If you plan to use the freeze-it-now, use-it-later plan, do have a good supply of freezer containers and freezer wrapping papers on hand: the quality of frozen food depends on a good, secure airtight wrap. It also depends upon storage in a zero-range freezer compartment. This means that the temperature in your freezer should not fluctuate beyond 0° F. and 10° F. Warmer temperatures would affect the quality of the food and its safekeeping. You can purchase an inexpensive refrigerator-freezer thermometer if you're not sure about the temperature of your freezing compartment.

If you want to be less committed to using the make-it-to-freeze plan of timesaving, you may find it convenient to double the recipe for a favorite dish: serve one and freeze the other to have a few weeks later.

## *Five Dinners for Four*
## *from Five Pounds of Ground Beef*

### BASIC MEATBALLS

> 5 *pounds ground beef chuck*  3 *tablespoons instant*
> ⅔ *cup fine dry bread crumbs*    *minced onion*
> 2½ *teaspoons salt*  3 *eggs, slightly beaten*
> ½ *teaspoon pepper*

Place beef in a large mixing bowl; in another bowl combine remaining ingredients; add to beef and combine thoroughly. With the hands shape meat mixture into 1-inch balls and place them on

ungreased cookie sheets. Cover meatballs with plastic wrap. Place covered cookie sheets in freezer until meatballs are firm, about 2 hours. Remove frozen balls from the cookie sheets and divide them into 5 equal portions; place each portion in a plastic bag or freezer container. Label each container with the contents and the date and return to the freezer. Makes 125 to 130 1-inch meatballs.
Your Time: About 45 minutes
*The meatballs may be kept 4 to 6 months in the freezer.*

## FONDUE

1 *package Basic Meatballs*     *Horseradish Sauce (recipe*
    *(about 25 meatballs)*       *follows)*
½ *pound cocktail frankfurters*   *Sweet-and-Sour Sauce (recipe*
3 *cups vegetable oil*          *follows)*
*Dill Sauce (recipe follows)*     *Curry Sauce (recipe follows)*

Remove 1 package of Basic Meatballs from the freezer to the refrigerator at least 5 hours (but not more than 24 hours) before serving time. Allow the meatballs and frankfurters to stand at room temperature 30 minutes before serving. Place oil in a fondue pot and place on the range over high heat (about 400° F.) until the temperature reaches 400° F. on a deep-fat thermometer. Then bring the pot to the table and place pot on its heat stand over high heat. Have sauces in small individual serving dishes at each place setting or use divided fondue plates. Each person spears a meatball or frankfurter on a fondue fork and cooks meat to desired doneness in the hot oil. The cooked meat is removed to the serving plate and dipped into one of the following sauces with another fork. (Do not use the fondue fork for eating the cooked meatball—it will be very hot.) Makes 4 servings.
Thawing Time: 5½ hours
Preparation Time: 10 minutes

### DILL SAUCE

½ *cup commercial sour cream*    2 *tablespoons prepared brown*
1 *medium-sized dill pickle,*        *mustard*
    *coarsely chopped (about ½*    ⅛ *teaspoon salt*
    *cup)*                 *Few grains pepper*

Combine all ingredients in a small bowl and stir to blend well. Cover and chill sauce at least 30 minutes. Sauce may be prepared several hours ahead. Makes about 1 cup.
Your Time: 5 minutes

## HORSERADISH SAUCE

2 tablespoons well-drained
  prepared horseradish
2 tablespoons light cream
1 teaspoon sugar
½ teaspoon freeze-dried
  chopped chives

⅛ teaspoon salt
Few grains pepper
3 tablespoons commercial
  sour cream

Combine all ingredients in a small bowl and stir to blend well. Cover and chill sauce at least 30 minutes. Sauce may be prepared several hours ahead. Makes about ½ cup.
Your Time: 4 minutes

## SWEET AND SOUR SAUCE

½ cup peach preserves
1 canned pimiento pod,
  drained and finely
  chopped

2 to 3 tablespoons white
  vinegar

Combine all ingredients in a small bowl and stir to blend well. Cover and chill sauce at least 30 minutes. Sauce may be prepared several hours ahead. Makes about ¾ cup.
Your Time: 5 minutes

## CURRY SAUCE

½ cup mayonnaise
3 tablespoons light cream
2 to 3 teaspoons curry
  powder

2 tablespoons finely chopped
  salted peanuts
¼ teaspoon Tabasco

Combine all ingredients in a small bowl and stir to blend well. Cover and chill sauce at least 30 minutes. Sauce may be prepared several hours ahead. Makes about ¾ cup.
Your Time: 5 minutes

## KABOBS

1 package Basic Meatballs
    (about 25 meatballs)
8 cherry tomatoes
2 medium-sized green peppers
1 4-ounce can tiny boiled
    onions
Vegetable oil
4 tablespoons butter or
    margarine

3 beef bouillon cubes,
    crumbled, or 3 envelopes
    instant beef broth mix
3 tablespoons flour
2 cups water
½ to 1 teaspoon bottled
    brown bouquet sauce
About 2 cups hot cooked rice

Remove the package of Basic Meatballs from the freezer to the refrigerator at least 5 hours (but not more than 24 hours) before preparation time. Wash and hull 8 cherry tomatoes. Remove stem, seeds, and inner white membrane from the green peppers and cut peppers into quarters and then each quarter into 2 squares. Drain onions and select 8 of uniform size. Slice the remaining onions lengthwise and reserve for sauce. Heat broiler. Arrange the kabobs in the following manner: On each of 8 6-inch skewers place 1 green pepper square, 1 meatball, 1 tomato, 1 meatball, 1 whole onion, 1 meatball and 1 green pepper square. Place kabobs on a broiler rack and brush them with oil; broil 4 inches from the heat 3 to 4 minutes; turn kabobs and broil 3 to 4 minutes on the opposite side. While kabobs are broiling, melt butter in a small saucepan over moderately low heat (about 225° F.). Add the bouillon cubes or the instant beef broth mix to the melted butter. Add the sliced onions and cook about 2 minutes. Blend in the flour. Gradually add the water, stirring constantly, until the sauce is thickened and smooth. Cook 1 minute. Add bouquet sauce to color sauce as desired. For each serving, place 2 kabobs on individual beds of rice and remove skewers if desired. Pour some of the sauce over each kabob. If there is sauce left over, pass it in a sauceboat. Makes 4 servings.
Thawing Time: 5 hours
Preparation Time: 30 minutes

## STROGANOFF

1 *package Basic Meatballs*
   *(about 25 meatballs)*
3 *tablespoons vegetable oil*
1 *4-ounce can mushroom*
   *stems and pieces, drained*
1 *medium-sized onion, peeled*
   *and thinly sliced*
3 *beef bouillon cubes*
1 *cup hot water*
½ *teaspoon salt*

2 *tablespoons catsup*
1 *teaspoon dry mustard*
2 *cups uncooked wide*
   *spinach noodles*
2 *tablespoons flour*
½ *cup cold water*
2 *tablespoons dry sherry*
   *(optional)*
1 *cup commercial sour cream*

Remove the package of Basic Meatballs from the freezer to the refrigerator at least 5 hours (but not more than 24 hours) before preparation time. Heat oil in a 10-inch skillet over moderate heat (about 250° F.). Add mushrooms and onion and cook until tender, about 5 minutes. Add meatballs and brown them on all sides. Add bouillon cubes, hot water, salt, catsup, and mustard; heat to boiling. Reduce heat to moderately low (about 225° F.) and simmer, uncovered, for 10 minutes. Cook noodles according to package directions; drain and set aside on a warm platter. In a small bowl combine the flour and water, and the sherry if desired, and stir until smooth. Gradually add the flour mixture to the meatball mixture, stirring constantly. Bring to a boil and cook 1 minute longer. Add sour cream and cook until just heated through. Do not boil. Serve on the noodles. Makes 4 servings.
Thawing Time: 5 hours
Preparation Time: 48 minutes

## ITALIAN SPAGHETTI AND MEATBALLS

1 *package Basic Meatballs*
   *(about 25 meatballs)*
2 *tablespoons olive oil*
½ *clove peeled garlic, crushed*
1 *tablespoon dried parsley*
   *flakes*
½ *teaspoon salt*
½ *teaspoon dried oregano*
   *leaves*

¼ *teaspoon dried basil leaves*
½ *teaspoon sugar*
1 *small can tomato paste*
1 *15-ounce can tomato sauce*
   *with tomato bits, onions,*
   *celery, and green peppers*
1 *16-ounce package thin*
   *spaghetti*
*Grated Parmesan cheese*

Remove the package of Basic Meatballs from the freezer to the refrigerator at least 5 hours (but not more than 24 hours) before preparation time. Heat olive oil in a Dutch oven or large heavy saucepot over moderate heat (about 250° F.). Add meatballs and brown them on all sides. Add the garlic, parsley, salt, oregano, basil, sugar, tomato paste, and tomato sauce; stir to combine and bring mixture to a boil. Reduce heat to moderately low (about 225° F.) and allow mixture to simmer, uncovered, 15 to 20 minutes. While the sauce is simmering, cook spaghetti according to package directions. Place cooked spaghetti on a heated platter and spoon the meatball sauce over the spaghetti. Sprinkle the top with grated Parmesan cheese. Makes 4 servings.
Thawing Time: 5 hours
Preparation Time: 40 to 45 minutes

## HEARTY MEATBALL SOUP

1  *package Basic Meatballs
   (about 25 meatballs)*
1  *cup uncooked elbow
   macaroni*
2  *10½-ounce cans condensed
   beef broth, undiluted*
2  *broth cans water*
¼  *teaspoon dried basil leaves*
¼  *teaspoon dried marjoram
   leaves*
¼  *teaspoon dried thyme
   leaves*

2  *carrots, peeled and thinly
   sliced (about 1 cup)*
½  *11-ounce package frozen
   peas or 1 8-ounce can
   peas, drained*
2  *large stalks celery, thinly
   sliced (about 1 cup)*
¼  *cup flour*
¼  *cup red wine (if desired;
   otherwise use water)*

Remove the package of Basic Meatballs from the freezer to the refrigerator at least 5 hours (but not more than 24 hours) before preparation time. Cook macaroni according to package directions; drain and set aside. In a large saucepan heat beef broth and the 2 broth cans of water over moderately high heat (about 275° F.) until it starts to boil. Add basil, marjoram, thyme, carrots, peas, and celery and cook, covered, 5 minutes. Drop meatballs, a few at a time, into the boiling broth, making sure that the broth keeps boiling. Cook, covered, 10 minutes. Combine the flour and the ¼ cup wine or water in a small bowl and stir until smooth. Stir some of the hot broth into the flour mixture. Gradually add the flour mixture to the rest of the

hot broth, stirring constantly so that no lumps form. Add the cooked macaroni and cook 2 to 3 minutes longer. Makes about 2 quarts soup, or 5 1½-cup main-dish servings.
Thawing Time: 5 hours
Preparation Time: 53 minutes

## BARBECUED RIBS

| | |
|---|---|
| 2 tablespoons olive oil | ½ cup water |
| 1 large onion, peeled and sliced | ¼ cup Worcestershire sauce |
| | ¼ cup prepared mustard |
| ½ cup dark molasses | 1 tablespoon salt |
| 1 cup catsup | 3 pounds beef short ribs |

Heat oil in a 10-inch skillet over moderate heat (about 250° F.). Add onion and cook until tender. Add molasses, catsup, water, Worcestershire, mustard, and salt. Simmer over moderately low heat (about 225° F.) 10 minutes. Heat oven to 350° F. Place short ribs in a 12-x-9-x-2½-inch aluminum-foil pan. Brush ribs on all sides with the barbecue sauce. Bake, uncovered, 1½ to 2 hours, or until fork-tender, basting with sauce every half hour. Turn ribs occasionally. Cool. Wrap pan for freezing and freeze. Place remaining barbecue sauce in a freezer container and freeze. When ready to use, thaw sauce in refrigerator overnight. Remove ribs from freezer and remove the freezer wrap. Bake ribs, covered tightly with aluminum foil, in a preheated 350° F. oven for 1 to 1½ hours, or until heated through, basting occasionally with some of the barbecue sauce. Place the remaining sauce in a small saucepan and heat over low heat (about 200° F.), stirring occasionally. Serve the hot sauce with the ribs. Makes 4 servings.
Your Time: 20 minutes
First Baking Time: 1½ to 2 hours
Thawing Time: Overnight
Heat-to-Serve Time: 1 to 1½ hours
*Barbecued Ribs and sauce may be kept in the freezer for 4 to 6 months.*

## BEEF RAGOUT

Salt and pepper
2½ pounds round steak, cut
    into 1-inch cubes
2 tablespoons vegetable oil
1 teaspoon soy sauce
½ cup dry red wine
2½ cups water
  ½ 10½-ounce can condensed
    beef broth, undiluted
1 large onion, peeled and
    thinly sliced

2 cups sliced mushrooms
¼ cup chopped fresh parsley
¾ teaspoon salt
½ teaspoon dried thyme
    leaves
1 10-ounce package frozen
    tiny peas
6 tablespoons water
3 tablespoons flour

Salt and pepper meat lightly. Heat oil in a large skillet or Dutch oven over moderately high heat (about 325° F.); add soy sauce. Gradually add meat cubes and cook until lightly browned on all sides; remove meat as it is browned and continue browning remaining pieces. Reduce heat to moderately low (about 225° F.). Return meat to pan and add wine, the 2½ cups water, beef broth, onion, mushrooms, parsley, the ¾ teaspoon salt, and the thyme; cover and cook for 2 hours, or until meat is fork-tender, stirring occasionally. Remove from heat and add peas, stirring until peas are just defrosted. Cool mixture and spoon it into a 12-x-9-x-2½-inch aluminum-foil pan or 2-quart foil casserole. Wrap pan for freezing and freeze. When ready to use, remove ragout from freezer and remove outer wrap. Bake, uncovered, in a preheated 350° F. oven for 1¼ hours, or until thoroughly heated. With a slotted spoon, remove meat and peas to a warm serving dish. Pour gravy into a saucepan. Pour the 6 tablespoons water into a jar with a tight lid, add flour; cover jar and shake until mixture is blended. Gradually add flour mixture to gravy and cook over moderately low heat (about 225° F.), stirring constantly, until gravy is thickened. Pour gravy over meat. Makes 8 servings.
Your Time: 45 minutes
First Cooking Time: 2 hours
Thawing Time: None
Heat-to-Serve Time: 1½ hours
*Beef Ragout may be kept in the freezer for 4 to 6 months.*

## BEEF LIVER AND MACARONI CASSEROLE

| | |
|---|---|
| 1 cup elbow macaroni | ¾ cup milk |
| 1 pound beef liver, cubed | 1½ tablespoons steak sauce |
| 1 tablespoon flour | 1 8-ounce can whole-kernel |
| 1 teaspoon salt | corn, drained |
| 2 tablespoons vegetable oil | 4 to 6 slices raw bacon |
| ½ cup sliced peeled onion | |
| 1 10½-ounce can condensed | |
| cream of mushroom | |
| soup, undiluted | |

Cook macaroni according to package directions; drain. Toss liver cubes with flour and salt in a small bowl, coating pieces well. Heat oil in a medium-sized skillet over moderate heat (about 250° F.). Add onion and liver and cook until lightly browned on all sides. Pour soup into an ungreased deep 2-quart casserole. Add milk and steak sauce and stir to blend well. Fold in macaroni, liver, onion, and corn. Cool. Wrap for freezing and freeze. When ready to use, remove from freezer and remove outer wrap. Thaw in refrigerator 18 to 24 hours; mixture will be almost thawed. Let casserole stand at room temperature 1 hour. Bake, covered, in a preheated 350° F. oven 1 hour. Meanwhile, cook bacon in a 10-inch skillet over moderately high heat (about 325° F.) until partially browned but not crisp. Drain bacon and place on top of liver mixture. Bake, uncovered, 30 minutes longer, or until heated thoroughly and bacon is crisp. Makes 4 servings.

Your Time and First Cooking Time: 35 minutes
Thawing Time: Overnight
Heat-to-Serve Time: 1½ hours
*This casserole may be kept in the freezer for 4 to 6 weeks.*

## CALICO-BEAN HOT POT

| | |
|---|---|
| ½ pound raw bacon, cut into | 2 teaspoons white vinegar |
| 1-inch pieces | ½ teaspoon salt |
| 1 pound ground beef round | 1 16-ounce can pork and |
| ½ cup chopped peeled onion | beans |
| ½ cup catsup | 1 16-ounce can lima beans, |
| ½ cup firmly packed | drained |
| dark-brown sugar | 1 16-ounce can kidney beans, |
| 1 teaspoon prepared mustard | undrained |

Heat oven to 325° F. Cook bacon in a 10-inch skillet over moderately high heat (about 325° F.) until crisp. Remove bacon from skillet and drain on paper towels. Drain off all but 2 tablespoons of the bacon fat and reserve drained fat. Add beef to skillet and cook over moderate heat (about 250° F.) until brown and crumbly, stirring occasionally. Remove beef from skillet and reserve. Add 2 tablespoons of the reserved bacon fat to the skillet. Add onion and cook until lightly browned. Combine beef and onion with remaining ingredients in a deep 3-quart casserole lined with heavy-duty foil with enough overlap for a double-fold seal. Stir mixture to blend well. Bake, uncovered, 1½ hours. Cool. Seal foil and freeze. When solidly frozen, remove foil packet from casserole and return packet to freezer. When ready to use, remove foil from frozen mixture and slip frozen block into the casserole in which it was frozen. Cover casserole with foil and bake in a preheated 350° F. oven 1½ hours, or until thoroughly heated, stirring mixture occasionally as it thaws. Makes 8 servings.

Your Time: 34 minutes
First Baking Time: 1½ hours
Thawing Time: None
Heat-to-Serve Time: 1½ hours
*This casserole may be kept in the freezer for 4 to 6 weeks.*

## CHICKEN À L'ORANGE

| | |
|---|---|
| 2  3-pound broiler-fryer chickens, cut into quarters | 1  cup sliced mushrooms |
| ½ cup flour | 2  cups orange juice |
| Salt | ¼ cup dry sherry |
| Pepper | 1  tablespoon dark-brown sugar |
| Paprika | ¾ teaspoon salt |
| 1  large onion, peeled and thinly sliced | 1  large orange, thinly sliced |
| ½ cup chopped seeded green pepper | 2  tablespoons water |
| | 2  tablespoons cornstarch |

Heat oven to 375° F. Wash and dry chicken; coat chicken with flour and sprinkle with salt, pepper, and paprika. Put one quartered chicken in each of 2 shallow 12-x-9-x-2½-inch aluminum-foil pans. Sprinkle half the onion, green pepper, and mushrooms over each chicken. Mix together orange juice, sherry, brown sugar, and the ¾ teaspoon salt in a saucepan; place over moderate heat (about 250° F.) until mixture comes to a boil. Pour half the orange juice mixture over each chicken. Arrange half orange slices over each chicken. Cover pans with aluminum foil and bake 1 to 1¼ hours, or until fork-tender. Cool and wrap pans for freezing and freeze. When ready to use, remove chicken from freezer and remove outer wrap. Cover pans with aluminum foil. Bake chicken in a preheated 350° F. oven for 45 minutes. Increase oven temperature to 400° F.; remove covers from pans and continue heating for 40 minutes, basting occasionally with the sauce in the pans. Place chicken and sliced orange on a warm platter. Drain gravy from pans into a saucepan. (There will be about 3 cups.) Skim off excess fat. Mix water and cornstarch together and gradually stir into the gravy. Cook over moderately low heat (about 225° F.), stirring constantly, until gravy is thickened. Serve over chicken. Makes 8 servings.

Your Time: 26 minutes
First Baking Time: 1 to 1¼ hours
Thawing Time: None
Heat-to-Serve Time: 1½ hours
*This casserole may be kept in the freezer for 4 to 6 months.*

## CHICKEN WINGS ORIENTAL

| | |
|---|---|
| *2 pounds chicken wings* | *1 8-ounce can tomato sauce* |
| *3 tablespoons vegetable oil* | *2 tablespoons soy sauce* |
| *½ teaspoon salt* | *1 teaspoon sugar* |
| *¼ teaspoon pepper* | *2 tablespoons cornstarch* |
| *2 chicken bouillon cubes* | *2 tablespoons water* |
| *2 cups boiling water* | *2 cups hot cooked rice* |
| *¾ cup sliced green onion or scallions* | *Chopped fresh parsley* |

Wash and dry chicken wings. Heat oil in a 10-inch skillet over moderately high heat (about 275° F.). Add wings and cook until browned on all sides, turning occasionally. Sprinkle with salt and pepper. Dissolve chicken bouillon cubes in the 2 cups boiling water. Pour liquid over wings in skillet. Reduce heat to moderately low (about 225° F.); cover and simmer 45 minutes, or until chicken is tender. Add onion and tomato sauce. Stir to blend well, and simmer 5 minutes. In a small bowl combine soy sauce, sugar, cornstarch, and water and blend well. Gradually pour into skillet, stirring constantly until mixture is thickened and smooth. Cool. Spoon mixture into a 12-x-9-x-2½-inch aluminum-foil pan. Wrap for freezing and freeze. When ready to use, remove from freezer and remove outer wrap. Bake, covered, in a preheated 350° F. oven for 1 hour. Uncover,

increase temperature to 400° F. and bake 40 minutes longer, or until heated through. Serve with cooked rice; garnish with parsley. Makes 4 servings.
Your Time: 25 minutes
First Cooking Time: 50 minutes
Thawing Time: None
Heat-to-Serve Time: 1 hour and 40 minutes
*This casserole may be kept in the freezer for 4 to 6 months.*

## DEVILED FLANK STEAK

2 *pounds flank steak*
1 *4-ounce can chopped mushroom stems and pieces*
½ *cup chopped peeled onion*
¼ *cup chopped fresh parsley*
4 *slices raw bacon, finely chopped*

2 *tablespoons vegetable oil*
2 *8-ounce cans tomato sauce*
1 *beef bouillon cube*
1 *teaspoon prepared mustard*
½ *teaspoon Worcestershire sauce*
1 *teaspoon sugar*
¼ *teaspoon pepper*

Score flank steak on one side in a diamond pattern, making cuts ⅛ inch deep. Drain mushrooms, reserving liquid. In a 10-inch skillet combine mushrooms, onion, parsley, and bacon and cook over moderate heat (about 250° F.), stirring occasionally, until onion is tender. Spread vegetable mixture evenly over unscored side of steak. Carefully roll up steak and fasten roll with string every 2 inches. Secure ends with skewers. Heat oil in a Dutch oven over moderately high heat (about 325° F.). Brown steak roll on all sides. Reduce heat to moderately low (about 225° F.). Add mushroom liquid, tomato sauce, bouillon cube, mustard, Worcestershire, sugar, and pepper. Simmer, covered, 1½ to 2 hours, or until fork-tender. Cool. Place steak and gravy in a 12-x-9-x-2½-inch aluminum-foil pan or shallow 2-quart foil casserole. Wrap for freezing and freeze. When ready to use, remove from freezer and remove outer wrap. Bake, covered, in a preheated 350° F. oven 1½ hours, or until heated through. Makes 4 to 6 servings.
Your Time: 30 minutes
First Cooking Time: 1½ to 2 hours
Thawing Time: None
Heat-to-Serve Time: 1½ hours
*This casserole may be kept in the freezer for 4 to 6 months.*

## BRIDE'S GOULASH

| | |
|---|---|
| 1 *pound broad egg noodles* | 1 *28-ounce can whole* |
| 3 *tablespoons vegetable oil* | *tomatoes, undrained* |
| 1 *large onion, peeled and* | 1 *16-ounce can stewed* |
| *finely chopped* | *tomatoes* |
| 1 *medium-sized green pepper,* | 2 *teaspoons dried oregano* |
| *seeded and finely chopped* | *leaves* |
| 1 *cup sliced mushrooms* | 2 *teaspoons salt* |
| 2 *pounds round beef ground* | ¼ *teaspoon pepper* |

Cook noodles in boiling salted water as directed on package. Heat oven to 350° F. Heat oil in large skillet over moderate heat (about 250° F.); add onion and green pepper and cook until tender. Add mushrooms and cook until tender. Place spoonfuls of the meat over the vegetables and cook and stir until meat loses its pink color. Combine cooked vegetable-meat mixture, whole tomatoes, stewed tomatoes, oregano, salt, and pepper. Stir in noodles. Spoon mixture into 2 12-x-9-x-2½-inch aluminum-foil pans. Cool and wrap for freezing; place in freezer.. When ready to use, remove goulash from freezer and remove outer wrap. Bake, covered, in a preheated 350° F. oven for about 2 hours, or until thoroughly heated. Makes 8 servings.

Your Time and First Cooking Time: 32 minutes
Thawing Time: None
Heat-to-Serve Time: 2 hours
*This casserole may be kept in the freezer for 4 to 6 months.*

## LAMB CURRY

| | |
|---|---|
| 3 *pounds boneless lamb* | ¾ *cup chopped celery* |
| *shoulder, cut into ¾-inch* | 1 *tablespoon curry powder* |
| *cubes* | ¾ *teaspoon salt* |
| ½ *teaspoon salt* | ¼ *cup flour* |
| 1 *quart boiling water* | 1 *apple, peeled, cored, and* |
| 6 *tablespoons butter or* | *sliced* |
| *margarine* | ¾ *cup bottled chutney* |
| ¾ *cup chopped peeled onion* | 4 *cups hot cooked rice* |

Cook lamb in the ½ teaspoon salt and the water over moderately low heat (about 225° F.) until tender, about 1½ to 2 hours. Drain and measure 3¾ cups of the stock. Melt butter in a large skillet over moderate heat (about 250° F.); add onion and celery and cook about 5 minutes, until tender. Stir in curry, the ¾ teaspoon salt and the flour. Add apple and cook a few minutes. Gradually add the 3¾ cups stock. Cook over moderately low heat (about 225° F.), stirring constantly, until thickened. Add cooked lamb and chutney. Cool and spoon into freezer containers and freeze. When ready to use, thaw curry in refrigerator overnight and heat in a saucepan over low heat (about 200° F.), stirring frequently. Serve over rice. Makes 8 servings.

Your Time: 25 minutes
First Cooking Time: 1½ to 2 hours
Thawing Time: Overnight
Heat-to-Serve Time: 20 minutes
*This Lamb Curry may be kept in the freezer for 4 to 6 months.*


## LAMB WITH LEMON SAUCE

| | |
|---|---|
| 1  teaspoon salt | ½ cup water |
| ⅛ teaspoon pepper | ½ cup dry white wine |
| ¼ teaspoon garlic powder | 2 tablespoons chopped fresh |
| 3 pounds lean boneless lamb |    dill |
|    shoulder, cut into 1½-inch | 2 tablespoons chopped fresh |
|    cubes |    parsley |
| 3 tablespoons vegetable oil | ½ teaspoon salt |
| 2 tablespoons butter or | 3 stalks celery with leaves |
|    margarine | 3 small zucchini, sliced |
| 1 large onion, peeled and | 4 egg yolks |
|    finely chopped | 6 tablespoons lemon juice |
| 2 tablespoons flour | |

Combine the 1 teaspoon salt, the pepper, and garlic powder in a small bowl. Add lamb cubes a few at a time and turn to coat pieces well. Heat oil in a Dutch oven over moderately high heat (about 275° F.). Add lamb cubes and brown meat on all sides. Remove meat with a slotted spoon as it browns. Add butter to Dutch oven and reduce heat to moderately low (about 225° F.). Add onion and cook until tender. Add flour and stir to blend well. Pour in water and wine and cook, stirring constantly, until mixture is thickened and smooth. Return meat to Dutch oven. Add dill, parsley, and the ½ teaspoon salt; cover and simmer 1 hour. Cut celery stalks diagonally into 2-inch slices. Chop celery leaves. Add zucchini and celery and leaves to Dutch oven. Cover and simmer 10 minutes. Cool. Pour mixture into a 2-quart freezer container. Freeze. When ready to use, thaw lamb mixture completely in refrigerator. Place mixture in a Dutch oven. Cook, covered, over moderately low heat (about 225° F.) 30 minutes, or until heated through. In a small bowl beat egg yolks until thick. Beat in lemon juice, 1 tablespoon at a time. Gradually pour 1 cup of the hot liquid from lamb mixture into the egg yolk mixture while beating vigorously. Slowly pour egg yolk mixture back into Dutch oven, stirring constantly, until mixture is smooth and thickened. Do not let mixture come to a boil. Makes 8 servings.

Your Time: 50 minutes
First Cooking Time: 1 hour
Thawing Time: Overnight
Heat-to-Serve Time: 35 minutes
*The lamb mixture may be kept in the freezer for 4 to 6 months.*

## HAMBURGER AND NOODLES STROGANOFF

¾ of an 8-ounce package
   medium egg noodles
   (about 3½ cups raw)
¼ cup butter or margarine
½ cup finely chopped peeled
   onion
1 4-ounce can sliced
   mushrooms, drained
1 pound ground beef round
1 tablespoon flour
½ teaspoon garlic salt

1 8-ounce can tomato sauce
   with tomato bits
¼ cup Burgundy wine
1 10½-ounce can condensed
   beef broth, undiluted
1 teaspoon salt
¼ teaspoon pepper
1 cup commercial sour cream
½ cup grated Parmesan cheese
Grated Parmesan cheese

Cook noodles as directed on package; drain. In a large skillet melt butter over moderately low heat (about 225° F.). Add onion and mushrooms and cook until tender. Add beef and cook, stirring occasionally, until brown and crumbly. Drain off excess fat. Stir flour into meat mixture and blend well. Add garlic salt, tomato sauce, Burgundy, beef broth, salt, and pepper and blend well. Simmer, uncovered, 10 minutes, stirring occasionally. Blend in sour cream and remove from heat. Line a 2-quart casserole with heavy-duty aluminum foil, leaving enough overlap for a double-fold seal. Arrange alternate layers of beef mixture and noodles in casserole. Sprinkle the ½ cup cheese over top. Wrap for freezing and freeze. When solidly frozen, remove foil packet from casserole and return packet to freezer. When ready to use, remove packet from freezer and remove foil from frozen mixture, slip solid block into the

casserole in which it was frozen. Bake, covered, in a preheated 375° F. oven 2 hours, or until heated through, stirring occasionally as it heats. Serve with additional cheese. Makes 4 servings.
Your Time: 30 minutes
First Cooking Time: 10 minutes
Thawing Time: None
Heat-to-Serve Time: 2 hours
*This casserole may be kept in the freezer for 4 to 6 months.*

## SPICY MEATBALLS

| | |
|---|---|
| 2 pounds lean round beef ground | 3 tablespoons water |
| 2 teaspoons salt | 1 12-ounce bottle chili sauce |
| ½ cup dark seedless raisins | 1½ cups water |
| 2 teaspoons sweet sherry | 1 8-ounce jar currant jelly |
| 1 teaspoon prepared mustard | ¾ teaspoon salt |
| | ½ cup water |
| | ¼ cup flour |

In a bowl mix together beef, the 2 teaspoons salt, raisins, sherry, mustard, and the 3 tablespoons water. Shape slightly rounded tablespoonfuls of mixture into balls and place in a 12-x-9-x-2½-inch aluminum-foil pan or a 2-quart foil casserole. Heat oven to 350° F. Mix chili sauce, the 1½ cups water, the currant jelly, and the ¾ teaspoon salt in a saucepan. Place over moderate heat (about 250° F.) and heat until boiling. Remove from heat and pour mixture over meat balls. Cover pan with aluminum foil and bake 1 hour. Cool and wrap for freezing and freeze. When ready to use, remove meatballs from freezer and remove outer wrap. Bake, uncovered, in a preheated 350° F. oven for 1 hour, or until thoroughly heated. With a slotted spoon remove meat balls and place in a warm serving dish. Pour gravy into a saucepan. Pour the ½ cup water into a jar with a tight lid; add the flour; cover jar. Shake until blended. Gradually add flour mixture to gravy and cook over moderate heat (about 250° F.), stirring constantly, until gravy is thickened. Serve gravy with meat balls. Makes 8 servings.
Your Time: 23 minutes
First Baking Time: 1 hour
Thawing Time: None
Heat-to-Serve Time: 1 hour and 10 minutes
*The meatballs may be kept in the freezer for 4 to 6 months.*

## POT ROAST WITH PINEAPPLE SAUCE

1 3½-to-4½-pound blade pot roast
Salt and pepper
1 large onion, peeled and thinly sliced
1 15-ounce can tomato sauce

1 13¼-ounce can pineapple chunks, undrained
2 tablespoons brown sugar
2 teaspoons salt
½ cup water (optional)
¼ cup flour (optional)

Heat oven to 300° F. Place pot roast in a 12-x-9-x-2½-inch aluminum-foil pan; sprinkle with salt and pepper. Arrange onion over meat. Mix together tomato sauce, pineapple, brown sugar, and the 2 teaspoons salt; pour over meat. Cover pan with aluminum foil and bake 2½ to 3½ hours, or until fork-tender. Cool and wrap for freezing; place in freezer. When ready to use, remove pot roast from freezer and remove outer wrap. Bake, covered, in a preheated 350° F. oven 3 hours. Uncover and continue heating for 30 minutes, or until thoroughly heated. If a thickened gravy is desired, remove meat to a warm platter. Pour gravy into a saucepan. Pour ½ cup water into a jar with a tight lid; add ¼ cup flour; cover jar and shake until blended. Gradually add flour mixture to gravy and cook over moderately low heat (about 225° F.), stirring constantly, until gravy is thickened. Pass the gravy separately. Makes 6 servings.
Your Time: 5 minutes
First Baking Time: 2½ to 3½ hours
Thawing Time: None
Heat-to-Serve Time: 3 hours and 40 minutes
*The pot roast may be kept in the freezer for 4 to 6 months.*

## MUSHROOM-ONION POT ROAST

1 3½-pound boneless beef arm roast
1 envelope dry onion soup mix
1 10½-ounce can condensed cream of mushroom soup, undiluted

6 to 8 medium-sized baking potatoes, washed (optional)

Heat oven to 350° F. Place a large sheet of heavy-duty foil in the bottom of a 9-inch square cake pan. Place roast in the center of the foil. Sprinkle the dry onion soup mix over roast. Spoon the can of mushroom soup over roast. Seal foil with a double fold and seal all edges well. Bake 3 hours. Cool. Wrap pan for freezing, with foil left intact on roast, and freeze. When ready to use, remove from freezer and remove outer foil wrap. Bake roast in its foil packet in a preheated 350° F. oven about 2½ hours, or until heated. If desired, place potatoes in oven with roast 1 hour before ready to serve. Makes 6 to 8 servings.

Your Time: 4 minutes
First Baking Time: 3 hours
Thawing Time: None
Heat-to-Serve Time: 2½ hours
*This casserole may be kept in the freezer for 4 to 6 months.*

## BAKED SPARERIBS AND SAUERKRAUT

1  *tablespoon salt*
½ *teaspoon pepper*
½ *teaspoon caraway seeds*
2  *27-ounce cans sauerkraut,*
    *well drained*

3  *pounds pork spareribs, cut*
    *into serving-size pieces*
2  *tablespoons butter or*
    *margarine*

Heat oven to 350° F. In a small bowl combine salt, pepper, and caraway seeds. In a 4-quart freezer-to-oven casserole or a Dutch oven arrange alternate layers of sauerkraut and spareribs, sprinkling each layer with some of the seasoning mixture. Dot top with butter. Bake, covered, 2 hours, or until meat is fork-tender. Cool. Wrap for freezing and freeze. When ready to use, remove from freezer and remove outer wrap. Bake, covered, in a preheated 350° F. oven about 2 hours, or until completely thawed and heated through. Makes 6 to 8 servings.

Your Time: 11 minutes
First Baking Time: 2 hours
Thawing Time: None
Heat-to-Serve Time: 2 hours
*This casserole may be kept in the freezer for 4 to 6 months.*

## SWISS VEAL CASSEROLE

| | |
|---|---|
| ¼ cup all-purpose flour | 1 small green pepper, seeded |
| 1 teaspoon salt | and sliced |
| ⅛ teaspoon pepper | 1 cup tomato juice |
| 2 pounds boneless veal steak, | 1 10-ounce package frozen |
| 1 inch thick | Fordhook lima beans |
| 3 tablespoons vegetable oil | 1 teaspoon salt |
| 2 medium-sized onions, | Few grains pepper |
| peeled and sliced | |

Combine flour, the 1 teaspoon salt, and the ⅛ teaspoon pepper in a small bowl and coat veal well with the mixture. Heat oil in a 10-inch skillet over moderately high heat (about 275° F.). Add veal and brown well on both sides. Place veal in an ungreased shallow 3-quart baking dish. Add onion and green pepper to skillet and stir to coat with the drippings. Stir in tomato juice and blend well. Pour over veal. Wrap for freezing and freeze. When ready to use, thaw veal in refrigerator 18 to 24 hours. Bake, covered with aluminum foil, in a preheated 350° F. oven for 40 minutes. While veal is baking, remove lima beans from freezer, open box, and let beans thaw partially. Separate beans and sprinkle around edge of baking dish. Sprinkle the 1 teaspoon salt and the few grains pepper over the beans. Re-cover the baking dish tightly with aluminum foil and bake 40 minutes longer, or until veal is fork-tender. Makes 4 to 6 servings.
Your Time and First Cooking Time: 30 minutes
Thawing Time: Overnight
Heat-to-Serve Time: 1 hour and 20 minutes
*This casserole may be kept in the freezer for 4 to 6 months.*

## *Main Dishes from a Pressure Cooker*

The third time-saving technique is to use an appliance called a pressure cooker (sometimes it's called a pressure pan). Pressure cooking takes about one-third the time of conventional cooking methods. If time is your scarcest ingredient when you prepare meals and you can't devote an afternoon to the preparation of such flavorful and economical dishes as chicken in wine, Sauerbraten, or a succulent corned beef, then pressure cooking may be your answer.

A pressure cooker looks very much like an ordinary saucepan with a lid and a handle. The difference begins with the rubber gasket (a sealing ring) that fits around the rim of the lid. When the pan is closed, the gasket makes a tight seal between the lid and the pan and prevents steam from escaping. A vent in the lid permits air to be expelled as the liquid in the pan comes to a boil. A control regulates the pressure of the steam as the cooking takes place. In a pressure pan, food is cooked at temperatures above the boiling point—the higher the pressure, the higher the temperature and the shorter the cooking time. The cooking takes place in steam, not air.

Pressure cookers may be electric or nonelectric. They are made of stamped aluminum, cast aluminum, or stainless steel. A rack is included that may be placed in the bottom of the pan for cooking certain foods; in most cases it is not used.

The first rule in using a pressure cooker is to follow the instructions that come with your cooker. If you've lost or mislaid your instruction book, write to the manufacturer, specifying the model number of your cooker, and get a new book. Pressure regulators vary on different models; for best results you should use the pressure recommendations for your particular cooker.

When you start using a pressure cooker, stick at first with the recipes in your instruction book until you're familiar with the workings of your cooker and with the amount of liquid specified for a given food. As you become familiar with your cooker, you can adapt some of your favorite recipes to pressure-cooker use. That's what we did in the pressure-cooker-tested recipes that follow.

### BLANQUETTE DE MOUTON

| | |
|---|---|
| 2 *tablespoons vegetable oil* | 1 *teaspoon salt* |
| 1½ *pounds boneless lamb, cut into 2-inch cubes* | *Few grains pepper* |
| | ½ *cup heavy cream* |
| ¾ *cup chicken broth* | 1 *egg yolk* |
| 1 *medium-sized onion, peeled and thinly sliced* | 1 *tablespoon flour* |
| 2 *shallots, peeled and chopped* | |

Heat an uncovered 4-quart pressure cooker over moderately high heat (about 375° F.). If electric pressure cooker is used, turn heat selector to 375° F.). Heat oil and cook meat cubes until lightly browned on all sides. Turn off heat. Add broth, onion, shallots, salt, and pepper; close cooker cover securely. Bring to 15 pounds pressure (as manufacturer directs) and cook 15 minutes. (For electric pressure cooker see following note.) Reduce pressure immediately. Remove meat to serving platter. Strain meat juices. In a bowl beat cream, egg

yolk, and flour together with rotary beater; gradually add meat juices. Pour mixture back into cooker; cook and stir, uncovered, over low heat (about 200° F.) until gravy is thickened. Serve gravy over meat. Makes 4 to 6 servings.
Your Time: 28 minutes
Cooking Time (includes bringing pot up to pressure): 25 minutes

*Note:* Set heat control at 425° F. When pressure is reached, turn dial slowly to left until pilot light goes out. Cook for same amount of time given for regular pressure cooker.

### POLYNESIAN SPARERIBS

| | |
|---|---|
| 1 8¾-ounce can crushed pineapple | ½ cup dry sherry |
| 1½ teaspoons dry mustard | 1 tablespoon cider vinegar |
| 2 to 3 pounds pork spareribs, cut into 2- to 2½-inch pieces | 1 tablespoon soy sauce |
| | 1 small clove garlic, peeled and crushed |
| 1 teaspoon salt | 1 tablespoon ground ginger |
| 1 tablespoon shortening | 2 tablespoons dark-brown sugar |

Drain pineapple and reserve juice. Rub dry mustard on spareribs. Sprinkle with salt. Heat an uncovered 4-quart pressure cooker over moderately high heat (about 350° F.). (If electric pressure cooker is used, turn heat selector to 350° F.) Melt shortening and brown spareribs on all sides. Turn off heat. In a bowl blend pineapple juice, sherry, vinegar, soy sauce, garlic, and ginger. Sprinkle ribs with sugar. Pour in pineapple-juice mixture. Close cooker cover securely. Bring to 15 pounds pressure (as manufacturer directs) and cook 15 minutes. (For electric pressure cooker see note on page 000.) Reduce pressure immediately. Stir in crushed pineapple. Makes 3 to 4 servings.
Your Time: 33 minutes
Cooking Time (includes bringing pot up to pressure): 25 minutes

## SWEET AND SOUR PORK

1½ pounds boneless pork
2 tablespoons vegetable oil
1 20½-ounce can pineapple
   chunks
3 tablespoons cider vinegar
1 tablespoon soy sauce
¼ cup firmly packed
   dark-brown sugar
½ teaspoon salt

⅓ cup thinly sliced peeled
   onion
½ large green pepper, seeded
   and cut into 1½-inch
   strips
2 tablespoons water
1 tablespoon cornstarch
2 cups hot cooked rice

Cut meat into thin strips, 3 to 4 inches long and 1 inch wide. Heat a 4-quart pressure cooker over moderately high heat (about 375° F.). (If electric pressure cooker is used, turn heat selector to 375° F.) Heat oil and brown meat on all sides. Turn off heat. Pour off excess fat. Drain pineapple and reserve juice. In a bowl mix pineapple juice, vinegar, soy sauce, brown sugar, and salt; pour mixture over meat. Close cooker cover securely. Bring to 15 pounds pressure (as manufacturer directs) and cook 15 minutes. (For electric pressure cooker see note on page 000.) Reduce pressure immediately. Add pineapple chunks, onion, and green pepper to pork; close cooker cover securely; bring to 15 pounds pressure and cook 2 minutes. Reduce pressure immediately. Remove meat, vegetables and fruit to a warm platter. In a bowl blend water and cornstarch together; stir into juices in cooker. Cook and stir over moderate heat (about 250° F.) until thickened. Add gravy to meat and serve over rice. Makes 4 servings.
Your Time: 38 minutes
Cooking Time (includes bringing pot up to pressure): 37 minutes

## VEAL MARENGO

2 tablespoons vegetable oil
2 pounds veal cut into
   1½-inch cubes
1 16-ounce can tomatoes,
   undrained and pressed
   through a strainer
½ cup dry white wine
¼ cup tomato paste
2 tablespoons chopped peeled
   onion

1 small clove garlic, peeled
   and crushed
¾ teaspoon salt
8 fresh mushroom caps
8 peeled whole small white
   onions
⅓ cup heavy cream
2 tablespoons flour

Heat an uncovered 4-quart pressure cooker over high heat (about 400° F.). (If electric pressure cooker is used, turn heat to 400° F.) Heat oil and brown meat quickly on all sides. Turn off heat. Drain off excess fat. Add tomatoes, wine, tomato paste, chopped onion, garlic, and salt, and mix well. Close cooker cover securely. Bring to 15 pounds pressure (as manufacturer directs) and cook 5 minutes. (For electric pressure cooker see note on page 000.) Reduce pressure immediately. Add mushrooms and whole onions. Close cooker cover securely. Bring to 15 pounds pressure and cook 10 minutes. Reduce pressure immediately. Remove meat and vegetables to a warm platter. Put cream and flour in a small jar with a tight-fitting lid; cover jar and shake until mixture is blended. Gradually stir jar into juices in cooker; cook and stir over moderate heat (about 250° F.) until gravy is thickened. Pour gravy over meat and vegetables. Makes 4 to 6 servings.

Your Time: 40 minutes

Cooking Time (includes bringing pot up to pressure): 45 minutes

# CHAPTER

# X

# *Timesaver Menus*

Once you've become acquainted with the recipes in this book, you'll be able to put together timesaving menus that match ingredients you have on hand, the number of people you expect for dinner, your own family's likes and dislikes, and the amount of time you'd like to spend in the kitchen. But meantime, you might practice your timesaving techniques with several of the sample menus from this chapter.

In the first six of the fifteen-minute meal plans you'll find an order of preparation along with recipes, also given in their order of preparation. This kind of list-making approach to a menu can help you save time once you've actually begun the meal. Then you will find several more fifteen-minute, thirty-minute, forty-five minute, and one-hour menus, all made with recipes in this book. (You'll find the page number for each recipe listed with the menus.)

Two special menu sections follow—especially designed for emergency use when there's no time to shop. There are last-minute meals from the pantry shelf and last-minute meals from the freezer. Have the ingredients for one or more of these meals on hand, replenish them when needed, and you'll never be caught with nothing for dinner.

# Fifteen-Minute Menus with Work Plans

## Dinner for Two

---

*\* Steak Diane*
*\* Saucy French Fries*
*\* Deviled Carrots*
*Cherry Tomatoes and Watercress*
*\* Waffle Strawberry Shortcake*
*Coffee      Milk*

\* Recipe follows

---

**Advance Preparation:**
   Remove strawberries from freezer and place in lower part of refrigerator to defrost.
   Wash and chill tomatoes and watercress.
**Order of Preparation:**
   1. Deviled Carrots.
   2. Saucy French Fries—heat potatoes and prepare sauce, but combine just before serving.
   3. Steak Diane.
   4. Waffle Strawberry Shortcake—just before serving.

## DEVILED CARROTS

2 tablespoons butter or
   margarine
1 16-ounce can small whole
   carrots, drained
1½ tablespoons light-brown
   sugar

1 teaspoon dry mustard
Dash of Tabasco
¼ teaspoon salt
Few grains pepper

Melt butter in a saucepan over moderately low heat (about 225° F.); add carrots and cook about 3 minutes until coated with butter. Add brown sugar, mustard, Tabasco, salt, and pepper; mix well. Cover and heat 5 minutes, or until serving time, stirring frequently. Makes 2 generous servings.

## SAUCY FRENCH FRIES

| | |
|---|---|
| 1 tablespoon butter or margarine | 2 teaspoons flour |
| 1 9-ounce package frozen French fried potatoes | ¾ cup commercial sour cream |
| ½ teaspoon salt | 1 tablespoon freeze-dried chopped chives |
| 1½ tablespoons butter or margarine | ¼ teaspoon dried marjoram leaves |

Melt the 1 tablespoon butter in a large skillet over moderate heat (about 250° F.); add potatoes and cook, turning frequently, about 5 minutes, or until lightly browned. Sprinkle potatoes with salt. Melt the remaining 1½ tablespoons butter in small saucepan over moderately low heat (about 225° F.); blend in flour. Stir in sour cream, chives, and marjoram; heat, stirring constantly, until smooth, but do not boil. Put potatoes in a serving dish and pour hot sauce over them. Makes 2 servings.

## STEAK DIANE

| | |
|---|---|
| 1 tablespoon butter or margarine | 1 tablespoon dried parsley flakes |
| 1 tablespoon chopped green onion or scallions | 1 tablespoon Worcestershire sauce |
| 1¼ to 1½ pounds thinly sliced sirloin steak | 1 tablespoon bottled steak sauce |
| 1 tablespoon butter or margarine | 2 to 3 tablespoons cognac |
| 1 tablespoon freeze-dried chopped chives | |

Melt the 1 tablespoon butter in a medium-sized skillet over moderate heat (about 250° F.); add onion and cook 1 minute. Add steak and brown quickly on both sides over moderately high heat (about 350° F.). Remove skillet from heat. Remove steak to a platter. Add the remaining 1 tablespoon butter, chives, parsley, Worcestershire, and steak sauce to skillet; heat over moderate heat (about 250° F.) until mixture bubbles. Add steak and any meat juices from platter; cook about 1 minute, or until steak is done to the desired degree of doneness. Add cognac and heat; ignite with a match to flame. Remove steaks to warm serving plates and pour sauce over them. Makes 2 servings.

## WAFFLE STRAWBERRY SHORTCAKE

*2 frozen waffles*
*1 9-ounce package frozen*
*strawberries, defrosted*
*⅛ teaspoon almond extract*

*2 tablespoons slivered*
*almonds*
*Ready-whipped cream*

Heat waffles as directed on package. In a bowl mix strawberries, almond extract, and almonds; spoon strawberry mixture over waffles and garnish with whipped cream. Makes 2 servings.

## Dinner for Four

*Glazed Ham Steak*
*Herbed Zucchini*
*Hearts of Lettuce Salad with Russian Dressing*
*Poppy-Seed Rolls*
*Butter*
*Crackers and Cheese*
*Coffee      Tea*

* Recipe follows

**Advance Preparation:**
  Wash and chill salad greens.
**Order of Preparation:**
  1. Herbed Zucchini.
  2. Glazed Ham Steak.
  3. Prepare salad.
  4. Arrange crackers and cheese.
  5. Arrange Poppy-Seed Rolls.

## HERBED ZUCCHINI

*2 pounds zucchini*
*Boiling salted water*
*2 tablespoons butter or*
*margarine*

*⅛ teaspoon dried marjoram*
*leaves*
*Salt and pepper*

Wash and cut zucchini into ¾-inch cubes. Cook in a saucepan in boiling salted water over moderately low heat (about 225° F.) 10 minutes, or until tender. Drain in a colander; mash zucchini slightly with back of wooden spoon to remove excess moisture. Put squash back in saucepan and stir in butter and marjoram. Season to taste with salt and pepper. Heat to serving temperature. Makes 4 servings.

### GLAZED HAM STEAK

2  *tablespoons butter or*
  *margarine*
1  *1½-pound center-cut ham*
  *steak, cut about 1 inch*
  *thick*

1  *16-ounce can apricot halves,*
  *undrained*
¼  *cup dark corn syrup*
¼  *cup chopped walnuts*

Melt butter in a medium-sized skillet over moderately high heat (about 300° F.); add ham steak and brown quickly on both sides. Remove skillet from heat. Drain apricot halves and reserve 2 tablespoons of the juice. Add corn syrup, walnuts, apricots, and the 2 tablespoons juice to steaks in skillet. Cover, return to heat, and simmer over moderately low heat (about 225° F.) 10 minutes, stirring occasionally. Arrange ham on platter with apricots around it. Makes 4 servings.

## Dinner for Four

---

\* *Barbecued Liver*
\* *Hominy*      \* *Buttered Spinach*
*Celery Hearts*
\* *Frozen Fruit Ice*
*Coffee*      *Tea*

\* Recipe follows

---

**Advance Preparation:**
  Prepare Frozen Fruit Ice at least 4 hours before serving.
  Clean celery hearts and chill in refrigerator.
**Order of Preparation:**
  1.  Frozen Fruit Ice (earlier in day).
  2.  Barbecued Liver.
  3.  Buttered Spinach.
  4.  Hominy.

## FROZEN FRUIT ICE

1  16-ounce can fruit cocktail,
   undrained
½ cup semidry white wine

2  tablespoons thawed,
   undiluted orange juice or
   lemonade

Pour undrained fruit cocktail into a freezer tray or loaf pan. Stir in wine and juice. Freeze about 3 hours, until firm. Makes 4 to 6 servings.

## BARBECUED LIVER

2  tablespoons butter or
   margarine
1  pound baby beef liver

⅓ cup bottled all-purpose
   barbecue sauce
⅓ cup water

Melt butter in a medium-sized skillet over moderate heat (about 250° F.); brown liver on both sides. Mix barbecue sauce and water; pour over liver. Cover and cook over moderately low heat (about 225° F.) 10 minutes. Makes 4 servings.

## BUTTERED SPINACH

Cook *2 10-ounce packages frozen chopped spinach,* following directions on package. Drain well and stir in *2 tablespoons butter or margarine* and a *few grains ground nutmeg.* Heat thoroughly over moderately low heat (about 225° F.). Makes 4 servings.

## HOMINY

Drain *1 20-ounce can hominy* and place in top of double boiler. Add *2 tablespoons instant minced onion* and *2 tablespoons butter or margarine;* mix well. Heat 10 minutes over boiling water, stirring occasionally. Makes 4 servings.

# Dinner for Four

*Jellied Consommé*
*\* Hobo Casserole*
*\* Mixed Vegetable Salad*
*\* Pound Cake à la Mode*
*Coffee        Tea*

\* Recipe follows

**Advance Preparation:**
    Put consommé in refrigerator to chill.
    Wash and chill salad greens.
**Order of Preparation:**
    1. Hobo Casserole.
    2. Mixed Vegetable Salad.
    3. Serve consommé.
    4. Toast Pound Cake just before serving.

## HOBO CASSEROLE

1  *15¼-ounce can ground beef*        1  *medium-sized tomato, cut*
   *in barbecue sauce*                   *into 4 slices*
1  *15-ounce can macaroni with*       1  *3½-ounce can French fried*
   *cheese sauce*                         *onions*

Preheat broiler. In a bowl mix together ground beef in barbecue
sauce and macaroni and cheese; spoon mixture into individual
casseroles. Place a slice of tomato on each. Place in broiler 4 inches
from heat and broil 10 minutes. Remove casseroles from heat and
sprinkle onions around tomato slices. Broil 2 minutes, or until onions
are lightly browned and mixture is well heated. Makes 4 servings.

## MIXED VEGETABLE SALAD

1  *16-ounce can mixed*            *Salad greens*
   *vegetables, drained*          *½ cup commercial sour cream*
3  *tablespoons bottled Italian*  *¼ teaspoon ground dillseed*
   *dressing*

In a bowl mix vegetables and Italian dressing together and let stand
5 minutes. Arrange vegetables on salad greens. In a bowl combine
sour cream and ground dill and serve over vegetables. Makes 4
servings.

## POUND CAKE À LA MODE

4  ½-inch slices pound cake   ¼  cup coffee liqueur or
1  pint coffee ice cream         chocolate syrup

Toast sliced pound cake until lightly browned. Arrange cake slices on individual serving plates and top each with a scoop of coffee ice cream and a spoonful of coffee liqueur or chocolate syrup. Makes 4 servings.

## Dinner for Four

*Tomato Juice*
\* *Chinese-Style Chicken*
\* *Asparagus Pimiento Salad*
\* *Cherry Shortcake*
*Coffee        Tea*

\* Recipe follows

**Advance Preparation:**
  Chill tomato juice.
  Wash and chill salad greens.
**Order of Preparation:**
  1.  Chinese-Style Chicken.
  2.  Asparagus Pimiento Salad.
  3.  Cherry Shortcake.
  4.  Pour tomato juice.

## CHINESE-STYLE CHICKEN

2  tablespoons butter or
    margarine
¼  cup frozen chopped onion
1  10½-ounce can condensed
    cream of mushroom
    soup, undiluted
½  cup water
2  5-ounce cans boned
    chicken, diced

1¼  cups thinly sliced celery
½  cup salted cashew nuts
1  3-ounce can chow mein
    noodles
1  11-ounce can mandarin
    orange segments, drained
1  teaspoon soy sauce

Melt butter in a skillet over moderate heat (about 250° F.) and cook onion until tender. Reduce heat to moderately low (about 225° F.); stir in mushroom soup, water, chicken, celery, cashew nuts, 1 cup of the chow mein noodles, ¼ cup of the orange segments, and the soy

sauce. Cover and simmer 10 minutes, stirring occasionally. Garnish top with orange segments arranged in a ring and sprinkle with the remaining noodles. Cover and heat 2 minutes. Makes 4 servings.
Your Time: 7 minutes
Cooking Time: 12 minutes

## ASPARAGUS PIMIENTO SALAD

| | |
|---|---|
| 1  *19-ounce can asparagus, drained* | *⅓ cup mayonnaise or salad dressing* |
| 4  *leaves lettuce* | 2  *tablespoons milk* |
| 2  *canned pimientos, cut into strips* | 1  *teaspoon dried parsley flakes* |

Arrange asparagus on lettuce on individual salad plates. Garnish with pimiento strips. In a small bowl blend together mayonnaise, milk, and parsley. Serve dressing over asparagus. Makes 4 servings.

## CHERRY SHORTCAKE

| | |
|---|---|
| ½ *cup whipped cream cheese* | 1  *15-ounce can cherry pie filling* |
| 4  *packaged dessert sponge cups* | *Ready-whipped cream* |
| ½ *teaspoon almond extract* | |

Spread cream cheese in centers of sponge cups, using about 2 tablespoons for each. Arrange sponge cups on individual serving plates. Add almond extract to cherry pie filling; spoon filling over sponge cups. Garnish with whipped cream. Makes 4 servings.

# Dinner for Six

---

* *Grilled Salisbury Steak*
* *Creamed Potatoes*
* *Scalloped Tomatoes*
*Bread and Butter*
* *Blushing Applesauce*
*Coffee        Tea*

\* Recipe follows

---

**Order of Preparation:**
1. Grilled Salisbury Steak.
2. Creamed Potatoes.
3. Scalloped Tomatoes.
4. Blushing Applesauce.

## GRILLED SALISBURY STEAK

2 tablespoons water
2 tablespoons dried
 vegetable flakes
1¾ pounds ground beef chuck
1 teaspoon salt
Few grains pepper
⅛ teaspoon paprika
¼ teaspoon dried basil leaves
Olive oil

½ cup chili sauce or catsup
1 tablespoon lemon juice
¾ teaspoon Worcestershire
 sauce
1 teaspoon prepared
 mustard
¼ teaspoon salt
Few grains pepper

Preheat broiler. In a custard cup combine water and vegetable flakes and let stand 3 minutes; drain. In a bowl mix together meat, drained vegetable flakes, the 1 teaspoon salt, the few grains pepper, paprika, and basil. Shape meat into 6 individual patties about ¾ inch thick. Place on broiler rack; brush with olive oil. Broil 4 inches from heat for 3 to 5 minutes on each side, depending upon degree of doneness desired. While meat is broiling, in a small saucepan mix together chili sauce, lemon juice, Worcestershire, mustard, the ¼ teaspoon salt, and the few grains pepper. Heat to serving temperature over moderately low heat (about 225° F.). Arrange meat on serving platter. Pour sauce over meat patties. Makes 6 servings.

## CREAMED POTATOES

2 packages onion sauce mix
Milk or water
2 16-ounce cans small white
 potatoes, drained

½ teaspoon dried parsley
 flakes

In a saucepan prepare sauce using milk or water as called for on package. Add potatoes and mix well. Cover and cook over low heat (200° F.) 10 minutes. Stir in parsley. Makes 6 servings.

## SCALLOPED TOMATOES

2  16-ounce cans tomatoes,          1½ cups seasoned stuffing
   undrained                            croutons
½ teaspoon salt                      1  tablespoon butter or
½ teaspoon sugar                        margarine
Few grains pepper

Mix together tomatoes, salt, sugar, and pepper in a saucepan; cover
and cook over moderate heat (about 250° F.) 5 minutes. Add
croutons and butter; heat 5 minutes longer. Makes 6 servings.

## BLUSHING APPLESAUCE

2  16-ounce cans applesauce      ⅓ cup dark seedless raisins
¼ cup strawberry-flavored        ¾ cup commercial sour cream
   drink mix                        Ground nutmeg

In a bowl mix together applesauce, strawberry-flavored mix, and
raisins. Spoon mixture into individual serving dishes. Serve garnished
with sour cream and a dusting of nutmeg. Makes 6 servings.

# *Fifteen-Minute Meals*

---

*Chilled Cranberry Juice*
\* *Scalloped Salmon* (recipe on page 88)
\* *Peas and Mushrooms* (recipe on page 151)
*Hearts of Lettuce*
*French Dressing*
\* *Coffee-Macaroon Pudding* (recipe on page 218)
*Beverage*


\* *Chicken Livers Tarragon* (recipe on page 77)
\* *Parsley Rice* (recipe on page 156)
\* *Creamy Onion Spinach* (recipe on page 157)
\* *Pound Cake with Fruit à la Mode* (recipe on page 202)
*Beverage*

* *Stirred Shrimp in Sherry* (recipe on page 83)
* *Parsley Potato Puffs* (recipe on page 153)
* *Fried Tomatoes* (recipe on page 159)
Fruit and Cheese
Beverage

* *Skillet Tomato-Rice* (recipe on page 101)
* *Deviled Carrots* (recipe on page 299)
Celery Hearts
* *Pears Flambé* (recipe on page 206)
Beverage

* (Recipes appear as noted in this book.)

---

# Thirty-Minute Meals

---

* *Chicken and Zucchini Casserole* (recipe on page 73)
* *Baked Corn on the Cob* (recipe on page 148)
* *Tomato-Mushroom Salad* (recipe on page 167)
* *Pineapple Rice Pudding* (recipe on page 221)
Beverage

* *Shrimp de Luxe* (recipe on page 82)
Rice
Danish-Style Frozen Vegetables
* *Watercress Salad* (recipe on page 168)
Ice Cream with Chocolate Sauce
Beverage

* *Baked Ham Steak* (recipe on page 110)
* *Orange-Glazed Sweet Potatoes* (recipe on page 154)
* *Savory Spinach* (recipe on page 158)
Crisp Celery and Carrot Sticks
* *Coconut Cake with Lemon Sauce* (recipe on page 243)
Beverage

* *Vegetable Meat Loaf* (recipe on page 103)
Shoestring Potatoes
* *Minted Tomato-and-Lettuce Salad* (recipe on page 168)
* *Sherried Fruit Sundae* (recipe on page 209)
Beverage

* (Recipes appear as noted in this book.)

---

# Forty-Five-Minute Meals

---

\* *Peanut Soup* (recipe on page 50)
\* *Oven-Fried Chicken* (recipe on page 72)
\* *Curried Scalloped Potatoes* (recipe on page 152)
\* *Herbed Zucchini* (recipe on page 301)
\* *Sesame Cheese Loaf* (recipe on page 183)
\* *Apple-Raisin Salad* (recipe on page 164)
\* *Blueberry Halo* (recipe on page 200)
*Beverage*

\* *Quick Hot Borscht* (recipe on page 47)
\* *Creamed Tuna in Patty Shells* (recipe on page 91)
\* *Festive Green Beans* (recipe on page 144)
\* *Quick Cheese Crescents* (recipe on page 178)
*Celery and Carrot Sticks*
\* *Baked Alaska Waffles* (recipe on page 210)
*Beverage*

\* *Potato-Cheese Soup* (recipe on page 50)
\* *Quick Corned-Beef Dinner* (recipe on page 129)
\* *Celery and Olive Salad* (recipe on page 167)
\* *Onion Bread Sticks* (recipe on page 182)
\* *Apple Crisp* (recipe on page 199)
*Beverage*

\* *Clam-Chicken Broth* (recipe on page 47)
\* *Lazy Man's Lasagna* (recipe on page 137)
\* *Classic Green Salad* (recipe on page 164)
\* *Seasoned Italian Bread* (recipe on page 181)
\* *Hot Apricot Sundae* (recipe on page 209)
*Beverage*

\* (Recipes appear as noted in this book.)

# One-Hour Meals

---

\* *Quick Onion Soup* (recipe on page 49)
\* *Company Seafood Casserole* (recipe on page 95)
*Cooked Rice*

* *Glazed Carrot Slices* (recipe on page 147)
* *Quick Cranberry-Apple Salad* (recipe on page 170)
* *Chocolate Cream* (recipe on page 217)
* *No-Bake Peanut Butter Squares* (recipe on page 253)
*Beverage*

* *Chilled Black-Bean Soup* (recipe on page 42)
* *Cheese Meat Loaf* (recipe on page 102)
* *Quickie Stuffed Potatoes* (recipe on page 153)
* *Company Brussels Sprouts* (recipe on page 146)
* *Vegetable Macedoine Salad* (recipe on page 176)
* *Crème de Menthe Ice Cream* (recipe on page 211)
* *No-Bake Wine-Nut Balls* (recipe on page 256)
*Beverage*

* *Pumpkin Soup* (recipe on page 51)
* *Veal with Herb Sauce* (recipe on page 116)
* *Potatoes Dauphine* (recipe on page 152)
* *Company Creamed Peas* (recipe on page 151)
* *Cheese-Bacon Crescent Rolls* (recipe on page 179)
* *Asparagus Salad* (recipe on page 165)
* *Strawberry Parfaits* (recipe on page 224)
*Beverage*

* *Greek Lemon Soup* (recipe on page 48)
* *Chicken Breasts Parmesan* (recipe on page 67)
* *Pineapple-Pecan Sweet Potatoes* (recipe on page 154)
* *Green Bean Casserole* (recipe on page 143)
* *Classic Green Salad* (recipe on page 164)
* *Peach Melba Parfait* (recipe on page 213)
*Beverage*

* (Recipes appear as noted in this book.)

# *Last-Minute Meals from Your Pantry Shelf*

* *Seafood Curry on Chow Mein Noodles*
*Chutney*
*Chopped Peanuts*
* *Asparagus Vinaigrette*

*Home-Style Canned Peaches with Cointreau, if Desired*
*Crisp Sugar Wafers*
*Beverage*

\* Recipe follows

---

## SEAFOOD CURRY ON CHOW MEIN NOODLES

1  *3-ounce can chow mein noodles*
1  *7¾-ounce can crab meat*
1  *5-ounce can lobster meat*
2  *tablespoons butter or margarine*
4  *teaspoons flour*
½  *cup instant nonfat dry milk*
2  *tablespoons nondairy powdered creamer*

⅛ *teaspoon pepper*
2  *teaspoons curry powder*
1  *13¾-ounce can chicken broth*
1  *teaspoon instant minced onion*
1  *teaspoon dried parsley flakes*

Heat oven to 350° F. Open can of chow mein noodles and place can in oven while preparing seafood mixture. Open can of crab meat; drain, remove any hard cartilage, and flake meat. Open can of lobster; drain, remove spiny pieces, and flake meat. Melt butter in a large skillet over moderately low heat (about 225° F.). Remove skillet from heat. Place flour, nonfat dry milk, nondairy powdered creamer, pepper, curry powder, and chicken broth in a jar with a tight-fitting lid; cover and shake until all ingredients are blended. Pour chicken broth mixture into the skillet. Add onion and parsley flakes; return skillet to moderately low heat (about 225° F.) and cook, stirring constantly, until mixture is thickened. Add crab meat and lobster and heat, uncovered, stirring occasionally. Serve seafood mixture over heated chow mein noodles. Makes 4 servings.
Your Time: 12 minutes
Cooking Time: 7 minutes

## ASPARAGUS VINAIGRETTE

Drain *1 19-ounce can asparagus spears* and place them in a shallow baking dish. Combine *½ cup bottled French dressing* and *1 teaspoon dried parsley flakes*. Pour dressing over asparagus spears. Cover and refrigerate about 30 minutes. Makes 4 servings.
Your Time: 2 minutes
Chilling Time: 30 minutes

---

*\* Vegetable Beef Burgundy on Noodles*
*Bread and Butter Pickles*
*Melba Toast*
*Canned Pineapple*
*Beverage*

\* Recipe follows

---

## VEGETABLE BEEF BURGUNDY ON NOODLES

1  16-ounce can mixed
   vegetables
1  16-ounce can small white
   onions
1  1½-pound can beef stew
½  cup burgundy wine
¼  teaspoon dried thyme
   leaves

¼  teaspoon pepper
1  10½-ounce can condensed
   beef broth, undiluted
2  cups water
1  8-ounce package fine egg
   noodles

Drain liquid from mixed vegetables and onions and pour liquid into a large skillet. Place skillet over moderately high heat (about 275° F.) and cook about 5 minutes to reduce liquid to half. Remove from heat. Add beef stew, drained vegetables, wine, thyme, and pepper. Place mixture over moderately low heat (about 225° F.) and cook, uncovered, for 15 minutes, stirring occasionally. While heating stew, place beef broth and water in a large saucepan with cover over moderately high heat (about 275° F.) and bring to a boil. Reduce heat to moderately low (about 225° F.); add noodles, cover, and cook for 8 minutes, or until noodles are tender, stirring occasionally. Serve beef stew mixture over noodles. Makes 4 servings.
Your Time: 8 minutes
Cooking Time: 20 minutes

---

*Tomato Juice*
*\* Pagoda Salad*
*Pilot Crackers*
*\* Quick Cookie Pie*
*Beverage*

\* Recipe follows

---

## PAGODA SALAD

¾ *cup packaged precooked*
*rice*
¾ *cup boiling water*
1 *7-ounce can tuna, drained*
*and flaked*
1 *5-ounce can water*
*chestnuts, drained and*
*sliced*
1 *16-ounce can mixed*
*vegetables, drained*

1 *16-ounce can bean sprouts,*
*drained*
2 *teaspoons instant minced*
*onion*
1 *cup mayonnaise or salad*
*dressing*
¼ *cup chili sauce*
¼ *teaspoon seasoned salt*

Prepare rice with boiling water as directed on package. In a large bowl mix together tuna, water chestnuts, mixed vegetables, and bean sprouts. Stir in hot cooked rice. In a small box mix together onion, mayonnaise, chili sauce, and seasoned salt. Stir mayonnaise mixture into salad. Cover and chill 1 to 2 hours before serving. Makes 4 servings.
Your Time: 10 minutes
Chilling Time: 1 to 2 hours

## QUICK COOKIE PIE

1 *4-serving-size package*
*chocolate pudding and pie*
*filling*

*About 31 vanilla wafers*
1 *2-ounce package dessert*
*topping mix*

Prepare pudding according to package directions; cool and chill until cold. While chilling pudding, arrange some of the vanilla wafers over bottom of a 9-inch pie plate. Cut some of the wafers into small pieces to fill up the holes. Cut remaining wafers in half (if some of the cookies break, reserve them for the pie topping); stand halved wafers around edge of pie plate. Prepare dessert topping mix according to package directions. Beat chilled pudding with a rotary beater until smooth. Fold the dessert topping mix into the pudding. Pour mixture into the prepared pie plate. Crush remaining wafers and sprinkle over top of pie. Chill pie several hours, or until set, before serving. Makes 6 to 8 servings.
Your Time: 17 minutes
Cooking Time: 10 minutes
Chilling Time: 3 hours

* *Pantry Shelf Cassoulet*
*Sliced Canned Brown Bread*
*Cold Dilled Green Beans*
* *Minted Applesauce*
*Chocolate Cookies*
*Beverage*

**\* Recipe follows**

## PANTRY SHELF CASSOULET

1  teaspoon dried parsley
   flakes
¼  s,teaspoon dried thyme
   leaves
½  teaspoon celery salt
½  teaspoon garlic salt
2  16-ounce cans pork and
   beans
½  cup frozen chopped onion

2  3½-ounce jars chopped
   junior lamb
1  12-ounce can luncheon
   meat
2  4-ounce cans Vienna
   sausage
1  8-ounce can tomato sauce
1  slice buttered white bread

Heat oven to 300° F. In a large skillet mix together parsley flakes, thyme, celery salt, and garlic salt. Mix in beans, chopped onion, and lamb; heat to simmering over moderately low heat (about 225° F.), stirring occasionally. Remove skillet from heat. While beans are heating, cut luncheon meat into thin slices and sausages crosswise into halves. Spoon about one-third of the bean mixture into the bottom of an ungreased deep 2-quart casserole. Top with half of the meats. Repeat layers once again and then top with the remaining bean mixture. Pour in tomato sauce. Cover and bake 1 hour. Remove casserole from oven. Increase oven temperature to 400° F. Cut bread into small cubes and sprinkle over casserole; continue baking, uncovered, for 10 minutes, or until crumbs are brown. Makes 5 servings.
Your Time: 13 minutes
Cooking and Baking Time: 1 hour and 20 minutes

## MINTED APPLESAUCE

Stir *1 tablespoon softened mint jelly* into *1 25-ounce jar applesauce.*
Makes 5 servings.
Your Time: 1 minute

*\* Spaghetti with Red Clam Sauce*
*Bread Sticks*
*Canned Artichoke Hearts with French Dressing*
*Canned Orange and Grapefruit Sections*
*Beverage*

\* Recipe follows

## SPAGHETTI WITH RED CLAM SAUCE

½ cup vegetable oil
1 medium-sized clove garlic,
    peeled and finely minced
1 8-ounce can tomato sauce
2 8-ounce cans minced clams,
    undrained
½ teaspoon dried oregano
    leaves

½ teaspoon dried parsley
    flakes
½ teaspoon salt
¼ teaspoon pepper
¾ of a 1-pound package or 1½
    8-ounce packages thin
    spaghetti

Heat oil in a large skillet over moderate heat (about 250° F.); add
garlic and cook until lightly browned, stirring occasionally. Reduce
heat to moderately low (about 225° F.). Add tomato sauce and
clams with their juice to the skillet and continue cooking for 15
minutes, stirring occasionally. Add oregano, parsley, salt, and pepper
to the sauce and cook 5 minutes longer. While sauce is cooking, cook
spaghetti according to package directions. Drain. To serve, toss
drained cooked spaghetti with sauce, or serve sauce over cooked
spaghetti. Makes 4 servings.
Your Time: 8 minutes
Cooking Time: 25 minutes

*\* Ham and Yam Bake*
*Buttered Green Beans*
*Whole Wheat Wafers*
*Chocolate and Banana Instant Pudding Layered in Parfait Glasses*
*Beverage*

\* Recipe follows

## HAM AND YAM BAKE

1  12-ounce can luncheon
   meat
1  12-ounce can sweet
   potatoes, drained
1  20-ounce can sliced apples,
   drained
2  tablespoons firmly packed
   dark-brown sugar

½  cup packaged corn flake
   crumbs
1  tablespoon melted butter or
   margarine
2  tablespoons firmly packed
   dark-brown sugar

Heat oven to 400° F. Remove meat from can; slice meat into 6 slices and arrange in bottom of an ungreased shallow 1½-quart baking dish. Slice sweet potatoes in half and layer over meat. Mix sliced apples and the 2 tablespoons brown sugar together in a bowl and spoon over sweet potatoes. Mix corn flake crumbs, butter, and the remaining 2 tablespoons brown sugar in a small bowl and sprinkle over apples. Bake, uncovered, 20 minutes. Makes 4 servings.
Your Time: 8 minutes
Cooking and Baking Time: 22 minutes

---

* *Chicken Polenta Pie*
* *Green Beans Parmesan*
*Mixed Sweet Pickles*
*Canned Apricot Halves with Toasted Coconut*
*Beverages*

* Recipe follows

---

## CHICKEN POLENTA PIE

¼  cup butter or margarine
½  cup frozen chopped onion
1  13¾-ounce can chicken
   broth
¼  cup flour
1  8-ounce can tomato sauce
1  12-ounce can whole-kernel
   corn, drained
1  cup pitted ripe olives, cut in
   halves

1  12-ounce can boned
   chicken
1  teaspoon chili powder
½  teaspoon monosodium
   glutamate
1  12-ounce package corn
   muffin mix

Heat oven to 400° F. Grease a shallow 2-quart baking dish with unsalted shortening. Heat butter in a large skillet over moderate heat (about 250° F.); add onion and cook until tender, stirring frequently. Remove skillet from heat. Pour chicken broth into a 1-quart measuring cup and add enough water to measure 2½ cups. Add flour to onion in skillet and stir until well mixed. Gradually add 1½ cups of the chicken broth mixture, stirring constantly. Add tomato sauce and cook mixture over moderate heat (about 250° F.) until thickened, stirring constantly. Remove skillet from heat. Add corn, olives, chicken, chili powder, and monosodium glutamate; mix well. Pour mixture into the prepared dish. Pour corn muffin mix into a medium-sized bowl and blend in the remaining 1 cup chicken broth. Pour cornmeal mixture in a thin stream over mixture in casserole to cover the entire top. Bake, uncovered, for 35 minutes. Makes 6 servings.
Your Time: 15 minutes
Cooking and Baking Time: 45 minutes

## GREEN BEANS PARMESAN

Spread *2 16-ounce cans whole green beans,* drained, in the bottom of a buttered shallow baking dish; sprinkle top lightly with *grated Parmesan cheese.* Place in oven with Chicken Polenta Pie for last 15-minutes of baking. Makes 6 servings.
Your Time: 1 minute
Baking Time: 15 minutes

# *Last-Minute Meals from Your Freezer*

-----

*\* Fillet of Flounder Bonne Femme*
*Frozen Hashed Brown Potatoes*
*Toasted English Muffins*
*\* Strawberry Cheesecake*
*Beverage*

\* Recipe follows

-----

## FILLET OF FLOUNDER BONNE FEMME

2  *10-ounce packages frozen*
   *cut green beans*
⅛ *teaspoon pepper*
2  *12-ounce packages frozen*
   *flounder fillet, thawed*
*Salt and pepper*
2  *10½-ounce cans condensed*
   *cream of mushroom soup,*
   *undiluted*

½ *cup dry white wine*
¼ *cup melted butter or*
   *margarine*
2  *teaspoons paprika*

Heat oven to 375° F. Cook beans according to package directions. Drain beans and spoon them into the bottom of an ungreased shallow 2-quart baking dish. Sprinkle beans with the ⅛ teaspoon pepper. Arrange fish fillets over beans and sprinkle fish lightly with salt and pepper. In a bowl mix soup and wine together until blended and pour over fish. In a small bowl mix melted butter and paprika and pour over sauce. Bake, uncovered, 30 minutes. Makes 6 servings.
Your Time: 7 minutes
Cooking and Baking Time: 40 minutes

## STRAWBERRY CHEESECAKE

Thaw *1 8-inch frozen cheesecake* and *1 package frozen sliced strawberries* according to package directions. Spoon strawberries over cheesecake and refrigerate until serving time. Makes 6 servings.
Your Time: 1 minute
Thawing Time: 1 hour and 20 minutes

---

*\* Frozen Beef Steaks*
*Frozen French Fried Potatoes*
*Frozen French Fried Onion Rings*
*Frozen Brussels Sprouts*
*Club Rolls*
*\* Orange Cream Tortoni*
*Beverage*

\* Recipe follows

---

## FROZEN BEEF STEAKS

Cook *steaks* according to package directions.
Your Time: About 4 minutes

## ORANGE CREAM TORTONI

12  1½-inch soft coconut          1  pint softened vanilla ice
    *macaroons*                              *cream*
½ of a 6-ounce can frozen
    *orange juice concentrate*

Heat oven to 400° F. Break macaroons into small pieces and spread
out on an ungreased cookie sheet. Place macaroons in oven to toast
for 10 to 15 minutes, or until lightly browned. When macaroons are
cool enough to handle, rub them into fine crumbs. Pour orange juice,
crumbs, and vanilla ice cream into the container of an electric
blender; stir with a spoon to blend slightly. Cover and blend about 2
minutes at high speed. Pour mixture into sherbet glasses and place in
freezer for 1½ to 2 hours, or until firm. Makes 5 servings.
Your Time: 17 minutes
Baking Time: 10 to 15 minutes
Chilling Time: 1½ to 2 hours

---

*Grape Juice*
\* *Eggplant-Cheeseburger Casserole*
*Frozen Potato Puffs*
*Soft Rolls*
\* *Chocolate Ice Cream with Crème de Cacao*
*Beverage*

\* Recipe follows

---

## EGGPLANT-CHEESEBURGER CASSEROLE

2  tablespoons butter or         ¼  teaspoon onion salt
    *margarine*                           4  *slices process American*
4  *frozen beef burgers*             *cheese*
1  *7-ounce package frozen*        1  *8-ounce can tomato sauce*
    *breaded eggplant sticks*             *with cheese*

Heat oven to 350° F. Heat butter in a large skillet over moderate heat (about 250° F.); add beef burgers and cook over moderately high heat (about 275° F.) until lightly browned on both sides, or about 10 minutes. Arrange eggplant in a layer in the bottom of an ungreased shallow 1½-quart baking dish. Place burgers over eggplant and sprinkle lightly with onion salt. Place a slice of cheese on each burger. Pour tomato sauce over burgers. Bake, uncovered, 25 minutes, or until cheese is melted. Makes 4 servings.
Your Time: 10 minutes
Cooking and Baking Time: 35 minutes

## CHOCOLATE ICE CREAM WITH CRÈME DE CACAO

Scoop *chocolate ice cream* into sherbet glasses and top each serving with *1 tablespoon crème de cacao*.
Your Time: About 2 minutes

---

*Veal Marsala*
*Frozen Macaroni and Cheese*
*Salt Sticks*
*Toasted Pound Cake with Butter Pecan Ice Cream*
*Beverage*

* Recipe follows

---

## VEAL MARSALA

4 to 6 tablespoons olive oil
½ pound fresh mushrooms, sliced
4 frozen breaded veal patties

1 small clove garlic, peeled and minced
½ cup marsala wine

Heat 4 tablespoons oil in a large skillet over moderately high heat (about 275° F.); add mushrooms and cook until lightly browned, or about 5 minutes. Remove mushrooms with a slotted spoon and set aside. Add veal and garlic to skillet and cook over moderately high heat (about 300° F.) until veal is lightly browned on both sides, or about 8 to 10 minutes, adding additional oil as needed. Reduce heat to moderately low (about 225° F.). Remove veal from skillet and drain off all but 1 tablespoon of the fat from the pan. Pour wine into

the skillet and stir to loosen any brown particles on bottom of skillet. Return mushrooms and veal to skillet and heat thoroughly. Makes 4 servings.
Your Time: 12 minutes
Cooking Time: 25 minutes


## TOASTED POUND CAKE WITH BUTTER PECAN ICE CREAM

Thaw a *frozen pound cake* and cut off 4 ½-inch slices. Toast slices in toaster and top each slice with a scoop of *butter pecan ice cream.* Serve immediately. Makes 4 servings.
Your Time: About 5 minutes

# INDEX